This book is due on the last date stamped below.
Failure to return books on the date due may result
in assessment of overdue fees.

FINES .50 | per day

ORPHANS' HOME

The Voice and Vision of Horton Foote

Laurin Porter

LOUISIANA STATE UNIVERSITY PRESS
BATON ROUGE

Cloth
12   11   10   09   08   07   06   05   04   03
5   4   3   2   1
Paper
12   11   10   09   08   07   06   05   04   03
5   4   3   2   1

Designer: Melanie O'Quinn Samaha
Typeface: Galliard
Typesetter: Coghill Composition Co. Inc.
Printer and binder: Thomson-Shore, Inc.

Library of Congress Cataloging-in-Publication Data:

Porter, Laurin, 1945–
    Orphans' home : the voice and vision of Horton Foote / Laurin Porter.
        p.   cm. — (Southern literary studies)
    Includes bibliographical references and index.
    ISBN 0-8071-2845-7 (cloth : alk. paper) — ISBN 0-8071-2879-1 (pbk. : alk. paper)
    1. Foote, Horton. Orphans' home cycle. 2. Fathers and sons in literature. 3. Texas—In
    literature. 4. Orphans in literature. 5. Family in literature. 6. Men in literature. I. Title.
    II. Series.
    PS3511.O344 Z84 2003
    812'.54—dc21   2002015759

For
Tom, Katie, and Molly—
all my world.

CONTENTS

ACKNOWLEDGMENTS

Though writing a book is a solitary task, it is never done alone. My work was helped immeasurably by the interest and support of Horton Foote, whom I first met in 1988 when he was the keynote speaker at my university's Katherine Anne Porter Lecture Series, devoted that year to Texas films and filmmakers. Since then, when I interviewed him for the first time, he has generously read and responded to various articles and conference papers as well as several chapters of this book and has granted me access to invaluable materials. His kind words of encouragement have meant a great deal to me, and I would like to publicly thank him here.

I am grateful to Dr. Harry Wilmer, then director of the Institute for the Humanities at Salado, in Salado, Texas, for inviting me to participate as a featured speaker, along with Foote, in a weekend seminar devoted to *The Orphans' Home Cycle* in 1993. The seminar provided me with a unique opportunity to deepen my understanding of these plays and their biographical, cultural, and aesthetic roots in many lengthy conversations with Foote, as well as in the formal sessions.

I am also indebted to the University of Texas at Arlington for Research Enhancement Grants in the summers of 1996 and '97, which allowed me to complete my research, and a Faculty Development Leave in the fall of 1998, during which I completed the manuscript. Without this gift of time and money, this book would still be years away.

I appreciate the generous assistance of Kay Bost, then curator of archives, manuscripts, and photographs, at the DeGolyer Library, Southern Methodist University, and the other members of the library staff during my research in the Foote Collection.

Finally, and always, I would like to thank my husband, Tom, beloved colleague, collaborator, and friend. From him and our two daughters, Katie and Molly, I have learned the deep lessons of the heart. What I know of families and the power of love begins with them.

ORPHANS' HOME

1

AN ORPHAN'S DREAM

In the final drama of *The Orphans' Home Cycle*, Horton Foote's nine-play cycle based on the life of his father, we encounter the following exchange between ten-year-old Horace, Jr., Foote's counterpart in the play, and his mother, Elizabeth. It takes place shortly after the drowning death of eighteen-year-old Gertrude, their black maid:

HORACE, JR.: Gertrude said she would like to be a nurse or a teacher someday to help her race.

ELIZABETH: Did she?

HORACE, JR.: I'd like to help my race, too. What can I do?

ELIZABETH: Well, I don't know. We'll have to think about it. Start by being a good man; that will help all the races.

HORACE, JR.: How do I be a good man?

ELIZABETH: God only knows, honey.

HORACE, JR.: Is Daddy a good man?

ELIZABETH: I think so. I know he tries to be.

HORACE, JR.: Was Papa? [his grandfather, who has just died]

ELIZABETH: Oh, yes. Very good!

HORACE, JR.: Why?

ELIZABETH: Because he was.[1]

---

1. Horton Foote, *"Cousins" and "The Death of Papa": Two Plays from The Orphans' Home Cycle* (New York: Grove Press, 1989), 149. Hereinafter this work will be cited parenthetically by page numbers in the text as *Two Plays*.

In this play young Horace has observed the death of his powerful and beloved grandfather; the death of Gertrude several days later; and the dissipation of his uncle, "Brother," a hopeless alcoholic who kills a man in a drunken brawl and is forced to leave home, probably for good. He has watched his father struggle to make the mortgage payments on his dry goods store, stubbornly refusing to accept help from his wealthy mother-in-law and insisting on treating his black customers with the same respect as his white patrons, even when it costs him business. He knows that his grandmother and uncle don't consider his father a good businessman, and even his mother, who is devoted to Horace, Sr., qualifies her praise. How is young Horace to sort all this out? How, to quote the play, can he "be good"? How can anyone?

These few brief lines, as much as any others, encapsulate Foote's enduring themes not just in this play or the *Cycle* as a whole but throughout his entire canon. By his own confession, Foote is a student of human behavior. Ever since he was a young boy, much like Horace, Jr., in *The Death of Papa*, listening to the stories of his parents and other family members and observing those around him, he has wondered what accounted for the differences in the way people's lives turned out. What makes some people successful and others failures; some capable of great heroism and endurance and others not; some brave in the face of adversity while others crumble?

These may seem naive questions. Philosophers, sociologists, and psychologists have proposed elaborate schemata that describe, categorize, and explain human behavior from every perspective imaginable, anatomizing "the good" and articulating ethical systems; one might reasonably ask what is left to unearth in this well-excavated field. Foote, however, is not interested in systems or solutions. His genius lies in creating people we come to know as we might our next-door neighbor or the man down the street, giving us the conditions of their lives—their family histories, their fears and worries, joys and sorrows—then setting them in motion and seeing what they do.

It is with a sense of humility and awe, the playwright's and our own, that we become co-observers, because at bottom, no matter how richly textured and detailed the portrait, a complete accounting for one life choice over another is impossible. Life in a Foote play ultimately remains mysterious. Horace's father tries to be a good man and Elizabeth, at least, thinks he is; her father, Horace, Jr.'s, grandfather, *certainly* was, she avers. But when Horace, Jr., asks why, the answer is simply, "Because." There is no further explanation. In the same vein, when Horace, Jr., asks how he can be good, his mother replies that only God knows. She's neither being disingenuous here nor putting her son off. The wisdom she has acquired in the course of her lifetime tells her that there are no formulae to pass down, no magic answers. Things simply "are."

This is not, perhaps, the kind of issue one would expect to draw big audiences on Broadway. Foote's plays have, in fact, been dismissed as sentimental and nostalgic by critics such as John Simon, Pauline Kael, and Richard Corliss, who see themselves as too sophisticated for such concerns. His characters have been described as ordinary and uninteresting, and his plots have been called flat. This, however, is a response that fails to see beyond the surface to a world which is fraught with pain. As commentator Marian Burkhart observes in a 1988 *Commonweal* article, "For all its ordinariness, Foote's world is neither calm nor orderly. What serenity exists—and serenity is, in a sense, his subject—exists against a background of endless violence." She illustrates with several examples: a distraught man facing financial ruin who murders his banker in front of the banker's daughter in *The Roads to Home,* a man who murders his cousin to defend the honor of a prostitute in *Cousins,* convict laborers murdering one another in *Convicts.* It is not the violence of these acts per se that is disturbing, however, as Burkhart points out, but their arbitrary, random, and pervasive nature. "Intelligent men of good family who drink themselves into irresponsible near-idiocy pepper Foote's plays," she writes, "and a child, hungry for knowledge, is forbidden to read. Such perversion is systemic. Those murderers—except for the convicts—incur no punishment. If they are brought to trial at all, they suffer at most suspended sentences and walk away from the courtroom to swill again the bootleg liquor that leads to further violence." Foote's central preoccupation, as she sees it, is the question, "When so much in human nature seems to relish chaos, how do some people succeed in achieving lives orderly enough to permit a civilized society to exist?"[2]

2. Marian Burkhart, "Horton Foote's Many Roads Home: An American Playwright and His Characters," *Commonweal,* February 26, 1988, pp. 110–12.

This book will examine this far-reaching and profoundly important question as it is presented in *The Orphans' Home Cycle,* which,
with Burkhart, I consider Foote's foremost dramatic achievement.
Written in the 1970s and published in three volumes by Grove Press
in 1988–1989, *The Orphans' Home* represents a unique achievement
in the canon of American drama as well as in Foote's personal
oeuvre. In the course of nine plays, each of which stands alone yet
which together tell a single story, he explores the life of a small-town
boy, Horace Robedaux, as he is transformed from a twelve-year-old
orphan to a husband and father, the patriarch of a family. While it
appears to be a relatively simple tale of a boy becoming a man, a familiar archetype, *Orphans' Home* raises questions of considerable
complexity which reverberate far beyond the confines of Horace's
small world. What, it asks, is the relationship of the individual to the
whole, whether family, town, or cosmos at large: How does the individual voice blend with others and yet remain unique? To what extent
can we exercise our freedom, given the strictures and limitations of
socially dictated roles and mores? Do we write our own histories or
are they written for us? And finally, how does the past impinge on the
present?

These are, of course, questions of identity formation. In these
plays as in all his dramas and screenplays, Foote is interested in what
makes people do the things they do, how they become who they are.
At the same time, the dramas raise complex questions about individual agency versus cultural conditioning and the shaping power of custom and tradition. Given those patterns of thought and habits of
seeing into which I am born, to what extent can I control who I am
and who I choose to become? And what do language, epistemology,
and the nature of "truth" have to do with these questions?

A native Texan, or as he would prefer, a native of Wharton, Texas,
Foote's approach to these matters is informed by his Southern sensibility. The key to questions of identity for Foote lies in family, community, and the legacy of the past. The action of the cycle is set in
Harrison, Texas, the fictitious counterpart of Wharton, during the
years 1902–1928. As Horace, newly orphaned at twelve, moves to his
coming of age, we come to know two extended families, his own and
that of Elizabeth Vaughn, his future wife, across three generations, as
well as numerous other townsfolk who weave in and out of Horace's

life. The end result is a highly complex construct of interconnected stories, subsumed within that of Horace, told in ways that recast conventional dramatic language and structure. In examining these plays, this book will explore both the philosophical issues Foote raises and the innovative ways in which he uses dramatic form to do so.

Horton Foote is unique among contemporary American artists in that he writes equally well for the stage and the screen. Nevertheless, the general public has principally identified him with his screenplays rather than his dramas. Al Reinert points out in a *Texas Monthly* article, for instance, that for three generations some of America's finest actors have done their best work in roles that he created. Gregory Peck (*To Kill a Mockingbird,* 1962) and Robert Duvall (*Tender Mercies,* 1983) each won best actor Oscars speaking lines that he put into their mouths, while Geraldine Page, who had previously been nominated seven times without winning, finally received the best actress Oscar for her performance in *A Trip to Bountiful* in 1985. "It's all your fault, Horton," Page said when she accepted the award. She had agreed to do the part without even reading it when she learned it was Foote's script, trusting his ability to write "real characters using real dialogue."[3] *To Kill a Mockingbird* and *Tender Mercies* won Oscars for Foote, as well, the first for best adaptation and the second for original screenplay; the screenplay for *Bountiful* was nominated, although it didn't win.

He actually began his career as an actor, however, studying at the Pasadena Playhouse in California for two years in his late teens and training for an additional two years at the Tamara Daykarhanova School for Acting in New York City from 1937 to 1939. His first play, a one-act entitled *Wharton Dance* written in 1939, came out of an improvisational exercise he did for the American Actors Company, which he had helped found the previous year. As Foote tells it, he started writing to give himself lead roles to play, but got so interested in writing he left acting behind. Several dramas followed in quick succession, including *Only the Heart* (1944), his first play produced on Broadway, and dance plays choreographed by Valerie Bettis and Martha Graham. The 1950s saw the beginning of a long and productive

3. Al Reinert, "Tender Foote," *Texas Monthly,* July 1991, p. 110.

tenure writing plays for television series during the so-called Golden Age of Television, including such critically esteemed programs as *The Philco-Goodyear Playhouse, Studio One, Playhouse 90, The Dupont Show of the Month, and The U.S. Steel Hour*.[4] In the '60s, a turbulent age given over to radical rhetoric, guerrilla theater, and on-stage nudity, when Foote's subtle style and realistic, character-driven dramas fell out of favor, he moved his family to New Hampshire. It is here, during the '70s, after the death of his parents, to whom he was very attached, that he began to write the plays that were to become *The Orphans' Home Cycle*. Based on the life of his parents, these nine plays are Foote's *Long Day's Journey into Night,* though their serenity stands in stark contrast to O'Neill's anguished valediction to his family.

Foote eventually returned to New York, where he wrote adaptations as well as original screenplays and dramas. Once again the awards began to appear, with his Academy Award for *Tender Mercies* in 1983 and the nomination for *Trip to Bountiful* in 1985. About this time he and his wife, Lillian, dedicated to bringing all nine of the *Cycle* plays to the screen, decided they could make better movies outside the constraints of Hollywood. They returned to Texas, raised a modest $1.8 million, and began filming in Waxahachie, a small town near Dallas. Although he has not yet reached his goal of filming all nine plays, his commitment to independent films inspired other independent filmmakers throughout the 1980s and beyond.[5] Now eighty-six years old, with over thirty-seven telescripts, thirty-eight screenplays, and sixty dramas to his credit at last count, Foote continues to crisscross the country, lecturing, participating in symposia, and appearing at the many film and drama festivals dedicated to his work; supporting young playwrights and artists; and, as always, writing new plays of his own. He is the recipient of many awards, including, along with his two Oscars, an Emmy, the Pulitzer Prize for drama, an Outer Critics Circle Award, and induction into the Theatre Hall of Fame. His stature in the film world is suggested by the fact that in 1989 he

4. Many of these telescripts were later transformed into dramas for the stage, including such works as *A Trip to Bountiful, The Traveling Lady,* and *Night of the Storm,* which would later become *Roots in a Parched Ground,* the first of the nine *Cycle* plays.

5. Reinert, "Tender Foote," 136.

was selected as one of the American Film Institute's first three recipients of an honorary doctorate. In 1998 he was elected to the American Academy of Arts and Letters as a member in the Department of Literature; the academy also conferred upon him the Gold Medal for Drama.[6]

It is perhaps ironic, given the range and stature of these accomplishments, that Foote, dramatist, screenwriter, director, and producer for over fifty years, is just beginning to achieve recognition from the academic community. Vincent Canby puts it succinctly in a *New York Times* review: "Mr. Foote has the curious distinction of being possibly the least well-known major American playwright today."[7] His genius has long been acknowledged by practitioners in the field. He found fervent supporters in the famous acting teacher Peggy Feury and the director and teacher Herbert Berghof, founder of the HB Theater in New York, where many of Foote's plays were first staged. Ted Mann, who as one of the five founders of Circle in the Square Theatre in New York has been called the father of Off-Broadway, says, "I've always considered Horton Foote to be one of the great contemporary American playwrights." In directing a Foote play, he says, you have to "quickly find the truth. There's no artifice in his plays. You have to find the 'music' of the play, the theme song for each character."[8]

This matter of Foote's distinctive voice comes up again and again. Film director and producer Alan Pakula speaks with deep respect of Foote's unique voice and artistic integrity: "He [Foote] has a specific voice, a specific style, and he has never abandoned it, even though it cost him. He has never cut his talent to the fashion of the time." Actor Robert Duvall, whose first film role was that of the silent Boo

6. For a more detailed account of Foote's development as an artist as well as further biographical background, see Marion Castleberry, "Remembering Wharton, Texas," in *Horton Foote: A Casebook,* ed. Gerald C. Wood (New York: Garland Publishing, 1998), 13–33. For a detailed Foote chronology, see pp. 7–11 in Wood, ed., *Foote: A Casebook.* For a bibliography of Foote's plays, teleplays, and screenplays, see Gerald C. Wood, *Horton Foote and the Theater of Intimacy* (Baton Rouge: Louisiana State University Press, 1999), 115–25.

7. Vincent Canby, "For Horton Foote the Pictures Speak Volumes," review of *Talking Pictures,* by Horton Foote, *New York Times,* October 2, 1994, p. H5.

8. Ted Mann, interview with the author, January 8, 1999.

Radley in Foote's adaptation of *To Kill a Mockingbird,* says, "You can't make too many false moves with his writing. You can't push it. You can't propel it. You have to just let it lay there. It's like rural Chekhov, simple but deep."[9] Actor and director Robert Ellermann writes, "Horton Foote is an artist of the rarest form of theatre. He is a dramatic poet: each play *is* the experience which formed it," and adds, "Horton Foote is our mystic in the theatre."[10] His ear for authentic language, reflected in his dialogue, has given the many distinguished actors associated with him over the years—Geraldine Page, Gregory Peck, Robert Duvall, Steven Hill, Kim Stanley, James and Matthew Broderick, and Hallie Foote, to name a few—some of their best lines. In a congratulatory letter on the occasion of Foote's winning the Alley Theater Award in 1991, Gregory Peck wrote, "Thanks for giving me the best role of my life."[11]

Like these actors and directors, theater critics and social commentators also acknowledge the power of Foote's work. Marian Burkhart concludes the article quoted earlier by saying, "Foote has assessed American character, American myth, and American ambiance more accurately than has just about any other figure in the American theater." Frank Rich writes in a *New York Times* review of *The Roads to Home,* "Any list of America's living literary wonders must include Horton Foote." Vincent Canby says that Foote's plays "are cut so close to the bone of reality, they're so uncompromising and clear-eyed in their quotidian concerns, that there's nothing much to date them except the times in which they are set." Fellow writers respond in a similar fashion. Novelist and poet Reynolds Price says of the *Cycle* that he is "confident it will take its rightful earned place near the center of our largest American dramatic achievements."[12] Harper Lee has

9. Alan Pakula, quoted in Samuel G. Freedman, introduction to *Two Plays,* xv; Robert Duvall, quoted in Freedman, *Two Plays,* xxiv.

10. Robert Ellermann, introduction to vol. 2 of *Horton Foote: Collected Plays,* by Horton Foote (Lyme, N.H.: Smith and Kraus, 1996), n.p.

11. Gregory Peck to Horton Foote, n.d., box 10, Horton Foote Collection, De-Golyer Library, Southern Methodist University, Dallas, Texas.

12. Burkhart, "Horton Foote's Many Roads Home," 115; Frank Rich, "1920s Lives That Leap into the Present," review of *The Roads to Home,* by Horton Foote, *New York Times,* September 18, 1992, p. C2; Canby, "Pictures Speak Volumes," H5; and Reynolds Price, introduction to *"Courtship," "Valentine's Day," "1918": Three Plays from "The Orphans' Home Cycle,"* by Horton Foote (New York: Grove Press,

commented that Foote's adaptation of *To Kill a Mockingbird* is so true to her novel that many assume the dialogue was lifted from the book (it wasn't), while William Faulkner, after seeing Foote's adaptation of his short story "Tomorrow," offered to share the copyright with him, a virtually unheard-of gesture.

It is perhaps surprising, then, given the respect Foote is accorded by his peers in the theater world, that the academic community has been slow to recognize the depth, complexity, and beauty of his dramas. It was, for instance, not until 1986 that the *MLA Bibliography* first mentioned his work, some forty years after he wrote his first play. Within the past decade, however, this has at last begun to change, beginning with the Grove Press edition of *The Orphans' Home Cycle* and Gerald C. Wood's edition of Foote's one-act plays in 1989. Articles analyzing his plays, teleplays, and screenplays have begun to appear with increasing regularity in academic journals, along with master's theses and dissertations dedicated to his work. In 1994–95, the off-off-Broadway Signature Theater devoted its entire season to four of his plays (the fourth of the Signature's single-playwright seasons), winning glowing reviews from the critics; at the end of the season, Foote was awarded the Pulitzer Prize for another play, *The Young Man from Atlanta*. In 1997, the first critical anthology dedicated to his work, *Horton Foote: A Casebook,* edited by Gerald C. Wood, was brought out by Garland Publishing, and two years later, the first single-author, full-length analysis of Foote's canon, *Horton Foote and the Theater of Intimacy,* also by Wood, was published.[13] Foote studies have begun to come into their own.

Though Foote's works encompass multiple genres, with plots that focus on everything from a woman who plays the piano at the silent movies (*Talking Pictures*) to a man who dreams of being an astronaut (*The Land of the Astronauts*), they are united by certain unmistakable characteristics that mark them as his own. This begins, as critics frequently note, with his highly specific evocation of place—here, rural

---

1987), xiii. Subsequent citations refer to this edition and will be given parenthetically in the text as *Three Plays.*

13. Rebecca Luttrell Briley's *You Can Go Home Again: The Focus on Family in the Works of Horton Foote* (New York: Peter Lang, 1993), based on her dissertation of 1990 and preceding Wood's *Theater of Intimacy* by six years, is more limited in its scope.

East Texas, specifically, the Gulf coast town of Harrison (read Wharton), with Houston providing the big-city alternative to which (or from which) characters flee. This is a world that Foote knows deep in his bones. He grew up hearing stories about his cousins and aunts and uncles, as well as the other inhabitants of Wharton, falling asleep every night listening to his parents exchange the local gossip as they sat on the porch outside his bedroom window. His intimate knowledge of the inhabitants of this small world provides a depth that allows his characters to avoid any tinge of regional quaintness. It is a tribute to both this deep understanding and his mastery of his craft that he is able to capture the nuances of character and custom that evoke with such clarity another time and place.

Foote's control of language is also a major factor in his success, since the texture of this world is conveyed largely in the characters' speech patterns. What is perhaps most interesting in this regard is not so much what Foote's personae say as what they don't say. Their diction, for the most part, is limited to the everyday speech of ordinary people. There are few highly lyrical passages or poetic speeches. Indeed, dialogue in a typical Foote drama is stripped down to the bare minimum, with many speeches consisting of only a few words: "Yes mam," "No mam."

Foote's plots, like his language, are also understated. Uneventful in the usual ways, they are sometimes seen by critics as undramatic. While it is true that Foote eschews the usual structures and devises that shape dramatic action—conflicting ideas or characters, suspense, intrigue, and the like, to say that nothing happens is to miss the point. The action in the *Cycle* plays, as in virtually all of Foote's work, is interior; the transformations take place within, not without. The young Horace of *Roots in a Parched Ground,* for example, realizes at the end of that play that he is no longer a child. His father has died; his mother has remarried and moved to Houston with her new husband and with Lily Dale, Horace's sister, leaving Horace behind. A monumental change has occurred, one which will alter his life irrevocably, yet this is observed dramatically only in a brief exchange Horace has with his friend Lloyd when he says about his new job on the Gautier plantation, "I'm on my own," and the conversation returns to another subject. Gerald Wood refers to this strategy as "dedramatization," commenting that Foote's plays "discover [their] subject[s] by mostly disregarding plot."[14]

A final distinguishing characteristic has to do with theme. At the heart of Foote's dramas, as well as his works for television and film, is a sense of the ultimate mystery of human experience: why some lives turn out well and others don't, why some people thrive while others, facing similar challenges, fall apart. Foote himself comments, "I have enormous compassion for the human condition. A great admiration for what people have to put up with and endure—the way they survive or don't survive." Or again: "I'm always amazed at the grace of people, how they take adversity, how they face afflictions and addictions, how they manage to meet impossible things. If you have to say there is a theme to my work, it's this theme of people's courage."[15] Where, his plays ask, does this special grace come from?

While there are no easy answers to these questions, to understand the contours of the problem one must begin with family, the sine qua non of Foote's dramas. Nowhere is this more apparent than in *The Orphans' Home Cycle*, the nine plays which Foote wrote from his retreat in the New Hampshire woods based on stories of his father's youth and young adulthood. Although all of Foote's characters to some extent emerge from his experiences growing up in Wharton, these nine plays are unique in his canon in telling the story of his immediate family. Written shortly after the death of his parents, the plays have characters and events that reflect, for the most part, the actual life story of his father and mother.

Foote wrote *The Orphans' Home Cycle* at a critical moment in his life, having lost both of his parents within a two-year period, and being in the full flower of his artistic powers. Like O'Neill's confronting what he called the "ghosts of his past" from the seclusion of Tao House high in the hills outside San Francisco, these plays, though not as haunted as *The Iceman Cometh, Long Day's Journey into Night,* and the mellower *A Moon for the Misbegotten,* reflect the retrospective

14. Gerald C. Wood, "The Nature of Mystery in *The Young Man from Atlanta,*" in *Foote: A Casebook,* 187.

15. Irv Broughton, ed., *The Writer's Mind: Interviews with American Authors,* vol. 2 (Fayetteville: University of Arkansas Press, 1990), 21; Samir Hachem, "Foote-Work," *Horizon,* April 1986, p. 40.

wisdom of a great artist looking back at his life. Sounding much like O'Neill, Foote says, "I wrote the Cycle plays without knowing whether they'd ever be staged. . . . I just became obsessed with them." Finding himself the patriarch of the family upon his parents' death, he said that he "suddenly had this enormous desire . . . to speculate about them. They had had, I thought, a very moving life."[16]

I mention O'Neill because I find significant parallels between the two dramatists. Not only do both artists write their greatest works in a mature phase of their careers, retrospectively examining their early life experiences and those of their immediate family members, writing in relative seclusion miles from the actual scene of these life events; and not only do both become obsessed with the writing, pushing on even when the eventual production of the plays was in question (or, in O'Neill's case, in the distant future). Both artists are attempting an achievement unique in the canon of American drama: a cycle of plays, each play being complete in itself, yet the whole cycle telling the story of both a family and the larger community of which it is a part. With the exception of August Wilson, who is writing the history of the black experience in twentieth-century America, with one play per decade, only O'Neill and Foote have attempted (in Foote's case, *completed*) a cycle of this scope.

O'Neill's projected cycle, *A Tale of Possessors, Self-Dispossessed,* which began with three plays and expanded eventually to eleven, was to trace the merger of two families, the New England aristocratic Harfords and the Irish Catholic immigrant Melodys, with the marriage of Simon Harford and Sara Melody. As he tracked this family through six generations, beginning in 1755 and ending with what was then the present, the early 1930s, O'Neill planned to simultaneously trace significant developments in the culture at large. Although he never completed this magnum opus, finishing only one play (*A Touch of the Poet*) to his satisfaction and accidentally leaving behind unfinished drafts of two more (*More Stately Mansions* and *The Calms of Capricorn*), scholars have been able to reconstruct the overall plot

16. Laurin Porter, "An Interview with Horton Foote," *Studies in American Drama, 1945–Present* 6, no. 2 (1991): 181.

line of what would have been, if completed, a work of enormous scope and power.[17]

Foote's cycle, while more limited in scope, functions in much the same way. The nine plays of *The Orphans' Home Cycle* trace the story of Horace Robedaux (based on Horton Foote's father, Albert Horton Foote) from the point at which he is orphaned at age twelve until he is a husband and father himself. Set in the Gulf Coast town of Harrison, it covers twenty-six years, from 1902 to 1928, a period which saw the decline of the cotton-dependent small town and the emergence of an oil- and industry-based economy, the transition from rural to urban life, and the tragedies of World War I and the flu epidemic of 1918.

It is a moving story, one which gathers momentum as it goes. By the final scenes the reader has encountered three generations and three families (those of Horace's mother, his father, and his wife) and learned a good deal about the other residents of Harrison, as well, with the town becoming a kind of extended family. As in Faulkner's Yoknapatawpha saga, with which it has been compared, Foote's cycle eventually extends beyond the story of the Robedauxs and Harrison, Texas, to the entire South, tapping finally the depths of human experience. The carefully detailed cultural and historical references, down to the period songs which Foote weaves into the action,[18] do more

17. For a detailed history of the composition of O'Neill's *Cycle* plays and a summary of the time period covered by each, consult Travis Bogard, *Contour in Time: The Plays of Eugene O'Neill*, rev. ed. (New York: Oxford University Press, 1988), 371–94 and Appendix 1, 471–77. For further information, consult Laurin Porter, *The Banished Prince: Time, Memory, and Ritual in the Late Plays of Eugene O'Neill* (Ann Arbor: UMI Research Press, 1988), 113 n. 6.

18. Like O'Neill, Foote is deliberate and accurate in his choice of songs, whether they serve as part of the action (for example, when Elizabeth in *Courtship* plays the sad ballad "Nellie Grey" on the piano while her sister Laura sings, the lyrics suggest the tragedy which will soon befall their friend Sybil Thomas), a backdrop or contrast to the action (the dance music which floats in from offstage in this same play reminds Laura and Elizabeth, who are not allowed to attend the dance, of all they are missing), or a reinforcement of theme (as with the patriotic World War I songs like "Over There" and "It's a Long Way to Tipperary," sung in *1918*). For a discussion of Foote's use of found music and the influence of Charles Ives on the composition of the *Cycle,* see Crystal Brian, " 'To Be Quiet and Listen': *The Orphans' Home Cycle* and the Music of Charles Ives," in *Foote: A Casebook,* 89–108.

than provide an interesting backdrop for the play's events. These plays, like O'Neill's, present as profound an understanding of a culture as they do a family.

To illustrate this point as well as the contrast between Foote and O'Neill, it might be helpful to provide a brief summary of the dramas before proceeding further for those readers who are unfamiliar with the *Cycle* or haven't encountered all nine plays. *Roots in a Parched Ground,* the *Cycle*'s first play, introduces twelve-year-old Horace Robedaux at a critical juncture in his life. His mother and father have separated, and the two families, the Thorntons on his mother's side and the Robedauxs on his father's, are at war. Horace and his younger sister, Lily Dale, are caught between two camps, each with its own version of the split. By the play's end, Horace's father, Paul Horace, has died, and his mother, Corella, has remarried a man named Pete Davenport, who has little use for her son. Deferring to her new husband, Corella moves with him to Houston, taking Lily Dale and leaving Horace behind with her grandparents.

He ends up moving to a desolate plantation in nearby Floyd's Lane, Texas, with his Uncle Albert, a story taken up in *Convicts,* the next play. Albert, one of the *Cycle*'s ne'er-do-well gambling addicts, is supposedly looking after Horace, but it's clear he's not. Working in the plantation's store, hoping to save enough money to buy a tombstone for his father's grave (one of the central motifs of the *Cycle*), Horace is befriended by the black servants Ben and Martha, who try to shield him from the violence that seethes beneath the plantation's surface as well as from the erratic, drunken owner, Soll Gautier. In the course of this play, Soll, like Paul Horace, dies, only this time Horace is present at the deathbed, at Soll's insistence. The death scene is treated almost comically, with Soll seeming to die, "rising" again, then dying for good, but the impression it makes on the sensitive boy is anything but funny.

Lily Dale takes up Horace's story six years later, when, at age twenty, he travels to Houston in a last effort to become a part of his mother's family. Rebuffed by Pete, he tries to leave but falls deathly ill and is forced to stay until he recovers. His exchanges with his pampered, spoiled, and self-centered sister, Lily Dale, reveal a striking contrast between her and Horace, a self-sufficient, reflective, and compassionate young man. We see these same traits in evidence in the sequel play, *The Widow Claire,* which presents another cul-de-sac in Horace's journey toward family. Though his courtship of Claire, widowed at twenty-eight, does not end in marriage, we see his sensitivity and kindness toward both Claire and her two children (whose ages are close to Horace's and Lily Dale's in *Roots*) and his determination to make something of himself: he will go to Houston as planned to take a business course, while Claire chooses to marry an older man for the security he offers.

This decision clears the way for Horace's marriage to Elizabeth Vaughn, which is set up in *Courtship,* the *Cycle*'s fifth play, and tracked throughout the remaining plays. In *Courtship,* we learn of the Vaughns' opposition to Horace and Elizabeth's marriage, and in *Valentine's Day,* which focuses on the early marriage of the young couple, that they had to elope. Their deep devotion to one another is clear, and in the course of this play, in which we learn a great deal about the other boarders in Horace and Elizabeth's rooming house as well as the newlyweds themselves, they are reconciled to her parents and await the birth of their first child.

At the beginning of *1918,* the seventh play, Horace and Elizabeth are happily married and the parents of a baby girl, Jenny, but the course of world events, specifically, World War I and the flu epidemic of 1918, plays havoc with their lives. By the play's end, although Horace recovers from his near-fatal bout with the flu, Jenny has died. Although there are elements of hope—the war ends, and Elizabeth is pregnant with their second child—the loss of their infant daughter is a devastating one.

The final two plays, *Cousins* and *The Death of Papa,* tell the story of Horace at middle age, now a proprietor of a dry goods store, struggling to provide for his family. In what can be seen as a mock-comic response to the issue of Horace as orphan introduced in *Roots,* in *Cousins* he is depicted as related to nearly everyone in town. This play tells the story of two of Horace's cousins, Cousin Lewis and Cousin Minnie, whose lives have turned out sadly, though in very different ways. Again, we learn much about Horace and the quality of his choices as we compare him with those who people his world. In *The Death of Papa,* as Elizabeth's revered and powerful father, Henry Vaughn, dies, Horace is increasingly regarded as the family patriarch, a role he resists accepting, even as Elizabeth's brother, another of

Foote's alcoholic ne'er-do-wells, botches the handling of the family estate. This play also introduces ten-year-old Horace, Jr., Foote's own counterpart in the play, an observant, sensitive boy and artist in the making.[19]

While the overt contours of O'Neill's and Foote's projects may strike us as similar, the tracking of two families over several generations set against a specific historical-cultural backdrop, the tone, texture, and style of the two playwrights could not present a sharper contrast. A quick glance at a passage of an O'Neill play compared to one of Foote's reveals, in the first instance, vast differences in their use of language. O'Neill's plays are rich in dialects, painstakingly crafted for accuracy as well as effect. Perhaps the most brilliant example of this is *The Iceman Cometh,* whose cast of characters includes a Briton, a Boer, an African American gambler, a Neapolitan American bartender, three "tarts" from the slums of New York, a graduate of Harvard Law School, and of course, the requisite Irishmen; critic John Henry Raleigh calls *Iceman* O'Neill's supreme "linguistic symphony." His language at its best, in plays like *Long Day's Journey into Night* and *A Moon for the Misbegotten,* for instance, achieves a level of intensity and lyricism beyond that of everyday speech. One thinks of Edmund's bowsprit speech or Mary's pronouncements about the past being the present. Foote's characters, on the other hand, all sound the same. Their lexicon and speech patterns, for all practical purposes, are interchangeable. And his language, rather than drawing attention to itself, seems to disappear. His style is characterized by a deliberate lack of poetic figures or imagery.

Their plots, likewise, stand in stark contrast. While O'Neill's are structured to reveal information gradually, building to a climactic confrontation of opposing forces, Foote's plots appear at first glance to be rather uneventful, as discussed earlier. There are no overt villains or even clearly opposing points of view, no secrets withheld that are revealed in the end, no sense of a strong climax which arrives at a resolution. The playwright with whom he's most often compared, not surprisingly, is Chekhov, another master of plays in which inaction seems to dominate.

---

19. See the appendix for a chart summarizing the time, place, and action of all nine plays.

Yet despite his stripped-down language and understated plots, Foote's plays achieve enormous power, both in their staged and in their filmed versions. The obvious question becomes, How is this accomplished? Surely these dramas are not as uncontrived as they appear. It is the question that Reynolds Price poses in his introduction to volume two of the *Cycle*. Pointing to the fact that when pressed, critics have been hard put to account for the power of such works as an Oriental scroll-painting, a Blake lyric, or an Appalachian ballad, he argues that "modern aesthetic criticism . . . has proved generally helpless in the presence of apparent 'simplicity,' the illusory purity of means and ends toward universally comprehensible results. Where is there a genuinely illuminating discussion of Blake's 'Tyger,' Gluck's 'Dance of the Blessed Spirits,' or Joan Baez's traversals of the Child ballads?—one that helps us understand *how* and, above all, *why* such complex but supremely satisfactory ends are achieved in such small and evidently transparent vehicles." The problem as he sees it is that "the mechanistic methods of modern critics require complexity of means before their intricate gears can begin to grind." He goes on to describe how profoundly he was moved by Foote's film, *Tender Mercies*, adding, "Explain to me how actors—even as perfect as those he found, even so resourceful a director—could employ so few and such rhetorically uncomplicated speeches toward the flawless achievement of such a calmly profound and memorable face-to-face contemplation of human degradation and regeneration. I confidently suggest that even St. Augustine in his *Confessions* went no further toward the heart of that luminous dark mystery than Horton Foote. And I—a novelist, poet, playwright, and critic—cannot hope to begin to tell you how he has made that longest and hardest of journeys."[20] The questions that Price poses, it seems to me, are precisely on target. What appears to be profoundly simple is, in the last analysis, simply profound. The purpose of the present book is to explore these matters as they are manifested in Foote's masterpiece, *The Orphans' Home Cycle*, examining the playwright's themes, issues, and concerns as well as the strategies he devises for fleshing them out.

Both content and form are of great importance in fully appreciating the nature of Foote's achievement. These plays raise issues of con-

20. Price, introduction to *Three Plays*, ix–x, xi.

siderable complexity, addressing problems that have challenged the great thinkers of Western history; Price's reference to St. Augustine is not inappropriate. At the same time, they do so in ways which redefine accepted notions about drama as a genre. Eschewing the standard literary tools that most contemporary dramatists employ—stage directions with explicit descriptions of setting and personae as well as blocking and cues about affect; complicated plot lines, with twists and turns, withheld information, and strongly opposed forces struggling for dominance; and poetic or at least heightened language—Foote recasts dramatic form to achieve his ends in unique ways, as the following chapters illustrate. Both in his structuring of the cycle as a whole and within individual plays, he employs devices that are more commonly associated with the novel than drama: recurring motifs, character doubling and tripling, parallel and inverted episodes, even the pairing of entire plays. In this interplay of character and image, of play against play, he breaks new ground, bending drama, that most restrictive of genres, in new and striking ways.

The following chapters consider the questions Foote's plays raise: How do we become the people we are? Why do some choose to "be good," to quote Horace, Jr., while others succumb to chaos and despair? What role do custom, tradition, and social mores play in the process of identity formation, and, conversely, to what extent is one free to choose one's life path? And finally, how do the plays' structure and form both shape and comment on these issues?

Chapters 2 and 3 focus on questions of identity from psychological and cultural perspectives. I begin with a discussion of family, where the process of identity formation begins and one's sense of self is most indelibly stamped. Chapter 2, "Horace, Son and Father: The Role of Family in Shaping Identity," considers the question of individual identity within the context of family relationships and pressures, focusing primarily on *Lily Dale, Cousins,* and *The Death of Papa.* In *Lily Dale,* the third play of the *Cycle,* when Horace is rejected by his stepfather, Pete, now orphaned symbolically as he was physically in *Roots in a Parched Ground,* he is forced to acknowledge that his family has failed him and left him to make his own way in the world. *Cousins* and *The Death of Papa,* the final two plays of the *Cycle,* take up Horace's story as a mature man, now a father and budding entrepreneur. *Cousins,* while on one level a comic treatment of the complicated nature of extended families, builds to a climactic confrontation between Horace and his mother, who lies in a Houston hospital near death, bringing to the surface feelings of abandonment and betrayal that Horace has harbored since his father died twenty-three years earlier. In *Papa,* as his wealthy and influential father-in-law, Mr. Vaughn, dies, Horace moves to the center of both families, the new if somewhat unwilling patriarch. Horace's movement from margin to center, orphan to patriarch, allows for an extended analysis of the ongoing role family plays in the individual life. Although our sense of ourselves is first derived from our family, whose values and life narratives we at least initially adopt without questioning, to grow as autonomous individuals we learn to challenge those values and rearticulate the narratives, making them our own. Through the lens of Horace's life, this chapter considers the ways in which family is both a positive and negative influence, expanding one's view of one's self and the world in some ways, limiting it in others.

Chapter 3, "Cultural Influences: Community, Language, and Identity," examines a wider circle of influence, that of the culture at large, focusing specifically on the ways in which Foote uses language to deal with the relationship between cultural and individual identity. Thus while identity can be regarded as a product of one's unique family of origin, an accident of fate unevenly parceled out, one must also factor in the leveling influence of the cultural-historical moment into which one is born—a less personal but still powerful determinant. This chapter examines Foote's use of language, arguing that it is unique in American drama. Limiting himself to the everyday language of ordinary, small-town folk, his language, sparse, unadorned, and restrained, reflects and embodies cultural codes which must be decoded by the audience in order to understand the action and the issues. Furthermore, no longer able to cling to the conventions of traditional theater, the audience—like the characters—must sift through the various retellings of community stories in an effort to discover the truth, or that version which most closely approximates what seems to be true. From this perspective, Horace's identity, like those of all of the personae, cannot be separated from that of the culture in which he lives. As the cultural and linguistic analysis of this chapter reveals, drawing upon *Roots in a Parched Ground* and *Courtship* in particular, Horace can in a sense only think the thoughts and speak the words that his culture provides—or at least, choose from among those thoughts and words. Though it is his unique life story that unfolds, the culture is speaking through him, as it were.

The next two chapters, Chapters 4 and 5, which focus on aesthetic principles of the plays, move the discussion to a slightly more abstract level. Foote's strategy in *The Orphans' Home* of situating self-contained individual plays within the larger context of the *Cycle* as a whole reflects the intersection of individual and collective identity examined in Chapters 2 and 3. As Horace is both an individual and a member of society, so each play simultaneously stands alone and is a part of something larger than itself. Having divested himself of two of the playwright's chief tools, imaged language and conventional plotting, Foote uses structure in innovative ways to communicate his themes. In Chapter 4, "Polyphonic Voices: Repetition and the Multiplication of Meaning," I outline three of these strategies: the use of recurring motifs, which like a musical leitmotif serve to unify the individual plays; the doubling of characters—orphans, gamblers, alcoholics, pairs of brothers (in one play alone there are *five* pairs); and parallel and inverted episodes—the death of infant daughters, for instance, and the orphaning of Horace, his father-in-law, and his stepfather at the same age. I end this chapter with an extended analysis of *Valentine's Day,* the sixth play in the *Cycle,* showing the ways in which these structural strategies stretch conventional dramatic form. I argue, moreover, that the intercutting of Horace's narrative with those of other family members and townfolk demonstrates Foote's belief in the interconnectedness of individual and collective identity. The fact that Horace's story subsumes and is subsumed in the life narratives of the other characters is reflected in the dramatic structure.

Chapter 5, "Point-Counterpoint: Paired Plays, Multiple Perspectives," carries this argument one step further, examining three sets of paired plays: *Roots in a Parched Ground* and *Convicts, The Widow Claire* and *Courtship,* and (in less detail) *Cousins* and *The Death of Papa.* Each pair focuses on a different stage and critical experience in Horace's life: childhood and the death of a father (*Roots*) and father manqué (*Convicts*), young manhood and the choice of a wife (*Claire* and *Courtship*), and adulthood and the death or near-death of a parent (*Cousins* and *Papa*). The strategy of pairing these plays—playing out different endings to the same story, essentially—focuses our attention on the multiple options present to Horace at each point and invites us to consider further the question of self-determination: What makes Horace choose one course of action and reject another? What factors come to bear at these crucial junctures? How free are any of us to compose our own life stories?

The final two chapters move to a still more abstract level in considering these questions. If Chapters 2 and 3 examine the *Cycle* plays from cultural and psychological perspectives and Chapters 4 and 5 focus on the contributions of their aesthetic and formal dimensions, Chapters 6 and 7 address questions of philosophical and spiritual import. Chapter 6, "The Presence of the Past: *The Orphans' Home Cycle* and the Nature of Time," considers the nature of the past's impact upon the present; that is, how time can work to either imprison us or set us free—a question which undergirds every issue raised thus far. I approach this matter by comparing Foote's understanding of the nature of time and its relationship to individual experience with that of Faulkner and O'Neill, the giants of Southern literature and American drama, respectively, contrasting their tragic views of time with Foote's more optimistic position. While for Faulkner time functions primarily on the mythic level as compared to the individual experience of O'Neill's characters, in Foote's *Cycle* time is embedded in the context of family. Foote's presentation of time and its impact upon individual experience is actually quite complex. The first and perhaps most obvious modality of time in the *Cycle* is the chronological, linear march of events, in this case Horace's movement from orphan/son to patriarch/father, a progression which is played out against the backdrop of historical events, most noticeably in *1918,* the only play to take its title from a date. Several motifs reinforce this progression and invite us to reflect on the relationship of past to present, the graveyard being a prime example.

But while time's linear nature is emphasized by the changes Horace undergoes as his life story unfolds, Foote shapes both individual scenes and the *Cycle* as a whole to reveal another dimension of time, one less rational and objective than the calibrating of years. As Horace becomes the repository of thousands of individual experiences, a kind of walking history, he "contains" the past within the present moment. In certain key scenes, this boundary between *then* and *now* breaks down as Horace (and Elizabeth, in other scenes) participates simultaneously in past and present in a phenomenon that goes beyond mere memory. A third layer of complexity, given the nature of the *Cycle*'s structure, is the audience's ability to read forwards and backwards, with our response to Horace's confrontations with Corella as an adult, for instance, colored by our image of Horace the orphaned son in *Roots*. Finally, in this chapter I contrast the role that the concept of the ideal and its loss plays in Faulkner and O'Neill with Foote's quite different version of the drama of paradise.

My final chapter, "An Orphans' Home: Family, Place, and Redemption," situates Foote squarely in the tradition of Southern literature, with its emphasis on the importance of place and family. Drawing upon his screenplays for *Tender Mercies* and *A Trip to Bountiful* as well as the *Cycle* plays, however, I argue that unlike other Southern writers, Foote's emphasis is not so much on returning home as on leaving it, and that "home" in his works is not defined so much by a specific locale as it is a network of relationships, a family. His dramas, like his films, are informed by the archetypal pattern of leaving home and returning again, of death and resurrection. Place, an amalgam of community and family, is ultimately only redemptive insofar as it is defined not in terms of a specific location but a geography of the heart. To this end, I argue, Foote's is not just a Southern but an *American* voice. In the tradition of many American writers before him, he explores the relationship between the one and the many, between self-reliance and mutual dependence, but from a twentieth-century perspective acquainted with alienation and despair. These nine plays, with their gentle, unswerving heroes, stand at the center of his achievement, presenting us with a world composed of orphans, but one which is nonetheless home.

2

HORACE, SON AND FATHER

The Role of Family in Shaping Identity

In the works of Horton Foote, any discussion of individual identity must begin with family. To a large extent, this emphasis can be seen as emerging from Foote's Southern roots. Cultural historians have repeatedly noted that in the South, one is identified in terms of one's family, one's "people," a fact which is reflected in the most common of social customs. The standard "How is your mother?" (or father or husband or wife), for example, follows quickly upon—and is tantamount to—"Hello." In a sense, it is a greeting, not a question, just as "How are you?" is not really an inquiry about the state of one's health. The emphasis placed on the family name, on family honor, reflects the high value the South places on history and tradition; reputation lies not as much in individual accomplishment as in the accumulated histories of those who have preceded you. One is known within the context of family.

This cultural phenomenon can have both positive and negative consequences. In the best case, it can provide individuals with security, stability, and a clearly defined set of values. A child raised within a family with generations which have preceded him or her, especially if within the same town or geographic area, enters a stream of life. A certain sense of security obtains from hearing stories of grandparents and great-grandparents, aunts and uncles, all of whom have been waiting, as it were, for the arrival of this newest family member. He or she becomes a part of an ongoing saga, taking up the story and carrying it forward. As a member of the clan, the child slips easily into a pre-formed identity, having his or her place already carved out within the community. Along with the security and stability which this confers comes a known set of values by which to organize one's experience. In the best case, these will be positive values which will help the child grow into a happy, well-adjusted, and productive adult, ready to assume adult responsibilities.

As we know, of course, it is seldom this easy. Family histories are not always salutary; the stories by which one comes to know life experience are often less than ideal guides. Nor are family values necessarily life-affirming. The daily newspapers are full of stories that demonstrate what happens when families fail to convey positive values to their children, fail to give them guidance and love. A different problem occurs with children who aren't born into stable family units, but rather families that are dissolved or broken; children without fathers or mothers or others committed to caring for them. If we come to know who we are through our interactions within a family unit, what happens if we have no family?

Finally, how does one go about defining oneself over against the pre-existing family values, attitudes, and ideals? If the strength of the family as a socializing unit derives from the established codes of behavior which it passes on to the next generation, it can also become a kind of moral and psychological straitjacket. How does the child, insinuated into a habit of seeing and being, learn to form his or her own judgments? Emily Dickinson takes up this matter in her poem "I'm ceded,"[1] when she refers to "The name They dropped upon my face / With water, in the country church" (ll. 2–3). It is a "name," an identity, which she rejects as an adult, preferring "*this* time—Adequate—Erect, / With Will to choose, or to reject, / . . . just a Crown—" (ll. 17–19, italics mine). As an adult, "adequate" and "erect," with knowledge, life-experience, and wisdom, one can make one's own philosophical and moral decisions, choose one's own identity. But how, precisely, does that rite of passage from dependent child to autonomous adult take place? And why is it that some children manage to negotiate the tricky passage to adulthood while others fail?

1. Emily Dickinson, *Final Harvest: Emily Dickinson's Poems,* ed. Thomas H. Johnson (Boston: Little Brown, 1961), no. 508.

On one level, this question shapes all nine plays in *The Orphans'*
Home Cycle, which trace Horace Robedaux's journey from child to
adult, son to father. While all the plays add to our understanding of
this process, three are particularly instructive: *Lily Dale, Cousins,* and
The Death of Papa. Lily Dale, the third play of the nine, takes up the
story of Horace as a young man of twenty traveling to Houston to
visit his mother, Corella, and sister, Lily Dale. Having lived on his
own since his father died eight years earlier, he hopes to become part
of their family in some fashion, in spite of his hostile stepfather, Pete
Davenport. In *Cousins,* the *Cycle's* eighth play, we witness the deep
love of Horace, now thirty-five, and his wife of eight years, Elizabeth.
A family man himself now, the father of two sons and a daughter who
died in infancy, he is struggling to make ends meet as the proprietor
of a men's store. The action centers around the near-death of Corella
and Horace's confrontation with her in a Houston hospital. Though
a serious matter, revealing Horace's deep pain at his mother's abandonment of him in his youth, it is embedded in a semi-comic context
of the complications of extended family, the "cousins" of the title.
The Death of Papa, the *Cycle's* final play, begins with the death of
Elizabeth's father, Henry Vaughn, three years later. In this play Horace, initially rejected by the Vaughns as too wild and irresponsible for
Elizabeth, moves to the position of family patriarch, replacing his
father-in-law, however reluctantly, when Elizabeth's ne'er-do-well
brother squanders the family fortune and ends up killing a man in a
drunken brawl. While these dramas trace Horace's search for a family,
the leitmotif of all nine plays, on a deeper level they reveal truths
about families per se and how they function to both nurture and stifle
individual identity. We learn about this process by tracing not just
Horace's story, but those of other family members as well.

This is the case with *Lily Dale,* for instance, a play which though
primarily about Horace is named for his younger sister (or perhaps,
in an evocative ambiguity, the song "Lily Dale," for which his sister
is named). The title invites us to focus on Lily Dale, who at eighteen
is pampered, spoiled, and self-centered, Horace's opposite in almost
every way. As we observe her response to Horace and his intrusion,
as she sees it, into their family unit, noticing the sharp contrast between the two siblings, we wonder how she became the way she is.
Why is she so shallow and self-absorbed, while Horace, facing much

greater difficulties, is gentle, kind, and self-sufficient? To what extent are they shaped by circumstances beyond their control and to what degree can we attribute their character to their own choices? And how, finally, does family figure into the equation?

A crucial element in Lily Dale's sense of herself and her place in her family unit is the fact that when Corella married Pete, shortly after Paul Horace, her first husband's, death, they took Lily Dale with them to Houston to live while Horace was left to fend for himself. We watch this take place at the end of *Roots in a Parched Ground* in one of the most painful scenes in *The Orphans' Home Cycle*. Awaiting his mother's first visit with her new husband, Horace anticipates moving to Houston with them and studying law, as he had promised his father before he died. When Pete rejects him curtly, saying "lawyers are a dime a dozen," and Corella, deferring to her husband, tells Horace that they don't have room for him, he quietly withdraws, later telling his friends in typical Foote understatement, "I'm on my own."[2]

Lily Dale, on the other hand, becomes the object of Pete's affection, as she is quick to remind Horace whenever possible. Shortly after he arrives in Houston for his first-ever visit to their home, for example, Lily Dale says, in reference to her piano, "When Mama and Mr. Davenport first got married, he said he had always wanted a daughter and though he weren't a rich man, he was going to spoil me in all ways and make up for the daddy I never had. And my heaven, he has. He got me a secondhand piano straight off, and then after I learned to play some, he said he wouldn't have me using a secondhand piano and he went out and bought this one for me" (*Four Plays* 177). She reiterates this idea later, describing how before the marriage Pete "came into the living room of the house we rented then and took me in his arms and he said he was going to be a daddy to me. He was going to see that nothing bad ever happened to me ever again" (*Four Plays* 217). In order to accept Pete, Lily Dale feels she must obliterate the memory of her biological father. In a confronta-

2. Horton Foote, *"Roots in a Parched Ground," "Convicts," "Lily Dale," "The Widow Claire": Four Plays from "The Orphans' Home Cycle"* (New York: Grove Press, 1988), 84. Hereinafter this work will be cited parenthetically by page numbers in the text as *Four Plays*.

tion with Horace, for example, who wants to talk about the past, Lily Dale shouts, in reference to their father, "I don't care about him. How many times do I have to tell you that? I don't care if I ever hear his name again. Mr. Davenport is my father. I want no other. You have no father, but that's not my fault. I have one—the only one I want" (*Four Plays* 231).

Yet as much as she insists that she's secure within this newly con-figured family unit, it's clear that she is confused and concerned about who her "real" family is. She has recurring nightmares about Horace being dead in his coffin, which she experiences as a deep loss, often waking up crying. She also dreams that she is kidnapped and when she returns years later, no one recognizes her. Fears of not being known, of being snatched away from her warm family nest, per-meate her thinking. She's afraid of gypsies, for example, and won't answer the door unless Corella is there. She desperately needs a clearly defined sense of family and her place in it: to know herself, she must know who her family is.

Her thinking on this subject is marked by ambivalence. At one point, after Horace, who has been seriously ill, faints in the heat of an argument, she holds him, crying, "Forgive me, please, please forgive me. . . . I loved Papa. Believe me, I did. Just as much as you did. I loved him, but it hurts me so to talk about him. And it scares me, too," adding, "You're all the family I have, Brother, you and Mama. And we must never leave each other. Promise me you'll never leave me and promise me you'll forgive me" (*Four Plays* 233). Yet a week later she has another dream in which Horace dies and she says, "It's about time." And when her mother plans to bury him in the family plot in Houston, Lily Dale says in her dream, "No we won't. I'll not have him buried with you and Mr. Davenport and me. I want him buried with his father where he belongs" (*Four Plays* 236). Though she disavows this comment when telling the dream to Will, her fiancé, one gets the distinct impression that it reveals her true feelings.

Her underlying hostility toward Horace is also suggested by her overdeveloped sense of competition and her either-or mindset. She tends to experience life in terms of competition, often a competition for everyone's undivided attention. When she plays the piano, for in-stance, which she does rather poorly, everyone must listen. Corella can't look out the window (*Four Plays* 196), Pete can't read his newspaper, no one can talk. She prefers to play her classical pieces, with lots of "runs" in them, even when others request her ragtime songs. On Horace's last night in Houston, when Corella requests that she play a piece that Horace can sing to because "he has such a sweet voice," Lily Dale refuses and manipulates the conversation so that in the end, everyone begs her to play her classical pieces. She uses her piano playing to dominate the scene, making herself the center of attention. It is the same strategy she used in *Roots,* at a crucial point in Corella and Pete's first visit home after getting married. When young Horace works up his courage to ask if he too can come to live with them in Houston, Lily Dale insists on playing the piano and his question gets brushed aside. The exchange, which encapsulates the family dynamic that will set the stage for Horace's future, is worth quoting at length:

> HORACE *(almost mumbling):* I kind of want to go to Houston and live with you, Mama.
>
> CORELLA: What, Son? I didn't hear you. I was listening to Lily Dale [who is playing the piano].
>
> PETE *(interrupting):* Shh . . . shh. . . .
>
> CORELLA: Tell me later, Son, when she's finished.
>
> (*Four Plays* 80–81)

When he does repeat himself at last, saying he wants to go to school in Houston, Lily Dale interjects, "Go to school in Houston? Why, they wouldn't even let you in the first grade in Houston" (*Four Plays* 81). It is typical of her to exclude Horace so that she can have all the attention herself.

Lily Dale's either-or thinking is also reflected in her limited understanding of relationships. She needs to be reassured that Corella loves her more than Horace, as if love is a finite commodity, and any love shown to Horace will mean less for her. She even wants to know, in that regard, when the subject of childbirth arises, who caused Corella more pain, herself or Horace. Everything becomes a competition. Thus she cannot tolerate the possibility that Pete might learn to accept Horace, since that would, in her mind, dethrone her, and at every possible opportunity, she conspires to prevent their rapprochement.

Lily Dale's habitual dichotomization carries over to her under-standing of her family and her relationship to the past. In an effort to define her position in this split family, she has demonized the Robe-dauxs, her father's side of the family, and cast her lot with the Thorn-tons, Corella's family, as well as with her stepfather, Pete. In an altercation with Horace, for instance, having accused him of being jealous of her, she says, "You should be ashamed of yourself for allow-ing yourself to be jealous. Mama said that's the Robedaux disposi-tion: jealousy, spitefulness, and vindictiveness. I don't have an ounce of it, thank God, and if I thought I did, I'd jump off the highest building in Houston and kill myself. Because that kind of disposition makes you miserable, Mama said" (*Four Plays* 216). In a later conver-sation, feeling remorseful for causing Horace pain and asking his for-giveness, she says, "I don't know what gets into me. I have a terrible disposition, Brother, a terrible disposition. It's the Robedaux coming out in me" (*Four Plays* 232–33). This tendency of denigrating her paternal heritage carries over to her feelings for her father, whom she villainizes. In the passage quoted above, Lily Dale tells Horace about a conversation she has with their cousin Minnie Robedaux, in which she says, "My mother is a living, unselfish angel and I won't have you say a word against her. You and your family mooched off her and my father and drove him to drink. So don't come around here anymore and ask me anything about my father. I only know one thing about him: he died and left us all alone in this world" (*Four Plays* 216). Elsewhere she calls him a drunkard and a cigarette fiend who broke their mother's heart.

This also explains her need to forget the past. Horace feels com-pelled to recall their shared childhood and incorporate memories of the past into his present experience, a need which is symbolized by his father's pocket watch, carefully wrapped in a cloth, which he carries in his pocket, along with Corella's wedding ring. Lily Dale, on the other hand, insists on minimizing the impact of their childhood years. When Horace asks her if she recalls the song "Lily Dale," which their father used to sing to them (this will become a motif of the play), she replies, "No, and I don't want to. Brother, you always want to talk about the past. I have no interest in it, really, at all. . . . I want to think of now" (*Four Plays* 215). It's not surprising that she doesn't remember what Paul Horace looked like and mistakenly recalls him referring to them as "Sister" and "Brother," instead of their Christian names. Similarly, she says that she loves Will Kidder, her fiancé, because "he only talks about the future—what he's going to do with his life, how much he's going to accomplish." "I have not heard him mention his mother or father or childhood once," she adds, "and he had just as difficult a time as we had" (*Four Plays* 216). Not mentioning the past is clearly a virtue in Lily Dale's view.

Her unqualified praise of Pete Davenport, her stepfather, is simply the obverse of her rejection of her father. In Lily Dale's opinion, Pete can do no wrong. She quotes him at every opportunity as the ultimate authority, praises him in his absence, and plays the part of dutiful daughter, fetching a pillow for his head when he comes home from work and playing his favorite pieces on the piano. She has learned her gender lessons well: choose the man most likely to take care of you and cater to his every whim.

To some extent, we can attribute Lily Dale's attitudes and behaviors to cultural factors. This is not a society which allows women autonomy or financial freedom. Opportunities for higher education or career opportunities are extremely limited, a fact which is abundantly documented throughout the *Cycle*. Thus a woman's choice of husband will determine not only her personal happiness but her financial well-being, as well. That the single most important choice any woman of this time and place made was her choice of mate is inescapable. In *Courtship,* this fact is emphasized by the discussions of family marriages: Mr. Vaughn's sister Lucy married a man twenty years her senior who left her a widow at thirty-two with four children to feed; if Elizabeth had eloped with her beau Syd Joplin, who dies during the course of the play, she would have been left a widow and penniless. This is much like the situation of Claire Ratliff of *The Widow Claire,* who marries at sixteen, becomes a mother at seventeen, and at twenty-eight is a widow with children ages nine and ten. Claire, being courted by Horace, whom she obviously likes in spite of the fact that he's six years younger, ultimately decides to marry someone who can provide for her and her children, a decision based more on practicality than love. She knows that as "an old married woman with two half-grown children" (*Four Plays* 278) she won't have many opportunities to choose, and she has to select wisely.

This helps us understand Corella's choice of Pete as a mate. It is clear that this is not a love match. Pete is cold and unfeeling, showing little warmth or affection to anyone except Lily Dale and outright hostility to Horace. Corella has to save her own money to send Horace train fare for his visit, a fact she hides from her husband, who is away on a trip to visit his family in Atlanta. When he returns unexpectedly, discovering Horace's presence, she is extremely nervous and asks Horace to leave at the first opportunity. When she defends him to Horace, all she can say is that he doesn't smoke or drink or have any "bad habits," that he is a good provider and "worships" Lily Dale (*Four Plays* 213).

The causal connection between one's choice of husband and financial and social status is perhaps most clearly illustrated by a bit of seemingly desultory conversation between Corella and Horace. Talking about a neighbor, Myrtle Harris, an old friend from Harrison who now lives across the street in "that big house with the stone lions in front," Corella mentions that when her sister Virgie met Myrtle at a bridge party, she complained that Corella hadn't returned her social call: "Virgie said I hadn't, she was sure, because I was always working. 'What does she do?' Virgie said she asked her. 'Takes in sewing,' Virgie told her. 'Oh, heavens!' Virgie said Myrtle said. 'Oh, heavens what?' Virgie asked her. 'You know she's as poor as you were when you lived here. She didn't happen to marry a rich husband.' Virgie said that shut her up." (*Four Plays* 210–11). This economic fact of life makes it a bit easier to accept Corella's decision to marry Pete in spite of his cruel treatment of her son, whom she is forced to abandon. It also explains the deference, even fear, that Pete seems to inspire in her. Only once in the entire play does she stand up to him, when he accuses Horace of only pretending to be sick: "He's sick and you know he's sick," she says; "You should be ashamed of yourself, Pete!" Interestingly, it is the only time in the play that she calls him by his first name (*Four Plays* 208). As the male and the provider, he holds all the power in this relationship.[3]

---

3. Corella's anecdote illustrates Foote's concept of "texture" as it applies to his plays. Susan Underwood quotes an interview with Gerald Wood in which Foote comments that "texture is revealed in the specifics. . . . It has nothing to do with the forward action of the thing, but it has to do with what enriches it." Underwood goes on to explain the importance of "moments during which plot is stopped and attention is placed upon seemingly inconsequential dialogue," for it is often in these moments that the "oblique complexities of their [the characters'] inner lives" are revealed. See Susan

The same is true for Lily Dale, who knows she must placate her stepfather in all things, just as she will have to obey her husband-to-be, Will. Thus on a cultural level, her intense loyalty to Pete can be understood as a survival strategy, however unconscious. To the extent that the family functions as a purveyor of cultural values, we can attribute Lily Dale's narrow-mindedness and either-or thinking to the family as cultural unit. But the family dynamics of this particular unit are also key in shaping her character. The fact that Pete spoils her, for example, and that both he and Corella indulge her whims gives Lily Dale a false sense of entitlement and teaches her to be manipulative. Her piano playing, as explained above, is typical of her need to be at the center of family gatherings. When she complains that she doesn't like school, Corella allows her to withdraw at age fourteen and "compose music" instead. When Pete refuses to let Will call on her, she cries until he relents. The examples abound. What they have in common is the fact that Lily Dale never has to deal with adversity or disappointment. Though this can partly be accounted for by the culture's gender rules, that is, by the implicit understanding that if she plays the role of dutiful daughter she will be rewarded, it is exacerbated by what in today's parlance we would call bad parenting on the part of Corella and Pete. Parents, responsible for nurturing their young and preparing them to assume adult responsibilities, do not always do a good job. Babying Lily Dale, not surprisingly, keeps her childlike and immature. The opposite holds true for Horace. Ironically, the fact that he has been, as he says, "on his own" since he was twelve has made him independent and resourceful. Having first worked at a plantation store under the "supervision" of his irresponsible Uncle Albert, fending for himself in a very tough environment (the labor is done by a chain gang of convicts), Horace now works as a clerk at a dry goods store in Glen Rose for three dollars a week. Seeking to improve his prospects, he comes to Houston hoping to take a business course so that he can someday own a shop himself. He speaks very matter-of-factly, without a shred of self-pity. He thinks

---

Underwood, "Singing in the Face of Devastation: Texture in Horton Foote's *Talking Pictures*," in *Foote: A Casebook,* 151–52. See also Gary Edgerton, "A Visit to the Imaginary Landscape of Harrison, Texas: Sketching the Film Career of Horton Foote," *Literature/Film Quarterly* 17, no. 1 (1989): 12.

nothing of walking into Harrison along the railroad tracks every Sunday morning to have dinner with one of his aunts, for instance, and getting up early Monday morning to walk back in time to open the store. When Corella asks him how long the trip takes, he says simply, "Three hours," then, "Aunt Virgie has taught me to dance" (*Four Plays* 182). He doesn't dwell upon what others might consider hardships; his focus, instead, is on the pleasure he takes in learning to dance. At this point Lily Dale interrupts, saying she's "not going to play [piano] anymore if you all are going to talk," cutting off the conversation. "We'll talk when Lily Dale finishes," Corella says. "She's very sensitive" (*Four Plays* 182–83).

As the above response suggests, Corella defers to Lily Dale as she does to Pete. This is perhaps as harmful ultimately to Lily Dale as it is to Horace. Though Corella's refusal to defy Pete on Horace's behalf causes Horace deep pain, he emerges from the experience with qualities that will serve him well: determination, inner strength, autonomy (though we hardly give her credit for this). Lily Dale, catered to and indulged, will remain a whining, self-centered, unhappy person throughout her adulthood, as we will see in *Cousins,* allowed to be a child because she is never forced to assume responsibility for herself. Again, this can be attributed to ineffective parenting, a malfunctioning or underfunctioning family. A different and perhaps even more damning example of this is when Lily Dale, now engaged to Will and beginning to contemplate her future, asks her mother where babies come from (it reveals a great deal about this culture that at eighteen she doesn't know). Corella's handling of this situation reads like a manual of how *not* to tell one's children about sex. "What do they do to you when you're married to make you have children?" Lily Dale asks. Corella evades the question, saying it's too late in the evening to discuss such things; when Lily Dale presses, saying that her friend Myra Kate says your husband "does terrible things to you," Corella will only say that it's "not so terrible." When she asks again what it is, Corella responds, "You'll find out" (*Four Plays* 229). Though her evasiveness and obvious embarrassment about discussing sex are bad enough, when the question of childbearing comes up, Corella's response is even more damaging:

LILY DALE: Does it hurt to have children?
CORELLA: Yes, and I pray to God you never have to go through that.

LILY DALE: Will wants children.

CORELLA: He's a fool, and don't you ever let him talk you into it.

LILY DALE: Women die in childbirth, don't they?

CORELLA: All the time. Every minute of the hour. While I was having you and your brother, I prayed I would die.

LILY DALE: Why?

CORELLA: Because it hurt so much. . . . I was in terror the whole time.

(*Four Plays* 229–30)

We're not surprised when Lily Dale tells Horace soon thereafter that she's not going to have any children and makes Will promise that they never will.

Thus to some extent Lily Dale can be viewed sympathetically, as manipulative and self-centered as she is, when seen as a victim of family dynamics that have not served her well. At the same time, we are aware that she makes choices for which she alone is responsible. Perhaps the clearest example of this and the one that stands most in contrast with Horace is her refusal to deal with anything unpleasant, which includes, in her mind, the past. Her steadfast desire to wipe the slate clean, to pretend, in effect, that her early childhood did not take place, becomes one of Lily Dale's defining characteristics. As mentioned earlier, in casting her lot with Pete and Corella, her new family, she feels compelled to minimize any love she feels for her dead father that might link her to her past. This is reflected in her disinterest in recalling the song "Lily Dale," which Paul Horace used to sing to her and Horace.[4] Early in the play Horace mentions the song to

4. The lyrics of this song, written by H. S. Thompson, are as follows:

> 'Twas a calm, still night, and the moon's pale light
> Shone soft o'er hill and vale;
> When friends mute with grief stood around the death-bed
> Of my poor lost Lilly [*sic*] Dale.
> *Refrain:*
> Oh! Lilly, sweet Lilly, dear Lilly Dale,
> Now the wild rose blossoms o'er her little green grave,
> 'Neath the trees in the flow'ry vale.
>
> Her cheeks that once glowed with the rose tint of health,
> By the hand of disease had turned pale,
> And the death damp was on the pure white brow
> Of my poor lost Lilly Dale.   *Refrain.*
>
> "I go," she said, to the land of rest," [*sic punctuation*]
> And ere my strength shall fail,

his sister, enlisting her help in recalling the ballad's lyrics. Though seemingly a bit of desultory conversation, it becomes clear as he brings it up repeatedly throughout the play that it is very important to Horace both that he reclaim this memory, putting words to the haunting melody that he recalls, and that Lily Dale participate somehow in the experience. Undeterred by her initial reaction, a rather angry disavowal of interest in the topic, he later asks Corella if she remembers the words; then brings it up to Lily Dale once more, singing the lyrics which he and his mother have pieced together. Still later he sings even more and asks Lily Dale to try to play it on the piano. The play closes with a scene after Horace has left in which Lily Dale, now in possession of the sheet music, which he has secured for her, plays and sings the song softly. (This intercuts with a scene on the train with Horace and Mrs. Coons, a fellow passenger, which will be discussed shortly.)

Horace's obsession with this song brings several interesting facts into focus. It's significant, in the first instance, that Paul Horace used to sing to the children, since great emphasis is placed on the fact that singing and dancing are associated with the Thornton side of the family; the Robedauxs, more cerebral in orientation, are associated with reading and Greek and Latin. In *Roots*, the first play of the *Cycle*, as Paul Horace lies dying and music floats through the window from the nearby Thornton home, his mother complains that it bothers her son; we later learn, interestingly, that he actually enjoys it. Here we see evidence of that same phenomenon, suggesting a point of intersection, something which Corella and Paul Horace might have had in common. To young Horace, who is seeking ways to bridge the gap between opposing factions in his family history, such a confluence, however trivial, takes on considerable significance.

His desire for Lily Dale to learn to play the song, tapping into her

---

I must tell you where, near my own loved home,
You must lay poor Lilly Dale.   *Refrain.*

'Neath the chestnut tree, where the wild flow'rs grow,
And the stream ripples forth thro' the vale,
Where the birds shall warble their songs in spring,
There lay poor Lilly Dale.   *Refrain.*

In Joe Mitchell Chappel, ed., *Heart Songs* (Cleveland: World Publishing Co., n.d.), 299.

interest in the piano, is a way to widen the circle and re-create, if only momentarily, a moment from the past when their original family was intact. That this song played a ritualistic function in their family is suggested by the fact that even Corella remembers Paul Horace singing it and that the song's title inspired Lily Dale's name. Typically, Foote uses this song to perform several different functions. The lyrics, which refer to the singer's "poor, lost Lilly Dale," who dies and is buried in a "little green grave / 'Neath the trees" near a wild rose bush, establishes a melancholy tone. Insofar as we link the character Lily Dale with the subject of the song, we see Lily Dale as doomed, a tragic figure. The mention of the graveyard recalls Horace's determination to buy a tombstone for his father's grave, a leitmotif which runs throughout the entire *Cycle,* as well as the later references to burying his infant daughter Jenny, who dies in the influenza epidemic of 1918; the reference to the rose bush provides a link with the flowers carried in Horace and Elizabeth's wedding, the flowers they plant in the yard of their first home, and the rose bush Mrs. Vaughn plants next to Jenny's grave.[5]

Most importantly, the singing of this song represents a moment of potential healing between Corella, Lily Dale, and Horace. Lily Dale's refusal to learn the song, based on her determination to forget the past, forecloses the possibility of her integrating into her present a loving, positive memory of her father and sharing it with her brother and mother. Though we learn that Lily Dale does play the song once for Horace before he leaves Houston, a scene which we don't see (typically, Foote leaves this to our imaginations), as Crystal Brian points out, "The healing which the song might have provided had it been played earlier is now impossible."[6] As the play closes, we see Lily Dale on one side of the stage beginning to play the ballad on the piano, interspersed with comments to Corella which indicate that she is still trying to sort out her sense of her own value and her place in the world. She compares herself to the picture of the girl on the cover

5. As was noted in Chapter 1, Foote's use of music is careful and deliberate, as Crystal Brian and Reynolds Price, among others, have pointed out. See also Marjorie Smelstor, " 'The World's an Orphans' Home': Horton Foote's Social and Moral History," *Southern Quarterly* 19, no. 2 (1991): 12–14.

6. Brian, " 'To Be Quiet and Listen,' " 103.

of the sheet music, asking Corella if she's prettier (the correct answer, of course, is "yes"); she asks her mother whom she loved more, Paul Horace or Pete, and whether she loves Horace more than her; she says she wants Will to move in with them when they get married and when Corella points out that wouldn't be practical, she insists that they'll live next door or at least "as close as we can" (*Four Plays* 247). She is still thinking in either-or terms, unable to make room for Horace in their family or her heart, and her remark about never leaving Corella suggests that she will be unable to separate appropriately from her mother. While perhaps all this cannot be attributed simply to Lily Dale's refusal to face her past, it undeniably plays a major role in her continued immaturity.

On the other side of the stage we see Horace returning to Harrison on the train in the "care" of Uncle Albert, Corella's brother and one of the *Cycle*'s hopeless gamblers. When Albert leaves Horace to play in a poker game in the smoking car, extracting a promise that he won't tell Aunt Virgie or his wife, Mrs. Coons, a middle-aged woman who had struck up a conversation with Horace on the train into Houston, once again appears. She has just taken her husband, an alcoholic, for another Keeley Cure (alcoholism, like gambling, occurs in various guises throughout the *Cycle*).

Although a minor character, Mrs. Coons plays an important function in rounding out this play, which begins and ends with the train-ride conversations Horace has with her. On the ride to Houston, when Mrs. Coons learns that Horace is just two months older than her own son, she begins asking questions which most playgoers would find intrusive, even offensive: whom he's visiting (she assumes it's his grandmother), why his mother and father aren't living together, and, when she learns that the house she's now renting in Harrison was Horace's childhood home, she asks, "Is it your daddy died a drunkard?" (*Four Plays* 171).

This conversation is perhaps one of the best examples of the economy of Foote's "texture" and bears close examination. A passage which seems not to advance the plot, it adds significantly to our understanding of the culture as a whole and, in the end, becomes important to the plot, as well. In the first instance, the fact that Mrs. Coons has heard the Robedauxs' tragic family history though she has only lived there two months is not surprising, given the small-town milieu of Harrison. This also helps explain why she and Horace are able to slip into conversation so easily, though they have just met. As Chapter 3 will discuss in detail, the small town of Harrison at the turn of the century is a coherent community, one where everyone knows the codes of behavior and accepts, more or less, the values which inform them. This is by no means to idealize it. It is a community which is racially segregated and struggling with class differences and other ills. What it does offer, however limited it may be, is a world in which relationships are clear and norms are known. Mrs. Coons easily falls into calling Horace "son," and he respectfully answers her questions, taking them as an expression of interest rather than an intrusion. When she asks him if he's a Christian and if he's been baptized, having proudly identified herself as belonging to the only Baptist church in Harrison, not only is Horace not offended, he takes her question to heart. In fact, when he becomes seriously ill with malaria in Houston, one of the first questions he asks his mother after a week of near-unconsciousness is whether or not he's been baptized. It's significant that Corella's attitude about this is much more cavalier than Mrs. Coons's; she just "never got around to it" (*Four Plays* 206). Horace does not simply drop the subject at this point. He tells Corella he was afraid he was going to die without being baptized and even tries to get up from his sickbed to find someone to baptize him.

This issue resurfaces at the end of the play, when he and Mrs. Coons meet on the train going back to Harrison. At this point, he simply asks her to pray for him and his mother and sister. This scene intercuts with that of Lily Dale playing the ballad "Lily Dale" on the piano. The irony is masterful. While Lily Dale plays the song which Horace had asked her to learn, but too late, asking her mother whom she loves best, Horace, having been rejected by his family, asks Mrs. Coons to pray for them:

> HORACE: Pray for me, Mrs. Coons.
> MRS. COONS: What do you want me to pray about? That you live until you're baptized?
> HORACE: No Ma'am. Just pray for me and my sister and my mother.
> (*Four Plays* 249)

When she agrees to include his mother and sister in her prayers, even though she doesn't know them, he insists, "Now, Mrs. Coons. Pray for us now. This very moment." His sense of urgency is unmistakable. When she begins what seems to be a general prayer, he interrupts her: "My mother and my sister and me. Pray for us, Mrs. Coons, pray for us." She asks their names, then begins, "Father, I've been asked to remember in my prayers this young man, Horace, and his dear mother, Corella, and his dear sister, Lily Dale. Father of mercy, Father of goodness, Father of forgiveness . . ." as the lights fade out slowly (*Four Plays* 249–50). Our last image is of Lily Dale singing in the living room, as the lights fade slowly on her, too.

It is significant, in this regard, that both the song Lily Dale plays and the references to baptism are linked with naming, with identity. In the first case, Lily Dale's given name is drawn from this song and the ballad itself becomes a part of family history, while baptism confers a place in the family of believers, the Christian community. Horace, ever resourceful, manages to create a space for himself in a larger family, drawing on whatever love and concern he is offered by Mrs. Coons, his aunts, the culture at large. He knows who his family is, even if he is not living with them: himself, his mother, and his sister.

Lily Dale, on the other hand, who has been included in Corella's new family, with Pete as the patriarch, has tried to reinvent herself as Pete's daughter and dissociate herself from the past. The payoff for this choice is financial security, a life of relative ease where she is the center of attention, indulged and doted upon; the price is her continued dependence and childlike behavior, as well as the loss of her past, which includes both her father and Horace. To the extent that she rejects Paul Horace she must reject Horace too, whom she identifies as a "Robedaux," unlike herself. Psychologically, Horace must be dead to her, but she feels too much guilt about this desire to acknowledge it; it comes out instead in the ways in which she undermines him with Pete, her competition with him for Corella's love, and her unwillingness to include him in their family. It's an either-or world to Lily Dale, which results ultimately in her lack of compassion and the capacity for love.

It is just the opposite with Horace. As we have noted, Horace looks for ways to integrate the past into his present experience. His determination to buy a headstone for his father's grave, so that Paul Horace's life will not be effaced, suggests both Horace's loyalty to his father and his need to preserve his Robedaux heritage. Similarly, his carrying his father's watch and mother's wedding ring reveals his desire to integrate both sides of his family history. (It is interesting in this regard that Horace seems to have inherited traits from both the Robedaux and the Thornton strains. Like his father, Horace loves to read, especially out-of-town newspapers; like his mother and his aunts, he loves music and dancing.) He is also self-sufficient, unlike Lily Dale, taking responsibility for his own decisions and trying to improve his station in life. His trip to Houston is a case in point. He hopes not just to become a part of Corella's new family, but to find a job or take a business course. When that doesn't work out, he matter-of-factly sets out to find an alternative. He is able to deal with disappointments and pain in ways that are realistic and clear-eyed. He does not delude himself about Pete's cruelty toward him; he says that he "can't stand" Pete and "despises" him (*Four Plays* 218, 220), the strongest words of anger that Horace utters in the entire *Cycle*. Likewise, he acknowledges the fact that Corella essentially abandoned him. When Lily Dale says that their father left Corella penniless "to go out into the world to work and support two children," Horace responds quietly, "She didn't support me" (*Four Plays* 215).

What is crucial is that he is able to forgive Corella, as the closing train scene illustrates. Unlike Lily Dale, who can never forgive her father for abandoning their family, as she sees it, Horace can accept both his mother and his sister in spite of their limited ability to love him. It is no accident that the play's last word is "forgiveness," and that it is uttered by Mrs. Coons, functioning here as a mother-substitute, on Horace's behalf. Horace's ability to accept the reality of his life as he sees it, to embrace its pain as well as its joy, and to forgive those who wrong him allows him to move forward with wisdom and compassion, while Lily Dale for all practical purposes remains a child, the "poor lost Lily Dale" of the ballad.[7]

7. Horace's lack of rancor and generosity of spirit are qualities of the playwright himself, a fact which quickly becomes obvious to anyone who knows him or reads his interviews. One with John L. DiGaetani will serve as an illustration. At several points in the interview, DiGaetani almost seems to be baiting Foote. When he comments that he often thought of Foote's work as a "victim of the sixties," the playwright responds, "I don't think of myself as a victim of anything. I felt the sixties was an interesting period, and I was an interested observer. I wasn't being actively produced in the sixties, but sometimes there's a time for quietness and reflection, and so I was very active myself." When DiGaetani responds that he "expected some bitterness on this point,"

The concept of family as both a positive and negative factor in shaping individual identity is continued in *Cousins,* the eighth play of *The Orphans' Home Cycle.* On one level, as the title suggests, the nature of kinship in general seems to be the subject of this play. In terms of overt conflict and issues to be resolved, the plot-line of *Cousins* is perhaps even flatter than those of the other *Cycle* plays. The action, such as it is, revolves around Corella's illness and hospitalization. The play opens at Horace's men's store, where Horace and Gordon, his cousin and clerk, are engaging in desultory conversation; business is slow, which is obviously a concern for Horace. The subject of Corella's health comes up, and we learn that she's had three serious operations. Mr. Vaughn, Elizabeth's father, enters with the news that he's received a phone call saying that Corella is seriously ill (Horace has no phone in his store) and that he will drive Horace and Elizabeth to Houston to see her in the hospital. The hospital scene reintroduces Lily Dale and her husband Will, who now have a son, along with a Cousin Monty and his wife, Lola. We observe Horace with his mother, stepfather Pete, Lily Dale and Will, and Elizabeth. In his exchanges with his mother, who fears she may be dying, the question of her abandoning him comes up; she seems to feel guilty about this and wants to assure herself that she has done nothing wrong.

This scene, which could well have been the climax of the action, passes uneventfully. Corella does not, in fact, die (though her near-death is played off against the actual death of Mr. Vaughn in the next play, a structural strategy I will discuss in Chapter 5), and the action returns to Horace's store two months later. Corella arrives for a visit with Horace and Elizabeth, accompanied by Lily Dale and Will; Monty and Lola also show up, home from a trip to Europe, and all

---

Foote simply says, "I've been on this earth too long to become bitter about things like that. I mean, things go in cycles, and there's no point in resisting the cycles—just wait them out."

Later in the interview, DiGaetani mentions artists whose style is quite different from Foote's, Robert Wilson and Franco Zeffirelli and Peter Sellars, and says, "I suspect you hate that approach to theater," to which Foote responds, "I don't hate anything. I learn from it." When he is asked if there are any playwrights he envies, Foote says, "There's some I admire very much," and then proceeds to list several. See John L. DiGaetani, "Horton Foote," in *A Search for a Postmodern Theater: Interviews with Contemporary Playwrights* (Westport, Conn.: Greenwood Press, 1991), 66, 70–71.

except Horace and Elizabeth go to Horace's Aunt Inez's home for a chicken dinner.

While they're alone, Horace's Cousin Minnie arrives, having taken the train from Houston. Minnie's efforts to contact Horace, mentioned several times earlier in the play, add a second strand to the action and provide the play's climax. Minnie, Horace's cousin on his father's side, has always taken the position that Corella was at fault in the breakup of the marriage and has denounced her bitterly. When Horace moves to Houston briefly as a young man to take a business course and Corella has no place for him to stay, Minnie takes him in and helps him through school. In the hospital bedside scene, Corella tells Horace that she encountered Minnie in the ladies' room of a local department store, and Minnie accused her of abandoning Horace, saying that she (Minnie) was the only one in the family who took an interest in him. Minnie has been trying to reach Horace to once again insist on her side of the story and finally takes the train to Harrison to see him. When she gets there, she decides that it's foolish to be concerned about something that happened twenty-five years ago and lets go of her anger. Her speech, which will be discussed later in this chapter, is the emotional and thematic climax of the play. It is very brief, just a few pages. Then she leaves to return to Houston.

The other major strain of the action is provided by a semi-comic character, Cousin Lewis, who murdered his cousin Jamie Dale in a drunken argument.[8] He appears several times at Horace's store, drunk and disorderly, endlessly rehearsing the details of this sad moment, which was clearly the turning point of his life. Lewis's exchanges with Horace and Gordon begin and end the play, bookending the action.

Thus the action per se is relatively uneventful: Horace goes to Houston to see his mother, she survives the operation, he returns home. Cousin Minnie tries to reach Horace to argue her case about the family, a life-defining issue for her, and Cousin Lewis endlessly relives his quarrel with Jamie Dale. The contours of this basic plotline are filled in with bits and pieces of desultory conversation that function like an impressionistic painting, with each brushstroke, though

8. This episode is based on an actual incident that Foote heard while growing up in Wharton. Foote, personal communication, n.d.

seemingly random in itself, contributing to a portrait of shimmering beauty. Like Monet's haystacks or cathedral series, the drama extracts a moment from the flux of time and, freezing it, allows us to contemplate this particular world at this point in time in all its uniqueness as well as its typicality.

The way in which familial relationships shape our lives, then, the focus of the play, is explored by examining various cousins and pairs of cousins as well as the married couples who populate this community. The title, in this regard, reverberates in multiple directions. In the first instance, it can refer simply to cousins in the generic sense of the word. Much is made of the fact, for example, that Horace has a vast network of kinfolk. Gordon says to Horace in the play's opening scene, "I thought I was kin to a lot of people. I thought I had a lot of cousins, but I said to Mama the other night: 'I believe Cousin Horace is kin to a whole lot more. Why, if all of Cousin Horace's cousins traded with him in his store he would have the biggest business in south Texas' " (*Two Plays* 8).

Similarly, a great deal of effort is expended to establish who is kin to whom as well as the precise nature of the relationship. In the scene quoted above, Gordon asks how Cousin Lewis and Jamie Dale were related, then says, "Cousin Lewis is my second cousin and your second cousin, isn't that right?" to which Horace replies, "No. Second cousin, once removed" (*Two Plays* 6). Such distinctions are important. In the hospital when Horace is visiting Corella, Lily Dale first learns that she's kin to a Mae Buchanan on her mother's side. "I certainly never knew that. We don't call her cousin," she says. Corella responds, "We don't call a lot of our cousins cousin" (*Two Plays* 42). Discussions such as these form a motif which unifies the seemingly desultory conversations throughout the play, emphasizing the central role that familial relationships play in shaping our view of ourselves and our place in the universe in both positive and negative ways.

The point is made, for instance, that one can't always count on one's family for support. Gordon comments that many of Horace's cousins go to Houston to trade instead of patronizing his business (largely a response to the fact that Horace welcomes blacks as well as whites into his store), and that his cousins haven't come to the dances he (Gordon) organizes: "I said to Mama this morning: 'What's the matter with our kinfolks? You'd think you could count on your kinfolks. Wouldn't you?' I mean look at all our cousins. You'd think kin-folks would stick together" (*Two Plays* 4).

The most striking instance of this fact, of course, is Cousin Lewis's murder of Jamie Dale, a story which is told and retold throughout the play. But there are other less dramatic instances which illustrate that family networks, like other relationships, are not always harmonious. While Horace is in Houston, Cousin Lewis comes into the store and, angered by something Gordon says, kicks in the glass hat case. It will be expensive to fix, and Horace, who can't afford it, will bear the cost; though Lewis's brother Lester assures Horace he will cover the damages, he's a liar, as Monty says: "He'll never pay for it. He owes everybody in town now" (*Two Plays* 49). He does, in fact, owe Horace fifteen dollars. What is worse, he twice tried to scam Horace by cashing bad checks.

Lester's financial irresponsibility comes up in another context early in the play, in a conversation between Horace and Gordon, a young man given to gossip. Alluding to the family feud that has caused enmity for several generations, Gordon says, "Cousin Lester doesn't drink at all [comparing him to his brother Lewis], no, but he don't pay his bills, Brother says, and he owes everybody in town. Brother is bitter because they ended up with land that Mama says belonged to us. That was stolen from our grandfather [Mr. Thornton, Corella's father]. Yours too, Cousin Horace. Are you bitter about it? Brother says they own near two thousand acres that should have been at least half ours. How did it happen they wound up with it? Did you ever get it straight?" (*Two Plays* 9). Horace's response is typical; he has learned not to hold grudges or dwell on perceived injustices: "No. And I don't lose any sleep over it and I advise you not to" (*Two Plays* 9). But the damage that is done by differing views of the past and the permanent rifts that can result are clear. Lester's refusal to assume his financial responsibilities toward Horace and his attempts to swindle him are made even more ironic by the fact that his branch of the family may have cheated the Thorntons out of their share of the inheritance. Foote is no sentimentalist. Families are not always forces for good, as we see here.

We also note that those who pay the price for Lewis's hurtful actions, literally and figuratively, are other family members: Horace, in the case of the broken hat case, and Jamie Dale's mother. Evidence of her bitterness is again provided by Gordon, who supplies much of the gossip in this play. He tells Horace that Jamie's mother, Miss Velma, had taken a tombstone to the cemetery for her son's grave with the inscription "Jamie Dale, murdered by his cousin, Lewis Higgins" (*Two Plays* 94). Although some prominent citizens of Harrison called on her and finally persuaded her to have the last six words removed from the tombstone, it is clear that although Cousin Lewis may have been exonerated by the law, in Miss Velma's heart, he is still responsible.

The specifics of that incident are worth repeating in some detail, since it becomes one of the principal leitmotifs of the play and is played off against the responsible behavior of Horace; one can, in fact, understand the title on a second level to be about specific "cousins," here, Horace and Lewis. We first learn about the incident indirectly, from Gordon, whose attitude establishes a perspective for the audience before Lewis himself appears on stage. Gordon says to Horace, "I swear Cousin Lewis hasn't learned anything. I mean he killed Jamie Dale, cut him in cold blood. And because he was drunk and Jamie Dale was drunk they let him off with a suspended sentence, which he pays no attention to and walks around day and night always at least half full, carrying a knife or a gun until I know and you know he will kill somebody else or get killed" (*Two Plays* 5). Gordon's comment reveals the tolerance this society has for alcoholism and violence, a theme which permeates the entire *Cycle;* like a permissive parent, the judge admonishes Lewis and sends him on his way, as if his being drunk somehow excused his murderous act. Thus when Lewis shows up several minutes later, drunk and belligerent (he says to Gordon, who politely introduces himself although he has known Gordon for years, "You're no cousin of mine, you ugly sonovabitch"), the audience is prepared to disapprove of him.

After some introductory questions about who is cousin to whom, Lewis recounts his version of the story. Although Lewis can be seen as a comic character, a kind of buffoon, the episode is a poignant one, made all the more so by its irony. It seems that Lewis and Jamie Dale, both drunk, were with prostitutes, and Jamie started referring to them as "whores," which offended Lewis's sense of propriety. As Lewis tells it, he said to Jamie, " 'I told you once, Jamie. I don't want you speaking that way to ladies in my presence.' " But he went on saying 'whore this and whore that' . . . just a lot of dirty words, you know. And I said: 'Now listen here, we weren't raised that way to talk that way [*sic*] in front of ladies, so shut up!'" (*Two Plays* 15). At this point, both men draw knives and Lewis ends up mortally wounding his cousin, later pleading self-defense. But his real argument, the one he repeats to anyone who will listen, is that Jamie had violated a sacrosanct Southern code: one doesn't use vulgar language in the presence of women. Ironies abound here—the frivolousness of this claim as justification for murder as well as the fact that the women they were with weren't, by their own social codes, "ladies" in the first place. These ironies are compounded by the fact that in the play's final scene, Lewis commits the same "crime" he killed Jamie for when he curses in front of Cousin Minnie, who, as a proper lady and a stranger to Lewis, should elicit the highest degree of social etiquette. Underlining the irony of this moment, Foote has Lewis say after she leaves, "Doggone . . . I never cussed in front of a lady in my life unless I was so drunk I didn't know it." Then he immediately asks Horace and Gordon, "Were you all kin to Jamie Dale?" When Horace says no, he continues: "He was my cousin. I killed him. I feel so bad about it, but it was him or me. I killed my cousin, my cousin Jamie Dale. He didn't care how he talked in front of ladies, you know" (*Two Plays* 96).

It's clear that this is the defining moment in Lewis's life. Like the Ancient Mariner waylaying the wedding guest so he can tell his story one more time, Lewis seems condemned to go through life reliving this tragic experience. Jamie's life was cut short, and the lives of both Lewis and Miss Velma are forever shattered. Yet Lewis seems to have learned nothing, as Gordon points out. He continues to drink and behave in an irresponsible and frequently violent fashion.

The example of Minnie functions by way of contrast. Her story occurs as a counterbalance to that of Lewis, referred to intermittently, like his, throughout the play; on this level, one can read the title as referring to either Horace and Minnie or Minnie and Lewis, both cousins of Horace. Like Cousin Lewis, Minnie seems to have a defining moment in her life, though strangely, it is one in which she is not directly involved: the breakup of Corella and Paul Horace's marriage some twenty-five years earlier. She and her mother, abandoned by Minnie's father, moved in with Corella and Paul Horace, as did his mother and two unmarried brothers, at a time when the young couple was struggling to provide for their own children. According to the Thorntons' version of the story, this put such a strain on Paul Horace that he began to drink heavily, causing marital problems that eventually led to their separation. Minnie, on the other hand, criticizes the Thorntons as frivolous and flighty and casts Corella as the villain in this chapter of family history. Taking her cue from her Grandmother Robedaux, she says that Corella was only interested in Paul Horace's money, and when he fell upon hard times, she left him.

Like Cousin Lewis, Minnie tells and retells this story for years. She is still rehashing it when she runs into Corella in a department store ladies' room twenty-five years later, as previously mentioned. Corella, facing a serious operation, has found it so troubling she brings it up when she is alone with Horace in her hospital room: "I ran into her [Minnie] at the ladies' room at Foley's and I tried to avoid her, but she cornered me. . . . She went back over my marriage to your papa and I said: 'Minnie, that's all past.' 'For you,' she said, 'but not for me. And Horace has never forgiven you for running off and leaving him.' And I said: 'Minnie, you are crazy. No one ever left anybody.' 'You did,' she said. 'You left your husband and you left your son' (*Two Plays* 39). Corella becomes so upset that she loses her temper: "I said terrible things about your grandmother and your uncles, and your father. I said things I had long ago forgotten. And she said she would never forgive me for the things I said. And that she was going to tell you all about it and she bet you would never forgive me" (*Two Plays* 39).

We learn, in fact, that Minnie has tried to contact Horace. She calls the hospital several times, trying to catch him in the waiting room and later takes a train from Houston to Harrison to once again tell the story as she sees it. In this piece of family history, one of the unifying narratives of the *Cycle*, Corella is variously cast as victim or villain, and it matters desperately to Minnie that her version be established as the authoritative one. As the audience, we wonder why it matters so much to her, since as Paul Horace's niece, she is only tangentially involved.

The key to the intensity of Minnie's response appears in another of the *Cycle*'s seemingly desultory conversations, this time in *Roots in a Parched Ground*, the opening play. In a conversation with her grandmother and Horace about what Horace would call his new stepfather, Minnie suddenly says, "My daddy ran away." When her Grandmother Robedaux denies this, saying that probably some "strange tragic accident . . . prevented his return," Minnie replies, "I think he's run away and I don't think he's ever coming back. But that's all right with me. There was nothing but fighting when he was here," adding that she is glad her mother never remarried because stepparents are "always mean and hateful and cruel to the poor orphaned stepchildren" (*Four Plays* 73). Like similar detours in Foote's dialogue, this brief exchange, while it does nothing to advance the plot, tells us much about Minnie. The fact that she perceives herself as a "poor orphaned stepchild" and feels abandoned by her father places her in a parallel position with Horace and Lily Dale, whose parents also quarreled and separated. In this equation, since she and her mother have attached themselves to Paul Horace, he becomes the "good father" who replaces her own absent father, with Corella symbolically identified with the mean stepmother. That she identifies intensely with Paul Horace is made clear earlier in the play, when she says to Horace and Lily Dale, about to enter their father's sick room, "I'm his favorite. I guess you know that." When Lily Dale responds that she's just his niece, not his daughter, Minnie replies, "Yes, but I'm smart and he admires that in anyone, he told me once" (*Four Plays* 33). She clings to this shred of evidence as proof of her favored status, even though as Lily Dale points out, she can't read Latin and Greek; she's just learning.

Minnie, we infer, feels that life has treated her unjustly, and she has transferred her sense of loss at her own father's abandonment to Horace's family history. None of this is said directly, of course. But the fact that she's told this story over and over, like Cousin Lewis's recitation about Jamie Dale's murder, suggests that it functions as the central episode of her life; all her griefs are crystallized in this narrative. Thus it becomes imperative that Corella admit that she was wrong, that Horace and Lily Dale agree to her interpretation of the facts. Then, perhaps, life will right itself. When Corella says to Horace in her hospital room, "I think she's half crazy, Son. She goes over all that all the time, like it happened just yesterday," we understand that on some level Minnie's life is frozen at this point in the past, and she is trying desperately to do something about it.

Minnie's visit to Horace, whom she was unable to reach in Houston, is yet one more effort to come to some peace with her past. She's told Will to tell Horace that she'll be coming to Harrison soon, as "she has some facts to put before [him]" (*Two Plays* 63). Her conversation with Horace when she finally arrives becomes the emotional and thematic climax of the play. What is remarkable, especially in contrast with Lewis's story, is that she is able to step back and see herself from a distance, admitting that it's senseless to hold on to something that happened long ago. In fact, she tells Elizabeth, who is alone in the store when Minnie arrives, that she almost turned around and went back home. "I've been trying every way in the world I could to get down here to tell him [Horace] about it," she says. "I teach school, you know. I only have the weekends. So, I said this weekend I'm bound I'm going and I did, but now I got here I don't know why I came. I don't want to bother him anymore now with what happened twenty-five years ago or more. So, I almost turned around and went back, but I thought, no. He's my cousin, the cousin I'm most fond of, and I'll just go and visit with him before I go back to Houston" (*Two Plays* 91). It is a freeing moment for Minnie. When Horace arrives, delighted to see her ("Well, look who's here. Cousin Minnie. You're just the one I wanted to see. I was awake half the night trying to remember Cousin Cal's oldest daughter's name"), she is able not only to let go of her anger at last, but to admit that in fact she envied the Thorntons all these years. Her speech is revealing, especially vis-à-vis the issue of the extent to which one's life is determined by family. After years of criticizing the Thorntons for not being serious and scholarly, like the Robedauxs, Minnie admits, "I pretended I thought they were foolish and frivolous, and I'm sure they were, but that's really how I wanted to be, to have beaux and go to dances and play the piano and sing songs with my family. Not study Latin and Greek and worry about becoming a schoolteacher. I pretended to despise them, but I envied them. . . . I wanted them so for my relatives" (*Two Plays* 93). Although she has indeed become a schoolteacher and scholar, like her uncles, whom the Thorntons criticized for having too *much* learning, at this point in her life Minnie can acknowledge her desires as an individual; she can see beyond the received wisdom of her Robedaux forebears and look at the world through her own eyes.

She has also recognized the mysterious, ephemeral nature of family. One can't choose one's family, as the above quote emphasizes. The particular configuration of individuals who will, as our family, have an enormous, perhaps critical influence on shaping our lives is totally random, beyond our control. And while it can seem palpable in its concreteness, as solid as a rock, as an institution it, too, is subject to change. In answer to Horace's opening question (Cousin Cal's oldest daughter is Delia, it turns out; she's married with three children, though Cal himself is dead), she says, "Dead. So many are dead. So many of the cousins. Of course, there are new cousins, their children, and their children's children, but I've lost track of most of them." Then, beginning to cry, she speaks what may be the most poignant words of the entire play: "A family is a remarkable thing, isn't it? You belong. And then you don't. It passes you by. Unless you start a family of your own" (*Two Plays* 92). Now an unmarried, middle-aged schoolteacher, Minnie is alone in the world except for a few distant cousins, most of whom she doesn't like very much. "I'm alone," she says. "I've no mother or father or sisters or brothers, no husband, no children, only cousins who don't want to fool with me. Cousins. Cousins" (*Two Plays* 92).

We realize, with Minnie, that you can't choose your family. It simply is, with both its strengths and weaknesses. One's path in life is shaped largely by what family you belong to; Minnie, for instance, becomes a schoolteacher, is "serious" and doesn't go to dances not because she wants to but because she's a Robedaux and that's part of her family value system. But she is eventually able to see that, to understand her behavior and her attitudes and move on, unlike Cousin Lewis and Lily Dale, both of whom will remain essentially children, refusing to take responsibility for their own decisions. Family is where you start from, but not where you have to end up.

It's interesting structurally that the play concludes with the overlapping of Minnie's and Lewis's stories. Lewis enters the store just as Minnie is leaving. While they are all there together briefly, Gordon tells sotto voce the story of Jamie Dale's tombstone, and Lewis, overhearing, says, "My name is Lewis Higgins. What the hell are you talking about Lewis Higgins?" thus cursing in front of a lady. As Gordon, Horace's cousin on the Thornton side, offers to take Minnie, a Robedaux cousin, to the train station, the symbology is subtle but appropriate; the two sides of the family are joined in this small gesture. The play ends with Lewis retelling his story one more time, after having asked once again if Horace is his cousin. He adds, reflectively, "The graveyard is full of our cousins. The town is full of them. We'll be in that graveyard someday, I'll be there and you'll be there. Why, the graveyard will be full of cousins" (*Two Plays* 99). His comment points to mortality and the fact that for all our striving, we all end up in the graveyard eventually.[9] Though Lewis is hardly capable of benefitting from this piece of wisdom, the audience is. In the last analysis this comic play, we realize, holds forth considerable wisdom.

One final motif and another lens through which to examine family is the concept of marriage. Like the seemingly endless pairs of cousins in this play, we are offered a considerable array of marriages to observe and compare. The proliferation of marriages underlines the importance of family as contributing to or detracting from one's well-being and happiness, although unlike other family members, one can choose one's marriage partner. As Minnie's speech indicates, this choice results in the creation of a new family and determines, to a large extent, the course of one's adult life. Thus the importance of this decision cannot be overestimated.

To illustrate this point, Foote reintroduces Lily Dale and her husband, Will, who, although they have been mentioned in plays subsequent to *Lily Dale,* have not actually appeared on stage. Now the parents of a four-year-old son, they are quite well off financially. Will has succeeded in business, and both he and Lily Dale take great pride in their new house, new piano, and two new Packards. The qualities we observed in Lily Dale as a young woman have solidified; it quickly becomes obvious that she is as self-absorbed and insensitive as ever.

9. References to the graveyard occur throughout the *Cycle,* becoming an important motif which serves to unify and comment upon the action. Foote's fascination with cemeteries, a fact frequently mentioned in criticism and interviews, stems from his childhood. He says in his interview with Ronald L. Davis, for instance, "I was fascinated by cemeteries, I was fascinated by seeing little children's tombstones, and I was fascinated by the legends. I knew the history of everybody in the graveyard by the time I was fourteen. I went with my grandmother often, because she grieved very deeply for my grandfather. She went out there almost every day. It was kind of a friendly place to me." See Davis, "Roots in Parched Ground: An Interview with Horton Foote," *Southwest Review* 73 (summer 1988): 299.

Shortly after Horace arrives at the hospital, having just seen his critically ill mother for the first time, Lily Dale asks him, "Have you heard about my beautiful new house which Will has furnished so lavishly?" adding, "I want him to take you over there to spend the night so you can see everything. I have the most beautiful piano in the city of Houston and my drapes are the most expensive he could find. And the rugs, Horace" (*Two Plays* 42). Her knowledge of Horace and Elizabeth's financial struggles does not prevent her from bringing up her wealth whenever possible, and she will not rest until they have been to her home to see it themselves. While Will is more generous in spirit than Lily Dale, his values, too, are defined in material terms.

They have settled into a comfortable existence. Since the birth of their son, Lily Dale refers to her husband as "Daddy," a pet name which suggests a paternalistic marital relationship rather than the partnership of two adults. Their relationship is based on a kind of exchange system: Will keeps Lily Dale happy, while demonstrating his economic status, by showering her with gifts; he has taken over the role which Pete Davenport played when she was a child. In spite of their financial success, however, Lily Dale is not content. She is obsessed with getting her music published, and even after her compositions have been rejected by ten different publishers, she pressures Will to move to New York for her "career." She is overinvolved with her mother, calling her five or six times a day; Corella says that if Lily Dale hasn't called her by seven A.M., she begins to worry. And she barely mentions her son, except when comparing him to Horace and Elizabeth's children; when a fortune-teller informs Lily Dale that her life will be changed in nine months, her reply is telling: "Oh, I hope . . . I'm not going to have another baby" (*Two Plays* 66).

In spite of her wealth and Will's success, she seems envious of Horace and Elizabeth, ironically, complaining to Corella that she finds Elizabeth cold and self-centered; "all she thinks about, it seems to me," she says, "is Brother and her children" (*Two Plays* 43). While this marriage is holding up for now, largely, we suspect, because Lily Dale and Will have not yet encountered any major crises, it is like the house built on sand of the biblical parable; one wonders how long it will survive.[10]

10. This matter will be taken up in *The Young Man from Atlanta*, Foote's Pulitzer Prize–winning play, which dramatizes the life of Lily Dale and Will years later, after the apparent suicide of their son.

Cousin Monty and his wife, Lola, also financially successful, seem even less content in their marriage than Lily Dale and Will. They live in Harrison, but keep an apartment in Houston; they travel to Europe and float aimlessly from place to place, seeking new pleasures and diversions. Like Will, Monty seems to define himself in terms of his wealth. Having heard that Corella is facing surgery and that Horace is coming to see her, he calls every hospital in town to discover where she is so that he can see Horace. When he finally encounters his cousin in the waiting room, moments after greeting him he says, "Well, Cousin Horace, I'm a rich man" (*Two Plays* 45). When Horace responds simply, "I know you are," Monty says, "I sure don't mean to rub it in, but I wish you had taken my advice." He goes on to talk about the time that he'd invited Horace to invest $500 in an oil venture which ended up making him rich. Horace declined, choosing instead to put his money in a rent house, which, because the renters don't pay up, has not been a profitable investment.

Monty and Lola delight in referring back to this moment, a turning point in their lives and potentially, in Horace's. Lola says to Horace, for instance, quoting her husband, "'Why, all of Cousin Horace's worries would be over by now if he had just listened to me and put in that five hundred dollars,' Monty keeps saying" (*Two Plays* 46). Like Cousin Lewis's Jamie Dale story and Minnie's accusations against Corella, this becomes a kind of refrain which Monty repeats at every possible occasion. Indeed, in spite of his protestation about not wanting to "rub it in," one gets the distinct impression that the reason Monty took such pains to see Horace at the hospital is to once again bring up this subject, which makes him feel superior and highlights his success by contrasting it with Horace's situation. Yet in spite of living a life of luxury, the friction between Monty and Lola and their overall discontent are obvious; they bicker and "snarl" at one another, the stage directions tell us. Their wealth is not a sufficient substitute for mutual love and respect.[11]

The marriage of Corella and Pete, likewise, though cordial and

11. Gerald C. Wood summarizes Foote's attitude toward materialism succinctly in his essay "Horton Foote's Politics of Intimacy": "In Horton Foote's imaginative world, obsessive materialism indicates a failure of the kindness and generosity that could transform society. When intimacy is not achieved the void is filled by a dark call to artificial security." See Wood, "Horton Foote's Politics of Intimacy," *Journal of American Drama and Theatre* 9, no. 2 (1997): 48–49.

pleasant enough, does not reflect deep love or devotion. Corella has had two failed marriages. She married Paul Horace for love, but when he began drinking, she left him; her marriage to Pete for financial security has left her emotionally and spiritually empty. Mae Buchanan, another well-to-do cousin of Horace's, has been married five times; Lola, in her typical snide fashion, refers to Mae and her "five four-flushers": "She must like them, marrying so many. I bet she's over there [Europe] right now looking for another four-flusher to marry," she says (*Two Plays* 82). Unhappy marriages, ranging from rancorous to merely sad and empty, are everywhere in evidence.

Thus the deep love of Horace and Elizabeth, which sustains and enriches both their lives, shines forth as all the more remarkable by way of contrast. One of the central themes of the last four plays of the *Cycle*, the depth of their commitment and mutual devotion is clear to all who come in contact with them. Before her operation Corella says to Horace, for instance, "I used to worry about you, but now you're married to Elizabeth and you have such a happy home," adding to Elizabeth, "You're a wonderful wife to him, Elizabeth" (*Two Plays* 56). In desultory waiting-room conversation Lily Dale says to Lola that Horace is "not close to anybody but his wife and his children." Lola responds, "He worships Elizabeth, doesn't he?" Lily Dale answers, "I guess so" (*Two Plays* 51). Lola's statement and Lily Dale's obvious envy, like Corella's comment, suggest that those around them sense the quiet depth of their love.

Foote also dramatizes this for us in the only scene in which Horace and Elizabeth are alone, late in the play. The scene is Horace's men's shop, and all the family, including Cousin Gordon, have gone to his mother Inez's house for a chicken dinner. Elizabeth elects to stay at the store and have a hamburger with Horace. In the course of their conversation, we see how their marriage functions to sustain them both. Elizabeth asks about the business, knowing that Horace is discouraged. The rain has ruined the cotton crop and business is bad; Horace has only taken in eighty cents that morning. She comforts him, saying that it isn't his fault and she knows they're going to make it; he in turn tells her he went to the bank and borrowed more money. Their pressing financial concerns are made bearable by the fact that they share them with one another. Elizabeth then tells Horace that her ne'er-do-well brother missed his train for Galveston because he was drunk and her father is "in a state." She secured a baby-sitter to take care of the children and "cleared out." "You spend the afternoon here with me," Horace says. When he asks how the children are, Elizabeth replies that they are "wonderful" (*Two Plays* 89). Their devotion to their children is a natural outgrowth of their love for one another.

As Horace leaves to get them a hamburger, Elizabeth says quietly, "Horace . . . I love you," and he responds with the same three small words, taking her in his arms and kissing her. It is not a scene of great passion. In typical understated fashion, Foote uses this brief exchange to suggest the extent of their love. Thus when Elizabeth says that "today is Jenny's birthday," referring to their infant daughter who died in the flu epidemic, and Horace answers simply, "I know," we understand that if they don't talk about their emotions it's because each knows how the other feels. Talk isn't necessary. Elizabeth says that she's planning to go out to the cemetery later to take a plant for Jenny's grave and adds, "I don't forget her. . . . It's like Mama says, you think of her differently than the others, but you think of her," and Horace, who understands completely, doesn't even need to respond. The stage directions say simply, "*Horace goes*" (*Two Plays* 90).

If the overarching action of the *Cycle* as a whole is Horace's finding a family, having lost his own, the arc is completed in his marriage to Elizabeth. Although this choice does not shape his identity in the way that family of origin does, since he enters marriage as an adult, it confirms the choices he has already made relative to his past: the decision not to dwell on past injustices, to forgive Corella and Lily Dale and move forward, to work hard and take responsibility for his own actions. For Horace, Elizabeth is clearly the right choice, bringing him rest and peace and contentment. Corella, Lily Dale, Mae, and Monty make their marriage choices based on their values, also, and, predictably, these marriages serve to solidify character traits already in place. Thus while marriage doesn't shape identity, it creates a place where one is known, where identity is confirmed. The sine qua non of human existence, family connects us to the cosmos.

Thus while *Cousins* on one level provides a comic treatment of family and the small-town milieu, with everyone being related to and knowing the business of everyone else, with feuds and long-standing family quarrels, it also dramatizes how this vast network defines the worlds of these individuals and connects them to the universe. They are all a part of something larger than themselves, for better or for worse. Even in the graveyard, they won't be alone.

Those who value family and realize its importance, like Horace and Minnie, at the same time that they acknowledge its power to limit and circumscribe, are the characters we identify with and admire. They provide the moral yardstick by which we measure the others. When Monty refuses to acknowledge that Mae Buchanan is his cousin, for example, because he doesn't want to be associated with her, or in an even more telling example, when Horace politely inquires about Pete's "people," and he responds, "What people?" (*Two Plays* 58), we regard Monty and Pete with suspicion. They don't appreciate the key role that family plays in personal happiness. It is not enough, however, to cling to family mindlessly, letting it constitute one's whole world, as Lily Dale does, remaining essentially a child. One must come to an understanding of one's self and one's role within the family, deciding ultimately how one wants to respond to it.

With *The Death of Papa,* the sequel to *Cousins* and the last of the nine plays, the *Cycle* comes full circle. While as the title suggests, the play tells the story of the death of Mr. Vaughn, Elizabeth's father, it also brings to a conclusion Horace's narrative and introduces the counterpart to the playwright himself, in the character of ten-year-old Horace, Jr.[12] Dealing with three generations and extended family, it, like the other *Cycle* plays, explores the ways in which family functions to shape individual identity. This is particularly clear in the case of young Horace, an inquisitive and observant child who spends much of the play asking questions, sorting through complex issues, and in general trying to understand his position in the universe. As before, Foote multiplies the meanings of these questions by playing off characters against one another: Horace, Sr., and Brother, Elizabeth's ne'er-do-well younger brother; Horace, Jr., and Horace, Sr., as we remember him from *Roots in a Parched Ground*; young Horace and Gertrude, the Robedauxs' eighteen-year-old black nurse; and even the two grandmothers, Corella and Mary Vaughn.

---

12. This is the only time in his entire canon that Foote employs a character who directly corresponds to himself.

The play begins with the sudden death of Mr. Vaughn, Horace, Jr.,'s maternal grandfather, an event which the playwright identifies as a turning point in his childhood.[13] Mr. Vaughn is a prominent member of the community as well as the patriarch of his family, and his death sends shock waves that reverberate throughout the town. Within the family, several changes occur, most notably Mary's decision to place financial decisions in the hands of Brother, hoping that this responsibility will straighten him out, and the gradual movement of Horace to the position of patriarch when this strategy fails. By the end of the play, Brother's schemes to modernize the cotton farms have failed and his investments gone sour, and he has killed a man in Galveston in a drunken brawl (recalling the hapless Cousin Lewis of the previous play). Though his mother's money and a tolerant judge have gotten him out of this scrape, he is forced to move from Harrison, while Horace remains to watch over the Vaughn estate.

The subplot, which focuses on the coming of age of Horace, Jr., introduces a new generation to the family history, inviting a comparison with the first play of the *Cycle*, in which his father, here called "Big Horace," was dealing with many of the same questions the youth faces. The parallels between the two plays are striking. Both plays, for example, are structured around deaths: in *Roots*, twelve-year-old Horace loses his father, Paul Horace; in *Papa*, Horace, Jr.'s grandfather dies. Both deaths are watershed events in the lives of the young boys. Observing the contrasts between these two events, espe-

---

13. Foote has often spoken of the death of his grandfather as a turning point in his youth and one of the central experiences of his life. In his introduction to *Two Plays*, for instance, Freedman quotes Foote as saying, "The event that always stuck with me, the event I've always been groping toward as a writer, was the day my grandfather died. . . . Until then, life was just magic. I never felt so secure in my life as sitting on the porch swing and knowing I was the grandson of one of the richest families in town and my grandfather was the most respected man in town." Foote then goes on to describe the actual event in some detail, which is almost identical to the action of the play, including the dove, a harbinger of death, that a black woman reports seeing on the house that morning. He concludes, "I think it was the turning point to my whole family. He was kind of the king. And from then on, we had many problems that he would've shielded us from. He was just such a symbol." Freedman, introduction to *Two Plays*, xvii, xviii.

His linking this autobiographical event with his life as a writer suggests the importance of this play to Foote personally and to the *Cycle* as a whole.

cially the nature of family dynamics in each case, brings into sharp focus the extent to which family functions to support or hinder individual development.

In *Roots,* the death of thirty-two-year-old Paul Horace from "whiskey and cigarettes" (the Thornton version) represents the sad end of a wasted life. He and Corella have been separated for some time, and the two families are bitterly divided; as Chapter 3 will detail, young Horace is split between the two warring camps. He barely knows his father; his last visit with him is tightly controlled by his grandmother, a selfish and self-righteous woman. The funeral is small, and Corella, still angry, refuses to go. The play ends with Horace essentially parentless, collecting whiskey bottles to sell and planning to help his Uncle Albert on a plantation worked by convicts, a fairly grim prospect.

Henry Vaughn's death, by way of contrast, comes at the end of a productive and successful life. A philanthropist beloved by all, his funeral is the biggest in the town's history; the funeral procession is three blocks long, and downtown businesses close to show their respect. Horace, Jr., though he mourns his grandfather, is sustained by a family united in grief. His Grandmother Vaughn visits the cemetery every day, taking Horace with her, and his maternal grandmother, Corella, comes from Houston to help out. This integration of the two branches of the family and Horace's secure place in this extended network contrast strikingly with his father's situation when *his* father died. Horace, Sr., has created a secure environment for his son, who starts out in life with all the security and love that he himself was denied. As Horace, Sr., moves to the position of patriarch, and Brother, ironically, becomes the orphan, moving restlessly from place to place, the trajectory of the *Cycle* comes to a close.

As usual, this close is not unambiguous. Horace, for example, too proud to accept help from his mother-in-law, is still struggling financially and will clearly continue to do so. Gerald Wood, in speaking of Foote's mature drama, says that the endings act "more as lulls than resolutions," an especially apt description of this play.[14] But the key conditions for happiness are in place: Horace and Elizabeth's love will sustain them, and their family unit remains strong. There is even a

14. Wood, "Nature of Mystery," 180.

baby on the way. Horace's journey from margin to center, from orphan to patriarch is complete.

As the *Cycle*'s final play, *The Death of Papa* raises many complex issues introduced in the earlier dramas, questions of race, class, culture, and, of course, family, the subject of this chapter. If *Cousins* presents extended family comically, locating Horace in a network of relations that seem to extend indefinitely in time and space, *Papa* shows extended family functioning at its best. Corella and her sister Inez (Gordon's mother), for example, come to watch the children during the funeral and lend whatever help they can. The easy camaraderie between Corella and Mary Vaughn, whose friendship goes back to their childhoods, contrasts with the animosity between the Thorntons and the Robedauxs seen in earlier plays.

It is instructive to compare the two grandmothers. Though she is very kind in her responses to Horace, Jr., Corella responds to his love of reading from the same skewed position that informed her attitude when Horace, Sr., was a boy. Her belief, based on her opinion of her brother-in-law, Terrence Robedaux, is that "overeducated" people are essentially useless, depending on others to support them. "I wish he wasn't reading books," Corella says to Inez early in the play. "It worries me to death. I'm afraid he is going to turn out to be like Terrence Robedaux. And he won't be worth killing then for sure. He'll just spend his life reading books and letting other people take care of him" (*Two Plays* 111). When Inez responds wistfully, "I wish we'd had some education, though. I wish Papa had made us finish school," Corella only says, "There's good and bad in everything," adding that it's "fortunate" that Big Horace outgrew his love of reading (evidently his fondness for reading newspapers doesn't count).

This issue, which crops up periodically throughout the play, eventually comes to represent the ways in which Corella failed Horace as a child. Near the end of the play, it precipitates a confrontation between Horace and his mother that makes explicit the things he didn't say to her in the *Cousins'* hospital room scene.[15] When Corella says

15. In including this scene, Foote is employing a strategy which he uses throughout the *Cycle,* namely, taking a single episode and playing out two different endings. In the hospital confrontation scene between Horace and Corella in *Cousins,* Horace deflects what could have been an opportunity to articulate the deep pain her actions have caused him. In *Papa,* he lets his emotions show in what for him is an impassioned speech.

that "overeducation is a curse. I can name you boy after boy that were overeducated like Terrence Robedaux and weren't worth killing," Horace responds, in words that for him are unusually strong and direct, "And I can name you boy after boy whose family had no interest at all in them or what they learned. Who no one cared if they went to school or if they didn't. What they had to bear, what they had . . . And some of them that did survive have to work like dogs to make ends meet and to make up for their total lack of education. I could tell you heart-breaking stories . . . about those boys" (*Two Plays* 189). His response, in spite of its deep emotion, is not direct enough to penetrate Corella's defenses, however; she is unable to link the generalized "boys" with Horace, saying only to Elizabeth after he leaves, "I swear I didn't mean a thing in this world. He is so sensitive. I swear I don't know why he is so sensitive." We observed a similar illustration of her denial in the *Cousins* confrontation scene. During that exchange, when Corella asks Horace if he told Minnie that she was the only member of the family that took any interest in him, he says that that wasn't true, then proceeds to cite the help he received from his aunts and his grandparents. "And I was always interested," Corella hastily adds. "Of course we lived apart and circumstances were such that I . . ." (*Two Plays* 40). Her sentence remains uncompleted. On some level, Corella clearly feels guilty for her abandonment of Horace, but she is never able to acknowledge her culpability or understand the extent to which Horace has suffered. Her disparagement of Horace, Jr.,'s reading underlines the fact that she is not able to learn from her mistakes. Her thinking, shaped by the dissolution of her first marriage and the events that led up to it, remains frozen and unbending.

We are all the more impressed, therefore, when Mary Vaughn, young Horace's other grandmother, is able to realize when she is being self-absorbed and takes responsibility for it. Grieving for her husband and focused on thoughts of death, she associates the month of March with the death of her husband. When Horace, Jr., points out that it's also the month of his birthday, she says, "Of course it is,

---

While here Foote plays out the same scene with different endings, one can see this same strategy in the pairing of entire plays, a structural device I will discuss at length in Chapter 5.

forgive me," holding him close to her. "Grief makes us so selfish. Forgive your grandmother. The day you were born was a very happy time for us all" (*Two Plays* 140). While she is not perfect (most notably in her repeated rescuing of Brother), her ability to see beyond her own needs and experiences reflects well on her, especially when compared to Corella.

Another set of paired characters is Horace, Jr., and Gertrude, the family's young black nursemaid. Gertrude's family functions as a kind of shadow family to the Vaughn-Robedauxs. Her Aunt Eliza is Mrs. Vaughn's maid, and her Uncle Walter is Mary's chauffeur; references to their extended family hint at another network of lives being lived out with its own joys and sorrows. This is, of course, most clearly emphasized with the tragic drowning of Gertrude midway through the play, echoing the death of Mr. Vaughn, which has set the play in motion. Though their ages are considerably different (Horace is only ten and Gertrude eighteen), both are at the beginning of their life journeys, attempting to make sense of their place in society. In a lengthy conversation between the two, we are able to observe not only the difference that family makes in identity formation, but also the impact of cultural and ethnic backgrounds. Horace has a much clearer understanding of his family history than Gertrude does, for instance, while her emphasis is on race; each absorbs the values stressed within his or her own family circle. While Gertrude says she doesn't have a father and knows nothing about her two grandfathers, Horace has collected all sorts of information about his ancestors, all the way back to his great-grandfather, who had a plantation and 120 slaves. He is almost totally unaware of race as a social determinant, since for him, growing up white, it has never been an issue. Gertrude's thinking, on the other hand, is almost entirely shaped by her racial identity. She is going to college to help her people, she tells Horace. His response is telling: "Who are your people? Your mama and daddy?" to which she replies, "No. My people . . . my race. That's what Professor McCann says we're in school for. To help our race. Isn't that what you go to school for?" (*Two Plays* 115).

She comments that her professor is as light-skinned as Horace and is aware that Horace, Sr., is "a good friend to all the colored people around here" (*Two Plays* 115). When he mentions his grandfather's slaves, she responds that she's glad she wasn't alive then. Again, Horace's ignorance is revealing. She has to explain to him that "colored people were the slaves." "But no more," she adds; "And you're not going to do to us what you did to the Indians." Horace asks, "What did we do to the Indians?" and she answers, "Killed them all off and moved them onto reservations" (*Two Plays* 117).

Another of Foote's seemingly extraneous conversations, this short exchange is actually very revealing. Both Horace and Gertrude have accepted without question the received wisdom of their tribe; both are finely tuned to what their families value and have not yet ventured outside those conceptual boundaries. As we watch the two of them trying to come to terms with complex historical issues—slavery, the "resettlement" of the Indians, and racial questions, we are aware that their young lives are shaped by those ideas to which they are exposed, both on a societal and a familial level. Further emphasizing the process of identity formation, Foote has Horace ask Elizabeth in a later scene how he can help his race, referring to Gertrude's comment about wanting to help her people, and we realize that he's been mulling over what she has said and trying to integrate it into his own experience. In the same conversation, he queries Elizabeth about the concepts of class and poverty, wondering who is considered poor and why, if they work hard, they remain so—complicated issues for a ten-year-old boy.

The intertwining of these two lives is cut tragically short by Gertrude's sudden death. Typically, Foote doesn't overdramatize this event. Gertrude mentions that she is going fishing the next day; later, Horace, Jr., tells his grandmother that Gertrude drowned—the boat overturned and she couldn't swim. He isn't allowed to go to the funeral, though he seems eager to go with Walter to "see" Gertrude when the offer is made. When Elizabeth returns from the funeral the following day, she cries briefly, saying that "life doesn't seem very fair to me sometimes. We have so much and they have so little" (*Two Plays* 178), and he tries to comfort her.

While that is all the information we're given, we know from observing Horace, Jr., that Gertrude's death registers deeply. Elsewhere in the play he grills Elizabeth on the nature of death: who goes to heaven and why, what happens when you die, whether his Grandfather Robedaux will know him when they meet. He also ponders the nature of time and its relationship to death. After noting the dates on his Grandfather Robedaux's grave, he comments that his father, now thirty-six, is four years older than his own father when he died, and that he himself is older than his older sister Jenny, who died as an infant. Death freezes time, mysteriously allowing a child to be older than his father.

Young Horace is a child on whom nothing is lost. Recalling Henry James's description of the artistic sensibility as a giant spider web, whose whole being vibrates when any one part is disturbed, Horace is the artist as a young man—watching, listening, thinking. Both he and Gertrude begin their lives full of hope and promise; only one of them will live to fulfill that potential.

A third character pair that illustrates how differently similar lives can turn out is Horace, Sr., and Brother. We have encountered Brother in two earlier *Cycle* plays, *Valentine's Day* and *1918,* and his dissipated ways are commented upon in *Cousins.* Seeing him as an adult in this final play is sobering, for the audience if not for Brother himself. While his drinking, gambling, and irresponsibility can be seen as boyish foibles in the earlier plays, it is clear in *The Death of Papa* that Brother is now a confirmed alcoholic, self-pitying and self-serving. In spite of his numerous promises to his mother that he will abstain, he continues to act in a drunken and irresponsible manner, frittering away the fortune his father had built up over a lifetime—making decisions in matters where he is ignorant and ill-informed, talking too much and listening too little, and trusting the wrong people (including a minor character named Will, an "old friend" of Henry Vaughn, who profits from Brother's ignorance in selling him a herd of cattle).

It is instructive to compare Brother, whose life is in a shambles, with Horace, steady, hardworking, honest, and respected. One thinks of the question that Foote says informs all his work: what makes one person succeed in life, even in the face of great hardships, while another crumbles? Here as elsewhere, family is a major contributor to the shaping of individual destiny. Brother is in many ways like Lily Dale—pampered, coddled, and excused from difficult or onerous responsibilities. Ironically, the Vaughns' wealth becomes a liability, enabling them to bail Brother out when he has problems, which they do all too frequently: paying gambling debts, subsidizing an abortion for a girl he has gotten pregnant, making good his delinquent loans,

and fixing his murder trial. The costs get steadily steeper, both financially and morally, as the magnitude of his mistakes increases.

As Brother's situation draws to a climax, his farms in a state of ruin
and his investments gone sour, he strikes out at his sister, his mother,
the tenant farmers, even his dead father. "You think it is so easy?" he
says to Mrs. Vaughn. "All I hear is, your papa didn't do it this way.
Your papa didn't do it that way. I'm sick to death of hearing about
how Papa did things. Was he so perfect? Was he some kind of god? I
didn't think he was so damn perfect. I thought he made plenty of
mistakes. Plenty. I was scared as hell of him, for one thing. He always
made me feel like I couldn't do anything. I was dumb . . . I was in-
competent" (*Two Plays* 157). Although he apologizes immediately
afterwards, we sense that he is speaking the truth when he says, "I'm
not Papa. I'm never going to be Papa. I don't want to be him, or like
him in any way . . . Not in any way" (*Two Plays* 157).

Although it may have been done out of a desire to help Brother,
in the last analysis the Vaughns' repeated decisions to bail him out of
trouble have not served him well. To this extent, Brother may be regarded as a victim of poor parenting—a dysfunctional family, to use
contemporary terminology. At the same time, we consider the hand
fate has dealt Horace, who was abandoned by his family at any early
age. He, like Brother, could have drowned his sorrows in drink, taking refuge in a victim stance. Indeed, he does drink and gamble before he marries Elizabeth; as Mrs. Vaughn points out in the play's
closing scene, that's why she and her husband opposed their marriage. "But you've changed," she says to him. "You're responsible
and hardworking. A good husband and father. How have you
changed?" to which Horace replies simply, "I don't know. I just did.
I loved Elizabeth and I did" (*Two Plays* 191).

Those three sentences may be the cycle's most concise articulation
of the ultimate mysteriousness of life. Horace offers no explanations,
takes no credit. He simply loved Elizabeth, and the transformation
followed. While it is not perhaps a sufficient explanation, it does point
to Foote's belief in the redemptive power of love. At the same time,
he acknowledges that some things defy rational explanations. When
Mrs. Vaughn asks him what she should do about Brother, he answers,
"I don't know. I only know when I got into trouble there was no one
I could turn to to help me out." "And that was a blessing in disguise,

do you think?" she asks, and Horace says simply, "I don't know now. There was a time I felt very bitter about it. I felt no one cared about me at all. Now I don't know" (*Two Plays* 181). Eschewing the easy answer, Foote doesn't make Horace a hero who pulled himself up by his bootstraps, while Brother plays the part of poor little rich kid. Horace acknowledges his bitterness and pain, as well as the fact that at this point, he himself can't account for the way his life has turned out, other than to say he "loved Elizabeth." Individual identity, then, while shaped by family values and attitudes, is also affected by the vagaries of whatever experiences life brings us. Gertrude dies, while young Horace lives. Brother sinks deeper into alcoholism and despair, while Horace becomes a productive citizen. Cousin Lewis remains frozen in time, while Minnie is able to move forward. We're left with these facts, and a sense of wonder.

The play ends on a note of uncertainty. In a passage that recalls the title of the *Cycle*, Brother, forced to leave Harrison because of the scandal he is embroiled in, says to Horace, "I used to feel so sorry for you when you would come and call on Elizabeth. I'd hear Papa and Mama talking and they said you were practically an orphan and had no home. Now you have a home and I don't. I expect someday you'll even be living in my home while I'm wandering around the world." When Horace demurs, saying, "This is my home," Brother replies, in the closing words of the play, "Don't be too sure. Don't be too sure about anything, big [*sic*] Horace. Not about anything in this world" (*Two Plays* 194). That the play and the *Cycle* conclude on this note of uncertainty is no accident. Indeed, it is Foote's point. While we can isolate factors and causes, motives and reasons, ultimately some corner of individual destiny eludes our explanations. What we can say for certain is that in the vast realm of life experiences, few things are as important as family and love. While it may not seem like much, it is truth enough to cling to.

One final point. It is interesting to consider who the protagonist of this final play is. On one level, of course, it is the last chapter of Horace's story; Brother's story, while an important strand of the narrative, functions primarily as a contrast to that of Horace, Sr. One might also argue with impunity that with the advent of young Horace, the focus subtly shifts to the next generation. In a sense, however, the real protagonist of the play is the town itself. While the death of

Henry Vaughn brings about a radical restructuring of his family, it also represents a seachange occurring in the town as a whole. Everything changes with the death of Papa. The Vaughn household breaks up. As the play ends, Mrs. Vaughn is moving away, leaving the home she has lived in all her married life, and Brother will become a permanent drifter. Only Elizabeth is left, and she is part of a new family unit with Horace. The town, too, is changing. Business is no longer conducted with a handshake and a man's word, as Brother finds out when he tries to collect debts owed his father. Unscrupulous men like Will Borden, twice saved by Mr. Vaughn when he was going under financially, swindle and cheat their supposed friends if they can profit by it.

This transition from the town as a kind of extended family to a colder, more impersonal milieu is perhaps best illustrated by the anecdote of the pecan tree. When Mr. Vaughn donated a large piece of land to the town so that a new road could be paved, he made the city fathers promise that they would not cut down a favorite pecan tree that grew there. After his death, the tree is chopped down, a deed which deeply hurts Mrs. Vaughn. In speaking of this with her mother, Elizabeth asks, "Did he have it in writing?" "No," she responds. "But they promised him. I remember" (*Two Plays* 179). It is, however, a brave new world, past the time when promises are enough.

The Death of Papa is thus a fitting end to the *Cycle,* which tells the story both of Horace Robedaux and his family and of Harrison as a whole. The precise nature of the nexus between individual, family, and society and the ways in which the culture, too, contributes to individual identity is the subject of the next chapter.

3

CULTURAL INFLUENCES

Community, Language, and Identity

In an interview with John L. DiGaetani that appears in DiGaetani's book *A Search for a Postmodern Theater,* Foote points out that in poems and plays he's especially fond of, the effects are often achieved by "suggestion rather than statement." When DiGaetani says, "You feel that understated language is important in the theater," Foote responds, "I think language in general is of enormous importance— language is everything to me." Later in the same interview he says, "Writing has been one of the great joys of my life. I love reading, I love being read to, I love words, I love writing—the whole process."[1]

In the emphasis he places on language, especially on telling and listening to stories, Foote keeps company with other great writers of the South who, as a group, tend to value the oral tradition more than their counterparts elsewhere. Marjorie Smelstor points to this fact, calling Foote's characters "storytellers," who have, as she puts it, "a constant need to narrate and listen to narrative." Quoting Reynolds Price, another Southern writer much admired by Foote, she continues, " 'A need to tell and hear stories is essential to the species *Homo sapiens*—second in necessity apparently after nourishment and before love and shelter. Millions survive without love or home, almost none in silence; the opposite of silence leads quickly to narrative, and the

This chapter appeared, in a condensed and slightly altered form, as "Subtext as Text: Language and Culture in Horton Foote's Texas Cycle," in *Horton Foote: A Casebook,* ed. Gerald C. Wood (New York: Garland Publishing, 1998).

1. DiGaetani, "Horton Foote," 68, 71.

sound of story is the dominant sound of our lives.'" Smelstor concludes, "Having said that he gets his ideas from sound rather than
pictures, and that he starts with hearing and with voices, Foote echoes both Price—and Eudora Welty, who describes the act of listening
in her book *One Writer's Beginnings* and who connects this experience of listening with home and family and memory." By his own
testimony, Foote grew up listening to stories. Freedman quotes
Foote as saying, for instance, "When I was growing up . . . I spent
half of my time in the house listening. I always loved old people, and
you know they always adored me, because I could sit and listen for
hours." To David Sterritt of the *Christian Science Monitor* he comments, "One thing I was given in life is a deep desire to listen. I've
spent my life listening. When we were children, my brother—who
preferred baseball—would ask me why I fooled with all these things!
I said I didn't know, but I was just fascinated."[2]

Given Foote's testimony regarding the importance of language in
his work, it behooves us to examine with care how it functions, particularly since in many ways he violates conventional dramatic practices and modes of expression. Consider, for example, the fact that
his plays contain almost no stage directions. We are given no physical
descriptions of the personae, no indications of their emotional responses, no suggestions as to movement or blocking.[3] Thus divesting
himself of one of the playwright's principal tools, Foote relies almost
entirely on dialogue to carry meaning. But in both its lexicon and its
overt emotional content, his dialogue is also restrained. In *The Orphans' Home Cycle*, as in all of his plays, Foote deliberately limits himself to the ordinary language of average people living in a small Texas
town at the turn of the century. Their diction is flat, sparse, and unadorned. There are very few long speeches, with many one- or two-
word responses: "Yes, Ma'am," "No, Ma'am." The following conver-

2. Smelstor, "Social and Moral History," 12; Freedman, introduction to *Two
Plays*, xx; David Sterritt, "Horton Foote: Filmmaking Radical with a Tender Touch,"
Christian Science Monitor, May 15, 1986, 36.
3. In speaking of his tendency to omit stage directions, Foote once said, "If I put
[*Smiling*] in a script, a good actor is going to scratch that out. If you write strongly
enough, it's apparent what the emotion is and the actor might find a moment that you
hadn't thought of." Foote, quoted in Hachem, "Foote-Work," 41.

sation taken from *Roots in a Parched Ground* that the twelve-year-old Horace has with Mr. Ritter, a drunken friend of his father, is typical:

> MR. RITTER: Were you with your father when he died, Son?
> HORACE: No Sir.
> MR. RITTER: Was anybody with him?
> HORACE: My grandmother.
> MR. RITTER: Not your mother?
> HORACE: No Sir.
> MR. RITTER: That's right—they were separated.
> HORACE: Yes Sir.
> MR. RITTER: Any hope for a reconciliation?
> HORACE: No Sir.
> MR. RITTER: Why not? There's always hope, I think.
> HORACE: He's dead.
> MR. RITTER: Oh, of course.
>
> *(Four Plays* 52)

Likewise, in *Courtship,* the fifth play of the *Cycle,* the first kiss of Horace and Elizabeth Vaughn, an event fraught with significance in their budding romance, passes unremarked by either of them. In the midst of a conversation on Elizabeth's front porch, the stage directions merely state, *"They kiss."* Though this will mark the turning point in both their lives, Elizabeth matter-of-factly resumes their conversation without comment. In Foote's plays, what is unsaid is often more important than what is said.

It is also significant that all of his *Cycle* characters use more or less the same vocabulary. With occasional exceptions, language is not used to indicate social class. Instead, it becomes a kind of leveler, a font into which all dip with much the same results. The homogeneity of their lexicon and syntax reflects a culture which, though not without its problems, is coherent, whole, of a piece. Unlike the characters in a Mamet play—*Glengarry Glen Ross* or *American Buffalo,* for example, of whom this same statement could be made—the linguistic sameness of Foote's personae does not indicate a cultural and spiritual poverty. Just the opposite. The reason language works so well to communicate in this world is that the characters share values and attitudes, social conventions, and individual and collective pasts.

Even though societal norms and expectations are never overtly articulated, they are nevertheless known to all, including those who rebel against them. Thus to decode the meanings residing in the dialogue, one must make explicit the cultural realities of this particular time and place. As we do so, it will become clear that undergirding the cultural matrix of these nine plays are three central issues: (1) How does the individual fit within the larger context: family, town, and world? (2) How does what is said, the bits and pieces of conversation, fit into a larger whole? and (3) How does one's cultural community both shape and circumscribe individual identity?

Roots in a Parched Ground, the opening play, tells the story that both announces the *Cycle*'s theme and sets it in motion. The title is taken from William Carlos Williams's poem "Raleigh Was Right": "Love itself a flower / with roots in a parched ground." The poem is an affirmation of Raleigh's parody of Marlowe's famous "Come Live with Me and Be My Love," a bucolic pastoral extolling the joys of peasant life. Williams (like Raleigh before him) takes an unsentimental look at love, knowing that though it blooms in unlikely and inhospitable soil, it often does not have the roots to sustain it. In this play Horace loses his father, who dies of alcoholism and broken dreams while still a young man. Paul Horace has been estranged from his wife Corella for several years owing to conflicts between their two families, and Horace is caught in the middle of these warring camps. By the time the play is over, Horace is for all practical purposes an orphan. His father is dead, his mother has remarried and moved to Houston with his sister, Lily Dale, and his paternal grandmother and her family have moved, as well. The final scene sees Horace looking for empty whiskey bottles to sell, vowing to save enough money to buy a tombstone for his father's grave. All the adults in his life, including two friends of his father who promised to take care of the boy, have failed him. Seeing himself as all alone in the world, Horace sets about finding a home, a quest that will be pursued through the next eight plays.

The play begins in obvious disorder. Horace is caught between two warring families, the vibrant, music-loving, warm, and unpretentious Thorntons on his mother's side and the highly refined and educated, somewhat cold and distant Robedauxs on his father's. The physical division of stage space reinforces this split, with stage right designated as the Thorntons' and stage left as the Robedauxs'. Hor-

ace moves uneasily between these two camps, literally and figuratively. His parents' separation several years earlier has solidified the
tensions and misunderstandings between the two families of which
Horace is a part, and the suffering which ensues as he tries to find
his place in the world is painful to watch. His father lies dying in the
Robedaux family home, while just a few doors away the Thorntons
are celebrating a reunion with singing and dancing. Corella, back
from Houston where she's been working making shirts, refuses to
speak to her estranged husband and later won't even go to his funeral, so bitter is she about the circumstances that ended their marriage, yet neither her feelings nor their origin is verbalized.

Horace's last visit with his dying father is a particularly poignant
scene, though understated in typical Foote fashion. The entire interaction is controlled by Horace's unfeeling, domineering grandmother, who summons Horace in, directs what he is to say, then
dismisses him. His only words are, "Hello, Papa," and "Goodbye,
Papa." Yet in the sequel play, Horace, in naming those who care for
him, can only think of his father. "My daddy cared about me, but
he's dead," he says matter-of-factly (*Four Plays* 97).

By *Root*'s end, Horace has come to the understanding that he's on
his own. The adults who should look after him have either died,
moved away, or failed him, and at twelve he is alone in the world. It
may not seem the stuff of great tragedy, but as a statement of the
existential condition it wields great power in its simplicity. Horace's
life is as drained of possibility as the empty whiskey bottles he seeks,
and the play's last action—his father's friend Mr. Ritter giving him a
dime—is painfully ironic.

In this play, as in all nine, what is left unsaid is often more important than what is said—a hallmark of Foote's style and the first rhetorical trait I would like to examine. In a scene early in act 1, for
example, when Horace talks to his dying father, it is clear both that
his father loves him and that he has been fairly uninvolved in his son's
life, though nothing is said directly about either fact. Paul Horace
asks Horace if he's been going to school and is concerned to learn
he's not, because his teacher (whose name Horace's father doesn't
know) thinks he's "dumb." He asks his son to bring his books the
next day so he can help him, he corrects his grammar (no one else
bothers to do so), and he answers all his questions—of which there

are many. Young Horace asks his father if he's a lawyer (it's interest-ing that he's not sure) and if Mr. John Howard is his partner, then inquires about a tragedy in John Howard's life (in five typically un-derstated exchanges, we learn that Mr. Howard's two children were killed in a fire ten years earlier, and his wife, now mentally deranged, hasn't left their house since). His father is the one person both wise and caring enough to guide Horace through the vicissitudes of child-hood to a productive adult life, but he is dying.

Thus it's doubly tragic that on his deathbed, as Horace is called in to say good-bye, the boy is not free to speak his heart to his father, primarily because, unlike the previous occasion, his Grandmother Robedaux is present and controlling what can and can't be said. We have observed in previous scenes that she is both negative and manip-ulative (she complains in her son's name of the music coming from the Thorntons' home, for example, and though Paul Horace himself says he enjoys it, she later complains a second time that it upsets him). In conversations about the disintegration of Paul Horace's marriage, it is implied that perhaps the key factor was his mother, two brothers, a sister, and her daughter Minnie moving in with the young, strug-gling couple. The burden of assuming their financial support drove Paul Horace to drink and ultimately broke his spirit. Thus we know both first- and second-hand that this woman, who sees herself as in-nocent, a long-suffering martyr, manipulates reality to suit her own vision.

When Horace, who has been summoned by his grandmother, en-ters the sickroom with his younger sister, Lily Dale, the scene is or-chestrated by Mrs. Robedaux, who draws the children to her and says, "Dear Lord, why have you brought this suffering on this pre-cious child of mine? Spare him, I pray you, for the sake of these two innocent children who so need a father's love and guidance" (*Four Plays* 35). When her son moves his lips, she says, "Speak to him, chil-dren." "What shall I say?" Horace asks, and she tells him to say hello. Those will be the only words he is allowed: "Hello, Papa," and when he is told to leave, "Goodbye, Papa."

We know Horace suffers deeply the loss of his father. When he learns of his father's death and observes his mother's bitter response to this news (more on this shortly), he doesn't comment, exiting quickly, ostensibly to check on his fishing lines. Lily Dale responds that he goes to the river to smoke, and his Grandfather Thornton grabs him and shakes him. The fact that he has just lost his father is evidently not as important as the possibility that he smokes or that he calls his sister a liar when she accuses him. Later, with his friends, when asked about his parents' separation, he remains silent; when his friend Thurman says, "I bet you feel sad about your papa dying," he simply leaves. Deep emotions are not articulated or publicly displayed; for the most part, Foote doesn't even allow them to be seen on stage.

Two other brief examples of this emotional restraint: When Corella is told by her brother Albert that her husband is near death, she merely says, "Oh?" and continues her sewing. We are, of course, given no stage directions to indicate her emotional response, nor Horace's as he sits there and watches; we're only told that after a moment he gets up and leaves (*Four Plays* 7). When Paul Horace actually dies, we get a bit more information, which helps us understand Corella's unemotional response. Her mother wonders whether they should pay their respects or send food, and Corella says (again, in front of Horace), "I'm not going near them. I'll not put my foot in that house." Though she thinks the children should go to the cemetery, she refuses to go herself: "I couldn't stand being near them and if I went and stayed apart from them . . . (*Pause.*) Well, you know. Oh, don't look at me that way, Sis. I am very bitter still and I can't help it" (*Four Plays* 42). Several observations here: First, proper forms must be observed; even if she cannot bring herself to attend the funeral, the children should pay their respects. Secondly, it's unacceptable even for Corella's own sister to pry into the reasons for this decision. Corella simply states her position, and no one gainsays her. To do so would violate an unspoken but ironclad code of behavior.

In terms of dramatic exposition, we note that Foote withholds both Corella's emotional response to Paul Horace's death and the reason for her bitterness toward his family. We have to piece together for ourselves from second-hand information the reasons for their failed marriage and Corella's subsequent rancor. In this, as in other matters, Foote's use of language forces us to do what the townspeople have already done: sift through the two families' versions of the story and come to our own conclusions (hence the effectiveness of dividing the stage space and action between the two opposing families). Cousin Minnie's reaction is perhaps the strongest—ironically, since she's of another generation and seemingly the least affected by her aunt and uncle's separation. Yet she refuses to call Corella by name, referring to her by pronouns only. When Lily Dale comes to see her dying father, Minnie says to her, "I'm his favorite. I guess you know that" (*Four Plays* 33). We gather that her identification with her uncle is strong, especially since she and her mother were abandoned by her own father. As we saw in Chapter 2, she blames Corella for the failure of the marriage, accepting at face value the version she has probably heard from her Grandmother Robedaux. "Your mama is to blame for it, you know," she says to Lily Dale. "She deserted him when he needed her. All she was ever interested in was money. When he got sick and couldn't work, she left him" (*Four Plays* 38).

Lily Dale, on the other hand, is told a different version by her elders. Trying to sort it out, she tells Horace, "Aunt Virgie says it isn't true. She says Papa is being killed by whiskey and cigarettes and worry. Worry because he has to feed and clothe his relatives. She says his family are all shiftless and lazy" (*Four Plays* 38). Then Lily Dale gives us the one account we have of the final, irrevocable split: "I won't ever forget it. Walking down the street at two in the morning in our nightgowns with the neighbors all watching from their windows, Minnie screaming at Mama, Grandma Robedaux crying, Mama crying . . . Uncle Terrence calling to everybody to be calm" (*Four Plays* 38). As readers, then, we must sift through various versions of the story, testing one against the other, judging the degree to which a given character is or is not prone to exaggerate, embellish, distort. Foote will neither give us a single, direct account of what happened nor allow the characters who are most involved to reveal their feelings. We, like the children, in this case, can only observe the adults and come to our own conclusions.

As we watch Horace trying to decide on a course in life, we see a final example of this phenomenon. Horace has noted his father's concern that he continue his education and become a lawyer, and when he learns that his mother and her new husband are coming to visit, he takes the notion that he'll move to Houston with them and study law. Even though he hasn't attended school for some time, he starts going regularly, checking his fishing lines at daybreak so he can make it to school on time. He also quits chewing tobacco when he learns that his stepfather doesn't chew. He tells his friend Larry, "He doesn't chew, he doesn't drink, he doesn't smoke. As a matter of fact, he doesn't have any bad habits at all" (*Four Plays* 74). He's obviously eager to please his new father and awaits the visit with great anticipation. Thus when he's rejected by Mr. Davenport, who dotes on Lily Dale but feels boys should work for a living as he himself once did, Horace's hopes are dashed. "Lawyers are a dime a dozen," Pete says; "I wouldn't let a son of mine study for the law" (*Four Plays* 82). Corella, sadly, is no help. When Horace works up his courage to ask if he can come live with them in Houston, she tells him they have no room, at which point Lily Dale insists on performing a piece on the piano and the subject is dropped.

Foote doesn't dwell on this scene. The lights fade quickly and come up again on Horace, down by the river smoking his pipe and saying to his friend that it's "too noisy" at his house; he prefers the quiet. He also states flatly that he's decided not to go to Houston (he "doesn't care" for cities) or to school, since "lawyers are a dime a dozen." When his friend asks him what he calls his stepfather (titles are important in this community), Horace simply says, "Mr. Davenport." In masterful understatement, to the question "Do you think you'll ever call him anything else?" Horace replies, "Nope." This is not to be his father. His life has changed forever in a few short moments. He's decided he'll go to the Gautier plantation and work with his Uncle Albert for "my grub, all the tobacco I want, and four bits a week," adding, "I'm on my own" (*Four Plays* 84). The turning point of his life, the end of his childhood, is contained in these four words.

What do these examples tell us about the cultural milieu which informs this play and the eight that follow? What Southern mores and linguistic conventions do they reveal, and how does Foote's language both shape and reflect these realities?

One of the most obvious axioms of behavior that we observe is that children must not question, challenge, or even take the initiative with their elders. Horace cannot challenge his grandmother's authority, for instance, even though his father is dying and he knows he may never see him again. Although he is a bit more free to take the initiative with his father when Mrs. Robedaux is not present, even then there are certain topics he does not bring up, things we assume he would like to know, like why his father and mother are separated (or even what "separation" means, since he clearly doesn't know), how his father feels about dying, what impact this will have on his own future. Horace must guess, surmise, and piece together from whatever information he can gather the facts of his past and his prospects for the future.

The cultural value informing this rule of behavior is that children should respect their elders. A closely related value which extends this conversational restraint to adults is that of privacy. Corella's sister Mary assumes it would be a violation of her privacy if she presumed to ask Corella her reasons for not attending her husband's funeral. While it may have some advantages, the dictate "Thou shalt not interfere" can also have negative consequences. One poignant example of this occurs at the end of *Valentine's Day,* the sixth play of the *Cycle,* which tells the story of Horace's marriage to Elizabeth. A seemingly desultory conversation occurs in the final moments of the play between Horace, Elizabeth, her father, and two residents of the boardinghouse where Horace and Elizabeth live. In typical style, this seemingly aimless discussion touches upon matters that range from joy to heartbreak: Horace and Elizabeth's wedding day (her parents, who disapproved of the match, had disowned her and refused to attend); the death of Elizabeth's two infant sisters over twenty years earlier; the suicide of Mr. George Tyler that very day; and the building of Horace and Elizabeth's first home, a gift from her now-reconciled parents. In the midst of all this, Mr. Bobby, a boarder whose own life is in disarray, mentions the time Mr. Billy Lee whipped his "sissy" son Edgar. In one of the few references to homosexuality in the *Cycle,* we see quickly sketched this tragic story:

> BOBBY: Edgar, Edgar Lee. Now what made me think of him? Oh, yes. We were talking about Mr. Billy Lee. *(There is silence.)* Mama saw Mr. Billy Lee whip Edgar once. She was over at Mrs. Lee's visiting one day and Mr. Billy came home and she said she heard him say, "Take that dress off," and then Edgar run across the yard in his sister's dress and Mr. Billy run after him and he grabbed him halfway across the yard and had his buggy whip and she said he beat him until she thought he would kill him. She said Mrs. Lee kept right on talking as if nothing had happened.

> *(Three Plays* 106)

Not only does Bobby's mother not interfere at the time, though we infer she was upset or at least dismayed at what she saw; no one at the boardinghouse comments on the episode, whatever their feelings may be. The next line is Mr. Vaughn's to Elizabeth: "What kind of flowers did you say the Norton girl carried at your wedding?" Billy Lee is at the mercy of his father. No one, not even his own mother, interferes in what each presumably believes is a father's right to "discipline" his child.

A third cultural commandment interdicts any display of deep emotion, except in the most private of situations. When after almost a year of refusing to speak to Elizabeth, who eloped with Horace on Valentine's Day, Mrs. Vaughn calls to ask if they can bring over some Christmas presents, not a word is said by either about their estrangement. Elizabeth tells Horace about their phone conversation: "It was Mama! She said, 'Do you know who this is, Elizabeth?' and of course I did and I said, 'Mama.' And she said, 'Yes,' and then she said, 'Merry Christmas,' and I began to cry. And she began to cry and then she said, 'May we come over in a few minutes? We have a few little presents for you.' And I said, 'Yes,' and that was it" (*Three Plays* 64). When her parents and brother arrive shortly thereafter, it is as if nothing has happened, and nowhere else in the *Cycle* do they ever discuss it. The Vaughns simply accept Elizabeth back into the fold, along with Horace, as if no explanation of their harsh, even cruel behavior is necessary. If either Elizabeth or Horace is bitter, we are never to know; their respect for their elders and their sense of propriety forbid their talking about it, perhaps even to each other (though again, Foote doesn't let us know this).

Similar examples abound. The first kiss Horace and Elizabeth exchange, mentioned earlier in this chapter, passes unremarked by either, although its significance is clear. At the end of that same play, though nothing seems to have happened except Horace's paying Elizabeth a call, she says quietly to her sister Laura, "I'm marrying Horace Robedaux":

LAURA: If he asks you.
ELIZABETH: If he asks me.

(*Three Plays* 49)

She has made a momentous decision, one which will change her life, and though we have seen it happen and can piece together, once again through scraps of seemingly desultory conversations, the issues that contribute to her decision, deep emotions are never displayed, only inferred.

In all these matters, social conventions and a degree of formality foreign to a contemporary audience provide a way of managing feelings which might otherwise overflow and destroy the apparent tranquillity of the community. Certain prescribed rituals characteristic of this time and place function as rituals do everywhere: as containers for emotion. Standard forms of address, for instance, are insisted upon. Children respond to their parents, as to all elders, with "Ma'am" and "Sir." First and last names are generally used in speaking of one another—Mr. John Howard, Mr. George Tyler—though if the relationship is fairly close, they address one another with the title and first name only: Mr. Bobby, Miss Ruth. These forms of address sometimes indicate class distinctions. Horace calls the black gravedigger "Sam" in *1918,* while he responds with "Mr. Horace" (if Sam weren't so comfortable with him, it would be "Mr. Robedaux"). Even married couples observe these formalities. Mrs. Vaughn addresses her husband as "Mr. Vaughn" and wouldn't dream of using a pet name in public. We observe the changes that come with time in Horace and Elizabeth, who call each other by first name only; Horace even kisses Elizabeth hello in front of Bobby Lee and Miss Ruth.

It is also standard to inquire after someone's family when speaking as a matter of course; it is assumed, given the great value placed on family in the Southern culture, that this is a question of paramount importance. Answers to questions are kept brief and to the point and must always be polite. It goes without saying that swearing and the use of obscenities are never permitted in the presence of a lady, and sexual matters are not considered appropriate topics of conversation. Though in the course of the *Cycle* we learn of infidelities, broken marriages, abortions, and babies born out of wedlock, these things are generally whispered about or implied rather than openly discussed. In this world, behavior as well as speech is strictly governed by rules of decorum.

Once again, these customs and the values they reflect cut both ways. When tragedy strikes, everyone responds in predictable and supportive ways: food is brought to families who have experienced a death or a loss; one goes to pay one's respects. Thus grief does not have to be endured in isolation. The community at its best functions as an extended family. Since everyone knows the rules, there is a degree of comfort and ease, of knowing where one fits in the network of relationships, knowing what is expected. Unlike today's world, which for the most part values spontaneity, individuality, and freedom from restrictive codes of behavior yet experiences the sense of social isolation that can accompany these values, the citizens of Foote's Harrison know who they are. "Identity crisis" is not a term that they would understand.

Yet they, too, must all find their way in the world, and while their strict and often restrictive mores provide a clear starting point, they can also get in the way. The taboo against talking about sexual matters, for instance, particularly evident in *Courtship,* can have devastating results.

The action of this play is deceptively simple. The title suggests that it will portray a couple engaged in some form of courting ritual which will eventually lead to a marriage, a standard plot structure of romantic comedy. Yet the only overt action that could be categorized as such occurs when Horace leaves the dance which Elizabeth and her younger sister Laura are forbidden to attend and comes to call. His brief conversation with Elizabeth on her front porch, along with an even briefer one later in the evening, are the only times Elizabeth and Horace are together that evening. Both episodes combined amount to no more than ten minutes of stage time. Indeed, the play is more about the difficulties of marrying happily than it is about romance; on one level "Non-Courtship" might be a more accurate title. To underscore this point, Foote has young couples, ostensibly at the town dance, waltz across the stage from time to time, "unseen" by the actors but reminding the audience of what Laura and Elizabeth are missing. Yet in spite of the brevity of their actual encounters that evening, by the play's end, Elizabeth has decided that she will marry Horace if he asks her. As with all the *Cycle* plays, the information which shapes this decision is conveyed between the lines, by implication and indirection; the essential action is interior. A close inspection of the dialogue reveals how Foote accomplishes this.

The central issue of *Courtship* involves the way in which one chooses a life mate, a critical decision for both men and women. The life of Mr. Vaughn's brother Billy, we are told, was ruined by his choice of wives—first the "vain, extravagant, foolish" Stella (*Three Plays* 29) and then the dissipated Asa, who led him into drink and debauchery. His sister Lucy married a man twenty years her senior who left her a widow at thirty-two with four children to feed. Other examples of failed or unhappy marriages abound. At different points in the evening, both Elizabeth and Laura pose the critical question "How can you ever be sure?" (*Three Plays* 22). An important question for anyone contemplating marriage, this issue was especially critical to young women of this era, as Foote once commented to me, since they were totally dependent on their husbands financially, and divorce was not an option if the marriage didn't work out. In this community, the selection of a husband was without doubt the most important decision of these young women's lives.

This issue is uppermost in Laura's and Elizabeth's minds, especially since their father has forbidden them to go to the dance and discourages their beaux, including Horace, from coming to call. We learn in the course of the evening that both Elizabeth and Laura, when spending the night with girlfriends, had sneaked out with boyfriends: Elizabeth and her friend for a buggy ride; Laura and Annie Gayle and their callers for a walk around the block—hardly shocking fare to a contemporary audience.

The dangers of this kind of behavior, however, of deceiving one's parents and acting on one's own impulses, are illustrated by two tragic events that function as a shadow plot to Elizabeth's story: the deaths of her friend Sybil Thomas and a former beau, Syd Joplin. Foote weaves these stories, like those of the other townspeople, into seemingly desultory conversations, though these two receive special emphasis, functioning as comments upon Elizabeth's pending decision. We first learn of Syd Joplin's recent death in a conversation between Laura and Elizabeth early in the evening. Laura asks Elizabeth if it's true that at one time she had planned to elope with Syd, since their parents forbade her to see him, and Elizabeth admits that it is:

LAURA: Are you still in love with him?
ELIZABETH: No.
LAURA: Were you ever really in love with him?

ELIZABETH: I thought so.

LAURA: Annie Gayle said he asked you to marry him.

ELIZABETH: He did.

LAURA: Do you think if you had married him you would have still loved him?

ELIZABETH: No.

LAURA: Wouldn't it be terrible to think you were in love with someone, marry them, and then find out you weren't?

ELIZABETH: Yes.

(*Three Plays* 7)

(Elizabeth's one or two word responses are typical of Foote's sparse style.)

The desire for certainty in the face of love's mystery is a theme which recurs throughout the play. It surfaces again at the second mention of Syd Joplin, this time in Elizabeth's conversation with Horace. Horace asks Elizabeth if she had been in love with Syd, and she replies that she thought so and almost eloped with him, but didn't because she was afraid her parents would never speak to her again if she did:

HORACE: Did you think they meant it?

ELIZABETH: Yes, I did.

HORACE: Is that why you didn't marry him?

ELIZABETH: I guess so. I guess I also wasn't sure myself.

HORACE: If you had been sure . . . would you have eloped?

ELIZABETH: I guess so. If I were sure. How can you ever be sure?

(*Three Plays* 22)

This conversation, which makes explicit the parallel between the two relationships, is typical of the pattern of communication throughout the *Cycle*. Both Horace and Elizabeth are aware that what they're really talking about is not Syd Joplin but their own relationship and whether Elizabeth would be willing to elope with Horace.

None of this can be said directly, however, nor can they speak of their feelings. Instead, they seek confirmation indirectly. Horace wants to know if she'll write (he is leaving shortly for a long business trip); she wants to know if he dates while he's on the road. They talk about how old their parents were when they got married, about his sister's marriage, and Sybil Thomas's hasty marriage that afternoon. Horace speaks of his goal to own a dry goods store, Elizabeth says she's wearing the ring he gave her, and in the midst of all this, they kiss, then go on with their conversation as if nothing had happened.

Syd comes up one more time at the end of the play during a climactic confrontation between Elizabeth and her father. Mr. Vaughn, discouraging Elizabeth from seeing Horace, points out that he'd been right in breaking off her relationship to Syd in spite of her protests, and even Elizabeth admits that in the end she was glad she didn't marry him. Yet she is about to make the same decision regarding Horace, who, like Syd, is considered "wild."

Their conversation is interrupted with the news that Sybil Thomas has just died. Elizabeth's friend Sybil, we learn, six months pregnant, had corseted herself tightly to hide her disgrace from her parents. When the truth came out, she and her boyfriend were hastily married (the reports of which are accompanied by all the usual jokes about shotguns); that evening, the night of the play's action, she goes into premature labor. The baby is born dead, and Sybil herself later hemorrhages and dies. The impact of this story is heightened by the way in which Foote allows the information to leak out gradually. At first we learn in a conversation between Laura and Elizabeth that Sybil is four months pregnant, then from Horace that she and her boyfriend Leo Theil got married that afternoon. This is followed by conflicting reports that Sybil has died, the baby has died and Sybil has recovered, and then finally that Sybil was actually six months pregnant and her labor induced fatal hemorrhaging—a sobering announcement which spreads quickly throughout the town. The dance is called off, and everyone immediately walks to the Thomas home, despite the late hour, to pay their respects.

This event, juxtaposed as it is with Elizabeth's pending decision about marrying Horace, reverberates on several levels. In the first instance, it suggests that acting on passion as Sybil did, defying societal mores and deceiving one's parents, can lead to disaster. The parallel clearly isn't lost on Elizabeth. Mrs. Vaughn, who has just learned about Laura and Elizabeth's illicit escapades, makes this connection explicit when she confronts her daughters late that evening. "Think about poor Sybil Thomas the next time you start slipping around with boys in a buggy in the middle of the night," she says (*Three Plays* 35).

At the same time one could argue that it is the very repressiveness of this society that killed Sybil in the first place, the tight corset functioning as a symbol of a rigid, restrictive society that refuses to accept or even acknowledge sexuality. Nowhere is Sybil's character impugned; Elizabeth describes her as "always jolly . . . [with] a very sweet disposition" (*Three Plays* 37). The reluctance of the adults of this generation to discuss sexual matters is illustrated by Laura's naive questions about abortion. When she asks Elizabeth how women "get rid of" unwanted babies and Elizabeth doesn't know either, Laura says, "I guess we'll never know. I don't trust Anna Landry [a contemporary] and I don't know who else to ask. Can you imagine the expression on Mama's face, or Aunt Lucy's or Mrs. Cookenboo's if I asked them something like that?" (*Three Plays* 42).

This same phenomenon is dramatized before our eyes when Mrs. Vaughn, sent by her husband, comes to have a talk with Laura and Elizabeth near the play's end. The news about Sybil is known, and Elizabeth has confronted her father about her feelings for Horace and her anger at his restrictive behavior, at which point her ring from Horace falls off its chain inside her dress and clatters to the floor. The parallels between Sybil, Syd, and Elizabeth are out in the open, and the Vaughns are fearful that Elizabeth is about to make a terrible mistake. In this frame of mind, Mrs. Vaughn asks her daughters if they have any questions. Immediately, Laura says,

LAURA: How did you know you were in love with Papa?

MRS. VAUGHN: I just did.

LAURA: How could you be sure?

MRS. VAUGHN: I just was. (*Pause.*) Elizabeth, do you have any questions?

ELIZABETH: No Ma'am.

LAURA: Elizabeth thought at one time she was in love with Syd Joplin. How come she wasn't?

MRS. VAUGHN: She was wrong.

LAURA: Why was she wrong?

MRS. VAUGHN: She just was.

(*Three Plays* 47)

At this point, Mr. Vaughn joins them and his wife reports, "The girls and I have had a nice talk." In her mind they have, yet Laura's question, arguably the key issue of the play, goes unanswered. It isn't that Mrs. Vaughn is willfully withholding information from her daughters; she doesn't know any more than they do. There are some things, she insists, "you just know," sidestepping the question of *how* one knows or tests this knowledge. She hasn't given this matter much thought, we gather. She fell in love and got married, and her history has taken on the aura of inevitability.

It should be noted that sexual questions are not even posed. Though clearly there is much that Laura and Elizabeth would like to know, they realize that their mother's invitation to ask questions doesn't include this topic. Once again, what is not said is more telling than what is.

The play ends with Elizabeth saying aloud to herself, "I'm marrying Horace Robedaux . . . if he asks me" (*Three Plays* 49). She has weighed carefully all that she has seen and heard this evening—the tabletalk of her Aunts Lucy and Sarah, a widow and "old maid," respectively; the news about Syd's and Sybil's deaths; her conversations with Laura, who is as terrified of being an old maid as she is of marrying the wrong man. Thus if we read carefully, even though nothing has been said overtly, we are prepared for the fact that these seemingly unrelated snippets of casual after-dinner conversation are actually key factors in Elizabeth's decision. The subtext is more important than the text. The true action of this play, as in all the *Cycle* plays, is interior.

It is important to understand that Foote's restrained, indirect use of language reflects the mode of communication common to the period and milieu he is depicting. The dialogue rings true precisely because it emerges from a specific cultural context. The values that it reflects are those of that time and place: proper forms of address (Ma'am and Sir, Mr. and Mrs.), emotional restraint, family, privacy, decorum. Subjects like sex, abortions, homosexuality, and illegitimate births are not discussed in polite company or if so, only in hushed voices when no children are present. All of these topics occur in Foote's *Cycle;* critics who dismiss him as sentimental are mistaking the era's rhetorical restraint for his own. His is a clear-eyed, unsentimental picture of the world he knew as a boy.

The uniqueness of Foote's style comes into even sharper focus when placed side-by-side with passages from other American playwrights. Compare, for example, the exchanges between Laura and Elizabeth and between the girls and Mrs. Vaughn quoted above with the following passage from Arthur Miller's *Death of a Salesman*, another play where family relationships are central to the action:

> BIFF, *at the peak of his fury:* Pop, I'm nothing! I'm nothing, Pop. Can't you understand that? There's no spite in it any more. I'm just what I am, that's all.
> *Biff's fury has spent itself, and he breaks down, sobbing, holding on to Willy, who dumbly fumbles for Biff's face.*
> WILLY, *astonished:* What're you doing? What're you doing? *To Linda:* Why is he crying?
> BIFF, *crying, broken:* Will you let me go, for Christ's sake? Will you take that phony dream and burn it, before something happens? *Struggling to contain himself, he pulls away and moves to the stairs.* I'll go in the morning. Put him—put him to bed. *Exhausted, Biff moves up the stairs to his room.*
> WILLY, *after a long pause, astonished, elevated:* Isn't that—isn't that remarkable? Biff—he likes me![4]

This scene, which occurs at the crisis of the play and leads directly to its climax with Willy's suicide, focuses upon the confrontation between Willy and Biff that the action has been building to. Biff, Willy's older son and his pride and joy, has once again come home penniless. Willy is convinced that Biff has failed just to spite him, knowing, as his wife Linda and younger son Hap do not, of the time Biff discovered him with another woman. Their relationship has been strained ever since, until this moment when Biff pours out his heart to Willy.

Putting aside for a moment the differences caused by Miller's expressionistic technique and nonlinear structure in *Salesman* and focusing exclusively on his use of language, we note several striking differences between his style and Foote's. In the first place, the relationship of language and action is substantially different in the two plays. In *Courtship* (as in all the *Cycle* plays), language by and large is not used to propel the action in a direct or causal fashion. The characters speak of one thing while they are thinking about another. After

4. Arthur Miller, *Death of a Salesman* (New York: Viking Press, 1949), 133.

a quiet evening of dinner with her family, filled with seemingly innocent gossip and aimless chatter, Elizabeth announces (to herself, mainly) that she is going to marry Horace, a momentous decision for both of them. If every drama has a single, overarching action, as Francis Fergusson argues in *The Idea of a Theater,* the movement in *Courtship* is toward this impending marriage (which will occur offstage, between plays), yet except for Elizabeth's final quiet statement, this action is not contained directly in the language.

In *Salesman,* on the other hand, the action is linked directly to the dialogue. Though there is some indirection, to be sure—Biff confesses that he's "nothing" and Willy hears "He likes me"—essentially this reconciliation is effected explicitly by Biff's confession, with its attendant deep emotion. Holding on to Willy, Biff begs him to accept him as he is and says, "There's no spite in it any more." He has forgiven Willy, relinquishing his resentment, and wants only for Willy to be well (the veiled "before something happens" refers to his knowledge of Willy's earlier suicide attempts). The words and the action are one.

We also note that unlike Foote, Miller allows his characters to express and reveal deep emotion. This scene moves from fury to sorrow to letting go on Biff's part; from fear to confusion to astonishment to joy on Willy's, all in a matter of minutes. It's a deeply moving scene, one which, if done well, effects the catharsis that Aristotle associates with tragedy. And it does so by dramatizing for us both the anagnorisis and peripeteia that Aristotle claims constitutes complex plots, those he considers superior.[5] Willy's insight or recognition (anagnoresis) that Biff loves him precipitates his change of heart ("reversal," as Aristotle puts it—the peripeteia). His anguish is transformed into joy at what he mistakenly perceives as an affirmation of his own life. He returns to his earlier dream ("that boy is going to be magnificent!" he says) and soon thereafter commits suicide to secure the $20,000 insurance money he feels will give Biff his start.

My point is that all this action, both interior and exterior, is contained in the language itself; in text, not subtext. It is also highly charged emotionally. The dialogue's direct precipitation of action is

5. *Aristotle's Poetics,* trans. S. H. Butcher (New York: Hill and Wang, 1961), 71–72.

mirrored by open displays of unrestrained, deep emotion, a phenomenon seldom seen on Foote's stage.

Equally contrasting is Miller's abundant use of stage directions. In this passage there are fifty-eight words of stage directions compared to only sixty-nine of dialogue. Thus nearly half the text consists of stage directions, which he uses to indicate emotion, gestures, even blocking. Like many American playwrights, Miller leaves nothing to chance.

His rhetoric also differs from Foote's, though at first it might not appear so. The syntax is not complex, and the lexicon is consistent with that of its uneducated, lower-middle-class characters. But within these self-imposed constraints, Miller is more "poetic" than Foote. Think of John Proctor's final speech about discovering his own goodness: "Not enough to weave a banner with, but white enough to keep it from such dogs." Or Eddie Carbone to Marco in *A View from the Bridge*: "Wipin' the neighborhood with my name like a dirty rag! I want my name, Marco. . . . Now gimme my name and we go together to the wedding."[6] These lines have Miller's unmistakable stamp on them, as do those quoted earlier from *Salesman*. He has a special gift for taking the everyday words of ordinary people and weaving them into poetry. Using metaphor, simile, repetition, and cadence, he crafts lines that are uncontrived, yet unforgettable. Recall Linda's "Attention must be paid" speech or Charley's "Nobody dast blame this man" in *Salesman*'s final scene—the list goes on and on.

Not so with Foote, who employs a similar level of diction and equally uncomplicated syntax, but to quite different effect. With a few notable exceptions, one doesn't recall whole speeches from Foote's plays, or even lines. During one of the rare moments in the *Cycle* when deep emotion is openly displayed, for instance, after Horace has learned in *1918* that his infant daughter has died in the influenza epidemic while he himself was sick and both he and Elizabeth are crying, Elizabeth turns to Mrs. Vaughn and says, "Mama, help us. How did you stand it when you lost your children?" She answers simply, "You just stand it. You keep going" (*Three Plays* 150). Or at the end of *Roots,* when George Tyler says to young Horace, "There's

6. Arthur Miller, *The Crucible* (New York: Viking Press, 1952), 144; Arthur Miller, *A View from the Bridge* (New York: Viking Press, 1955), 111.

been some changes, haven't there? Your daddy's dead, the Robedauxs moved, your mama's married again—a lot of changes. Well, we have to get used to change, Son. All of us" (*Four Plays* 87), Horace merely turns his head away and begins to cry. The only time we see him show emotion, it is over very quickly, as he leaves to look for empty whiskey bottles and the curtain falls.

In both cases, no heightened or intensified language is used to underscore the characters' deep feelings, just as no stage directions tell the actors how to deliver their lines. Foote trusts his actors as he trusts his audience. The lines—simple, declarative, unadorned—stand alone.

To cite one more example, consider Eugene O'Neill's *Long Day's Journey into Night,* another play which turns on family relationships. Like Miller, O'Neill relies heavily on stage directions, including them with nearly every line of dialogue, as a quick glance at the text of *Long Day's Journey* reveals. A second contrast with Foote is O'Neill's characters' propensity for long speeches, compared to Foote's personae's typical abbreviated responses. But perhaps the greatest difference is the haunting quality that O'Neill, like Miller, brings to his prose. Despite his reputation in some quarters as a poor stylist and his own self-deprecation in that regard, there are passages in his plays that rank with the best in this country or abroad.[7] Recall, for instance, Edmund's famous bowsprit speech in act 4, or his description of the fog shortly before: "Everything looked and sounded unreal. Nothing was what it is. That's what I wanted—to be alone with myself in another world where truth is untrue and life can hide from itself. Out beyond the harbor, where the road runs along the beach, I even lost the feeling of being on land. The fog and the sea seemed part of each other. It was like walking on the bottom of the sea. As if I had drowned long ago. As if I was a ghost belonging to the fog, and the fog was the ghost of the sea. It felt damned peaceful to be nothing more than

---

7. Foote, in fact, an admirer of O'Neill, says in the Broughton interview quoted in Chapter 1 that O'Neill has a "tin ear." "Someone can be an effective writer and not be a great stylist," he adds. "There is no more effective play to me in the English language than *Long Day's Journey into Night*—there he comes nearest to hopefully achieving a style. But you take *Strange Interlude,* or even *Ice Man Cometh* [*sic*]. *Ice Man Cometh* certainly works theatrically but to me it works in spite of the style of writing." Broughton, *Writer's Mind,* 19.

a ghost within a ghost."[8] The oxymoron that O'Neill uses to structure this passage, that of truth being untrue, along with the double ghost metaphor, gets to the heart of Edmund's dilemma: the desire to escape from the reality of his life and the impossibility of doing so. The ghost reference also functions as a reminder of his mother, Mary, deep in her morphine trance at this point, whose footsteps from upstairs haunt the three lost souls below. The fog and the sea images, along with the reference to drowning, recall the water imagery that occurs throughout the play, with the fog also functioning as a symbol for the movement toward increasing isolation of the family as a whole as well as the individual members from one another. The rhythm of the sentences, the repetition of words and phrases—all are carefully crafted to cast a spell upon the audience. Indeed Tyrone, listening to his son, responds, "You have a poet in you." Though it's true that Edmund is better educated than most of Foote's *Cycle* characters, one can find a similar phenomenon, with the appropriate adjustments in dialect and lexicon, in Hickey of *The Iceman Cometh,* Yank in *The Hairy Ape,* Erie Smith in *Hughie,* and so forth, all of which provide a stark contrast to Foote's terse style.

As one compares these three playwrights, then, it becomes clear that both Miller and O'Neill, in their own ways, use the ordinary speech of individuals from every walk of life and craft it into memorable, even poetic prose. Not so with Foote. Though his love of language is just as intense, as the DiGaetani interview quoted earlier attests, he has a different end in mind. His language is not meant to call attention to itself, but to disappear. It is a vehicle for conveying themes and feelings, but one which trusts the actors and action to carry the weight of the meanings and the audience to read between the lines. What is remarkable about Foote's style, I would argue, in the root sense of that word, what one should remark or note, is the way in which his language reflects the practices and cultural values of the era he depicts as well as his own epistemology.

This brings me to my final point: the matter of epistemology, the discernment process. Language has great power in Foote's world, but a power of a different sort from that of other American playwrights.

---

8. Eugene O'Neill, *Long Day's Journey into Night* (New Haven: Yale University Press, 1956), 131.

His characters are all storytellers of one kind or another; they delight in anecdotes, family legends, local gossip. It is one of his most Southern characteristics. In a lecture Foote once gave entitled "The Artist as Myth Maker," he told of his own childhood, growing up listening to the talk on his front porch summer evenings like today's children watch television:

> Although I've always liked to read, I grew up in a place and time when there was no radio, no television, no VCRs, and no movies on Sundays, and strictly rationed during the weekdays, so people often entertained themselves by talking. In my family the talk was often about the past as in Miss [Katherine Anne] Porter's *Old Mortality*—my mother had been to Kid Key College and was certainly bright enough, read occasionally, but mostly she loved to talk, and my father loved to talk, and my grandmother, and my great aunts and great uncles, and my aunts and uncles, and my cousins—all loved to talk. And I often found their talk more interesting than the books I was reading.

These stories became a sort of oral history. "They told their stories endlessly," he said: "Their families had all come to Texas early, none later than 1836, and they seemed to me to remember everything that had ever happened to them."[9]

He quickly learned, however, as he went on to explain, that the versions of these stories changed slightly with each teller. Referring to Porter's work again, Foote said in his lecture:

> Miss Porter has written: No legend is ever true, but I believe all of them are founded on some sense of truth. And even these truths appear in different lights to every mind they are presented to, and the legend is that work of art which goes on in the human mind, adding to and arranging, harmonizing and rounding out, making larger or smaller than life, and holding the entire finished product in a good light and asking you to believe it.

He goes on to add, "It is true, no memory is really faithful, it has too far to go, too many changing landscapes of the human mind and heart, to bear any sort of really trustworthy witness, except in part."[10]

9. Horton Foote, "The Artist as Myth-Maker," unpublished lecture, University of Texas at Arlington, Arlington, Texas, November 16, 1988, p. 4.

10. Ibid., 6. Katherine Anne Porter, another Texas writer, has had a profound influence on Foote's work, perhaps even more than other playwrights. When one recalls

This vision of experience and the impossibility of ever knowing in any objective, verifiable fashion what really happened at any given moment in time is reflected in Foote's plays. For the most part, information is not conveyed in a direct, linear, cause-and-effect fashion. Bits and pieces of family conversations, stories that are told and retold by various personae must be added to whatever action is dramatized on stage in order to get some sense of the whole. Moreover, one must be careful to weigh the veracity of the storyteller, to take into account his or her stake in the story, proximity to its occurrence, and so forth in order to determine to what extent it is or isn't "true." Is Minnie's version of Paul Horace and Corella's breakup more accurate than Lily Dale's? Is Mr. Vaughn's judgment of Horace more trustworthy than Elizabeth's? He was, after all, right about Syd Joplin; he has the advantage of experience and a broader, less emotional perspective. What really happened to unbalance George Tyler in *Valentine's Day?* What caused the death of Paul Horace? To what extent is Lewis Higgins responsible for the death of his cousin Jamie in *Cousins?*

The impossibility of ever knowing with certainty the answers to these and countless other questions reveals a much more complex (and less sentimental) epistemology and worldview than Foote's critics have heretofore recognized. Truth in these plays is constantly shifting, changing, taking different shapes.

Comparing *The Orphans' Home Cycle,* written between 1971 and '77, with earlier examples of his work indicates that Foote arrived at this indirect style over time. A 1961 version of *Roots in a Parched Ground* provides an illuminating example of this. After Foote completed the other eight plays of the *Cycle,* he returned to an earlier version of *Roots* (originally presented on television's *DuPont Show of the Month* under the title *The Night of the Storm*) and rewrote it in its entirety. If one compares the plot, characterization, and dialogue of the '61 version with the final one, the effectiveness of his later style comes into sharp focus.

Horace's mother Julia is, to begin with, much more sympathetically portrayed than her counterpart Corella in the final version, as

---

her themes—memory and the past, families and the ways in which they both liberate and imprison, the importance of place in shaping life experience—it is not hard to understand why.

both the action and dialogue reveal. Corella, who is seen only from the outside, appears distant and insensitive at worst; at best she is simply unaware of Horace's pain. In the scene where Horace asks her if he can come live with her and Pete Davenport in Houston, for instance, she seems oblivious to the extent of his loneliness and his desire to be included in her new family. Screwing his courage to the sticking point, Horace says, "*(almost mumbling)*: I kind of want to go to Houston and live with you, Mama," to which she replies, "What, Son? I didn't hear you. I was listening to Lily Dale" (*Four Plays* 80). All conversation stops as Lily Dale plays a new piece on the piano; Corella's "I didn't hear you" is true both literally and figuratively.

Julia, on the other hand, is cast in a much softer light. The action of this play begins before she has moved to Houston, when she and her sister Callie are struggling to keep their boardinghouse afloat, at great personal and psychic cost. We watch her preparing and serving meals to "common" boarders with poor manners, who complain about the service and ultimately give notice, leaving Julia and Callie with no means of support. Callie pressures Julia into asking for financial assistance from her mother-in-law, having heard that Terrence Robedaux just sold the family-owned newspaper and arguing that the money is rightfully hers. When Julia asks why, Callie says, "Because you and your husband fed Terrence and his Mama and his sister and her children so they could use the little money they had to buy this paper for him. You scrimped and saved and half starved to do for them. Now let them return it. Now you go over there and without apologizing ask for what's due you." Callie's account, whether accurate or not, makes Julia appear the victim and increases our sympathy for her. It is confirmed by a statement made earlier by Paul Horace himself, who says to his son, "It was a mistake their all coming here in the first place. I realize that now. But Mama had such a hard time raising all of us after my father died, and when my sister was left widowed with all those children, I just thought we could all help each other. But your Mama resented having them here and I can see now why she should. This house was certainly too small for all of us, and we got on each other's nerves, and I began drinking too much and neglecting my law practice and your Mama and you children."[11]

Two points here. This version of what happened to their marriage clearly tips the scale in Julia's favor, as do other details of her characterization. Thus when she ultimately leaves Horace behind and goes off to Houston, we understand her reasons for doing so, seeing her as torn between her love for Horace and her need to support herself. Her motivation is made explicit, whereas in the later version of the play we can only guess. Similarly, the 1961 version provides direct information about the failure of the marriage, and from two sources which are more or less in agreement. In the rewritten play, we can only infer what might have happened, and that from conflicting sources, none of them directly involved. "Truth" in the first *Roots* is considerably easier to ascertain than in the subsequent one.

It is also easier to assign blame. Paul Horace is portrayed as impractical, a dreamer. He allows his mother and siblings to move in although there isn't enough room or money to go around. He has a soft heart, which may be endearing at times but often has unfortunate consequences. Paul Horace promises Horace, for instance, that when he recovers his health, he'll take him, Lily Dale, and Julia on a cruise—a dream that Horace clings to. His hopes, of course, are dashed when Julia moves to Houston and his father dies. Although Julia is not without responsibility—she allows herself to be manipulated by Callie, for instance, and is perhaps overquick to remarry for financial security—it is easy to see her as having limited choices, which makes her final abandonment of Horace (softened still further by instances of her worrying, fussing, and crying over him throughout the play) seem less cruel.

The revised play is much more clear-eyed in its presentation of Corella. Though there is almost always something to identify with in any Foote character, its portrait of Horace's mother is not as sentimentally painted as that of the earlier version. This allows us not only to focus on Horace's deep sense of loss, but also, in limiting what we

11. Horton Foote, *Roots in a Parched Ground* (New York: Dramatists Play Service, 1962), 25, 14.

know about her, replicates Horace's experience of his mother for the viewer.

A second major difference of the original play concerns Foote's willingness to display deeply felt emotions on stage. Consider, for instance, the two endings. In the '61 drama, Horace runs away from home when he learns that Julia plans to move to Houston. He has a chance to go along with his mother, aunt, and sister, but chooses to stay in Harrison with his dying father. He disappears for two months, and when he resurfaces and Mr. Ritter, now staying alone in the boardinghouse, calls Julia with the news of his return, she makes the long trip from Houston to see him. While he was gone, Horace's father has died and his mother has remarried, settled now in Houston with Lily Dale and her new husband. Unfortunately, there is no room for Horace in their small house; he must live on with Mr. Ritter, into whose hands Julia entrusts her son. As his mother leaves for the train, Horace calls after her in language more direct than anything we find in the revised version of the play, "Don't leave me. Please, Mama. Don't leave me. I don't want to be left alone. I went all through Papa's house and it's empty and desolate. I don't want to be left alone." It's a poignant scene, one that ends with Mr. Ritter and John Howard helping Horace with his math. Horace repeats to Mr. Howard the promise that when he's fourteen he can move to Houston and learn a trade, then adds, "I don't care about a trade, or being a lawyer. I want my Mama and my Daddy, and I want us all living together in one house . . . in one town . . . in one world," whereupon Mr. Howard consoles him with the thought that we can't always get what we want in the world so we focus upon what we can get.[12]

Although it is certainly touching, in my judgment this conclusion does not achieve the power of that in the revised play, which once again operates with indirection and implication, letting the audience observe and draw its own conclusions. In this version we see Horace with his peers, saying that he's through with school, he doesn't plan to go to Houston, and he's "on [his] own." The closing scene gives us Horace looking for empty whiskey bottles to sell when Mr. Ritter happens by. When asked how he likes his new stepfather, Horace replies, "He's all right," adding immediately, "How much does a

12. Ibid., 40, 41.

tombstone cost?" (*Four Plays* 86), establishing a motif which will be carried throughout the other plays, that of placing a tombstone on his father's grave. The only emotion he shows is after Mr. Ritter, in his usual tactless fashion, says, "There's been some changes, haven't there? Your daddy's dead, the Robedauxs moved, your mama married again—a lot of changes. Well, we have to get used to change, son. All of us." At this, Horace turns his head away, not wanting Mr. Ritter to see him cry. After a few clichés about being brave, he sends Horace away with a dime, telling him to "buy [himself] something" (*Four Plays* 87). Horace's last words and the closing words of the play, a polite "thank you," are painfully ironic. His loneliness is dramatized, not articulated, with a life as empty as the whiskey bottles he seeks. At least the previous play leaves him with Mr. Ritter and Mr. Howard (who dies in the final version), the two friends of his father who promised to watch over Horace. Here he is completely alone.

Along with a more sentimental presentation of character and motive and more direct displays of emotion, the earlier version includes considerably more stage directions than the later play. Most of these are blocking cues, indicating movement and actions for the actors. While it may be that these are remnants of the television version, it is interesting and not insignificant that Foote omits almost all of them in the revised *Roots* written expressly for the *Cycle*. Foote himself commented when asked about the nature of his revising process (speaking here specifically about *Valentine's Day,* the sixth play of the *Cycle*), "To me, the ideal is always through elimination. In other words, to get rid of what is excessive or what is unnecessary—which is kind of a constant pruning—or getting down to the essence of the work, and that's really all I did. I just found certain things now that were unessential." Later in that same interview when asked what being a Southerner contributes to his writing, Foote responded, "I think it gives you a language. . . . I think the main strength of the South is the oral tradition."[13] Indeed. It is his ear, his gift for the authentic language of ordinary people and his ability to present it in a manner that seems straightforward, conversational, and unplanned though it is actually carefully crafted that makes Foote's *Orphans' Home Cycle* the masterpiece it is.

13. Broughton, *Writer's Mind,* 14, 19.

When Eudora Welty says, speaking of the *Cycle,* that "these gentle plays . . . can make your hair stand on end,"[14] it recalls Emily Dickinson's definition of poetry as feeling as if the top of one's head were taken off. In his own way, though he would be the first to deny it, Foote is a poet—if one of a very different sort. His use of language is anything but ordinary, establishing in its own way the connection between the Me and the Not Me, the one and the many, the individual and society. A bit like Emerson's sentences, each of which seems to stand alone yet cannot be separated from its paragraph without loss to the whole, Foote's characters, through his dialogue, create a world both familiar and strange. As readers and audience, we, like the characters in these plays, must sift through their stories, consider the sources, make judgments and connections, and draw our own conclusions. It is like piecing together a puzzle, except that the pieces are presented so quietly and unobtrusively we're not aware that we're assembling them. His language works in new ways to help us rediscover ancient truths.

At the same time, in re-creating this particular time and place, Foote gives us the story of a culture as well as an individual. Horace's story is subsumed in that of the town, and vice versa. It is a seamless construction: we can't know Horace completely without understanding the world from which he emerges. Consideration of this element adds another layer to our understanding of identity formation. If family provides the foundation on which identity is built, society at large undergirds each individual family, dictating customs, mores, and norms of behavior. All of these are reflected in the language, both its content and form, and account for the emphasis which Foote places upon it when he speaks of his work. To return to the interview which begins this chapter, we can now appreciate more completely what Foote means when he says, "Language in general is of enormous importance—language is everything to me."[15] As we contemplate the bits and pieces of conversation that constitute these plays, all seemingly of little import in themselves, we understand that they both reflect and constitute individual identity, which in turn emerges from and defines itself over against both family and culture. These

14. Eudora Welty, frontispiece, *Four Plays.*
15. DiGaetani, "Horton Foote," 68.

plays tell the story of Horace Robedaux, an individual, yet one shaped by his world—a unique human being who is at the same time typical of his society.

In Chapter 4, which examines several of the structural devices Foote employs to unite the *Cycle* as a whole, we will look at yet another way in which the relationship between the one and the many is explored. Faced with the challenge of writing plays that stand alone yet when linked together tell a single, unified story, Foote, by instinct or design, has stretched drama as a genre in new and innovative ways, at the same time mirroring the theme of the individual and the larger group of which s/he is a part.

4

POLYPHONIC VOICES

Repetition and the Multiplication of Meaning

We have said that in writing *The Orphans' Home Cycle,* Foote divests himself of many of the tools available to him as a dramatist—detailed stage directions, for instance, to describe characters' appearance or emotional responses, or plots driven by conflict and suspense—the very elements that make drama *dramatic.* He also eschews poetic or emotionally intensified prose, writing instead in the everyday language of ordinary people. If one reads his plays, they can appear flat and prosaic on the printed page, almost like transcriptions of conversations overheard in the grocery store or a church social. But although it is true that Foote has an unusually good ear for dialect and speech patterns and is perfectly capable of sociologically accurate reporting, his apparently artless plays are actually very carefully crafted. While any given passage may seem the stuff of ordinary life, simple and unadorned, taken as a whole the plays weave together character, image, and scene in a technically innovative fashion. The previous chapter concerned itself with Foote's linguistic style, examining the way he embeds cultural codes in language, revealing meaning both in what is said and what is unsaid. In this chapter I would like to focus on another facet of Foote's style, his use of repetition to multiply meaning.

In undertaking the daunting task of writing not just one but a cycle of nine plays, tracking a single life history that encompasses three generations and three families within a twenty-six-year time frame, Foote took on some fairly significant challenges. If each of the plays is to be self-contained, that is, capable of being lifted out of the *Cycle* and produced independently (which was Foote's intent), all the information to understand that play's issues, the history, the background, the relationships and identities of various family members, must be present within its pages. Unlike a chapter in a novel, for instance, it must be a complete narrative in and of itself, with its own beginning, middle, and end. At the same time, it must function as part of a larger narrative of which it is only one segment.[1]

Writing each play as a self-contained unit is perhaps the lesser of Foote's difficulties, although the compression required to convey the complex network of family relationships and accumulated histories in each one is formidable. But how does one connect them, make them cohere, without relying on mechanical summaries of episodes in an earlier play, for instance, or other equally artificial devices? A related issue is the matter of selection. What experiences from Horace's life, taken together, will convey his journey from child to adult, orphan to husband and father? And how are these experiences related to one another? What is the spine of the story, the organizing principle?

In solving these thorny problems, Foote has employed narrative strategies more commonly encountered in novels than in drama. Three in particular stand out, all involving repetition of some sort: the use of recurring character types, an intricate network of intercutting images and symbols, and a series of parallel and inverted events that occur throughout all nine plays. These structural and stylistic devices both intensify meaning within individual plays and establish resonances which reverberate between and among the plays. This is not to say that Foote is unique in deploying these strategies. Other dramatists obviously use imagery and symbolism, as well as stock character types: the repressed spinster in Tennessee Williams, the promiscuous rebel in Beth Henley, the drifter in Sam Shepard. What is singular about Foote's approach is his use of repetition to create connections

---

1. Although it is true that as a part of the whole narrative each play on one level can be seen as similar to a chapter in a novel, Foote composed them out of sequence and has never produced them in sequence. He says in an interview with Davis, interestingly, "I haven't really wanted them to be thought of as a group. I've always wanted them to stand on their own." To say that he didn't want them to be thought of as a "group" is not to deny their interconnectedness, however, which is apparent. Davis, "Roots Interview," 313.

both within and among a discrete group of plays—a kind of inner- and *inter*textuality, carrying it to greater lengths than heretofore seen.

In many ways, the *Cycle* is perhaps even more akin to a musical composition than a novel in this regard. Like a symphony, which announces a musical motif early in the first movement and then employs variations on that theme through the rest of the work by inverting it, assigning it to various instruments, changing its tempo and volume, foregrounding and backgrounding it, and the like, these plays revolve around variations on two or three central themes and motifs. Critics have frequently noted that Foote has been influenced by music from the very beginning of his career, when he worked closely with composers and with dancers like Martha Graham and Valerie Bettis. Foote himself testifies to how profoundly he was influenced by the work of modernist composer Charles Ives when he was writing *The Orphans' Home Cycle*. In his interview with Crystal Brian, for instance, he says, "I guess I'd always been looking for a kind of kindred spirit. And I stumbled on Ives; and, the minute I heard him, I knew this was my boy." In her perceptive essay *"The Orphans' Home Cycle* and the Music of Charles Ives," Brian provides an in-depth analysis of the parallels between Ives's use of "found music," blending fragments of hymns, spirituals, folk songs, and popular tunes into his own melodic constructions to capture an authentic, particularized moment, with Foote's blending of various stories and voices as well as actual music—hymns, popular melodies, chain gang songs, and so forth—to construct his plays. Reynolds Price's oft-quoted introduction to the second volume of the *Cycle* also makes this connection, calling Foote "the supreme musician among our great American playwrights."[2]

Foote's adaptation of musical techniques in the shaping of his plays, then, works both as a means to structure entire plays and even pairs of plays, a subject which will be discussed in the following chapter, and to create unity within and among plays by using repetition, parallelism and inversion, and variations on a common theme. The *Cycle*'s title provides a clue to several of these motifs. The phrase *Orphans' Home* comes from "In Distrust of Merits," a meditation on

2. Brian, "To Be Quiet and Listen," 91; Price, introduction to *Three Plays*, xi.

war and death by Marianne Moore. The lines from which Foote
draws his title read as follows:

> The world's an orphans' home. Shall
> we never have peace without sorrow?
> without pleas of the dying for
> help that won't come? O
> quiet form upon the dust, I cannot
> look and yet I must.[3]

The verse concludes, "If these great patient / dyings . . . / can teach
us how to live, these / dyings were not wasted" (ll. 66–70). The tensions implicit in these few lines inform the entire *Cycle*, particularly
the tensions between orphan and home and home and world. The
word *orphan* suggests being cut off from society, abandoned, alone;
its opposite conjures visions of family, connectedness, roots, belonging—all subsumed in the image of home. The motif of an orphan
seeking a home provides the organizing principle for the action of the
play, namely Horace's search for a family, his desire to be a part of
something larger than himself.

Over against the concept of family and home, with its connota-
tions of the private and the personal, is that of the world at large. In
these plays, set in a rural, cotton-dependent community, the world is
embodied primarily in nature: the land and the river, drought and
rain, flowers and vegetation, though larger social forces—World War
I, the flu epidemic, racism, and poverty—also intrude on individual
life experience. Nature, then, provides a second matrix from which
Foote draws his imagery, establishing recurring patterns and motifs.
A third motif is that of the graveyard, which combines the concepts
of family and nature. Who is buried where, whether or not a grave is
marked by a tombstone, what the tombstone says—all these are matters of significance in the world of Harrison. For all practical purposes, the cemetery in this small community is an extension of the
town. Families are buried together, awaiting those who are to come,
and the living, with their frequent visits, pay tribute to those who

3. Marianne Moore, *The Complete Poems of Marianne Moore* (New York: Macmillan-Viking, 1981), 137–38.

have gone before. Thus as a symbol, the cemetery has a strong societal component. At the same time, it can be seen as representing the ultimate triumph of nature. Dust turns to dust again, and in the end, nature reclaims its own. As the black caretaker Ben says at the end of *Convicts* at the burial of Mr. Soll, the plantation owner, "The trees and the weeds, and the cane, will take everything. . . . The house will go, the store will go, the graves will go, those with tombstones and those without" (*Four Plays* 163). These three motifs, then, orphans and families, nature, and the graveyard, provide a matrix from which Foote draws many, if not all, of the character types, images and symbols, and events that unify the *Cycle* as a whole.

Of the character types that occur throughout these plays, four in particular stand out by virtue of the frequency of their occurrence: orphans, fathers and father-substitutes, alcoholics, and brothers. Turning first to orphans, we note that in addition to Horace, the *Cycle* includes *three* men who lost their fathers as young boys: Will Kidder, Lily Dale's husband; Henry Vaughn; and Pete Davenport. (To emphasize the connection between these men, Foote makes each of them twelve years old when their fathers die.)[4] Because losing their fathers appears to have been a life-shaping event for all of these characters, we are given a frame of reference for evaluating Horace's experience. Both Will and Mr. Vaughn seem to have emerged relatively unscathed, eventually becoming self-sufficient as well as financially secure, serving as poster boys for that most American of ideals, the rags-to-riches myth. Pete Davenport seems to be the most adversely affected by being orphaned. He works at a low-paying, menial job at the railroad, with nothing more to look forward to than coming home each evening and tending his garden. This in itself is not necessarily an indicator of failure, of course. It is his bitterness about his impoverished childhood and his inability to show love and compassion for others that suggest the extent to which being orphaned has permanently scarred him. When he first meets Horace, for instance, who is twelve at this point and proud of the fact that he hasn't missed a day of school in three weeks, Pete says, "I went to work when I was ten. I worked twelve hours a day at my first job. Seven days a week."

---

4. In *Roots in a Parched Ground,* Pete says that he was ten when his father died, though elsewhere it's reported as twelve.

Corella explains that when his father died, Pete got a job and supported his mother and four siblings. He goes on, squelching Horace's sense of accomplishment at completing all his lessons, "I wouldn't let a boy of mine go to school. I would put him to work as soon as he was able. I think work makes a man out of anybody" (*Four Plays* 79–80).

This insistence on the value of pulling oneself up by one's bootstraps becomes a kind of mantra for Pete, who intones it, with variations, whenever the occasion allows. In *Lily Dale,* for instance, discovering that Horace has accepted money from Corella for the train fare to Houston, he says, "You're a grown man. Aren't you ashamed to take money from your mama? When I was your age, I had been supporting my mother and my brothers and sisters for eight years. Nobody ever gave me anything and I never asked for anything. What kind of man are you gonna make, taking money from a woman at your age?" (*Four Plays* 192–93). Later he says, relative to Horace's search for employment, "He'd better not ask me for a job. Let him get his own job. Nobody ever helped me get a job. I've never asked anybody for anything. Not one solitary thing" (*Four Plays* 202).

While Pete clearly takes pride in what he sees as self-sufficiency, the audience understands that his inability to connect with others in a meaningful way is actually a liability. It's not insignificant that he is even detached from his family of origin. He returns from his visit to his family in Atlanta a day early, and when Corella asks him, "How were your people?" he sums up his visit in two words: "All right" (*Four Plays* 191).

Character doubling, a device often employed by novelists to either parallel or contrast the experience of the protagonist, is used here by Foote in much the same way. Hearing the various stories of struggle and hard work, deprivation and loneliness from an array of orphans, we appreciate more fully the challenge Horace faces as he sets out to fend for himself as a young boy. Both Mr. Vaughn and Will Kidder, as positive examples, parallel Horace's success and thus underline the extent of his achievement in maturing into a responsible, hardworking adult. Pete, by way of contrast, illustrates how Horace might have turned out and makes all the more remarkable his ability to form deep, loving relationships as a husband and father.

Buddy, the ten-year-old son of the Widow Claire in the play by that name, affords yet another variation on this theme. Like Horace and Lily Dale, Buddy and his younger sister Molly have lost their father to an untimely death; their young, widowed mother has to provide for herself and her children as best she can. While *Roots in a Parched Ground* contrasts Horace as a boy with an adult "orphan," Pete Davenport, *The Widow Claire* reverses this construct, showing us Horace as an adult responding to the orphaned ten-year-old Buddy. The contrast is instructive on two levels. Buddy, like the young Horace, obviously suffering from his father's death, tries to make sense of his life as a variety of suitors come to court his mother. Unlike Horace at that age, however, he responds with manipulative behavior, wheedling gifts and money out of Claire's callers and lying about it afterwards—a striking contrast with Horace's fishing and his hunting for empty whiskey bottles to sell. Horace as an adult also compares favorably in contrast with Pete in the earlier play. He responds to Buddy and Molly with sensitivity and kindness, even though their presence interferes with his courting Claire.[5]

This play also presents a striking parallel to the situation Corella and her children face in *Roots* and helps us understand more completely the challenges confronting a young widow in this society. Claire ultimately takes the safe course, marrying the older, financially established Ned to provide stability for herself and her children, much as Corella marries Pete. Neither is a love match. Knowing how Corella and Pete's marriage turns out, we fear for Claire; at the same time, we understand the exigencies that inform her choice. By providing this parallel situation, Foote presents us with a cultural context which helps us see not just individual case studies, but societal patterns at work. In the same fashion, with the proliferation of orphans in the *Cycle* we see Horace's story writ large, appreciating more fully both the degree of pain he must contend with and the depth of character he exhibits in his response to his fate.

The abundance of father figures associated with Horace serves a similar function. In *Roots* alone there are five adult males who fail Horace in one fashion or another. Paul Horace can't help the fact that he is dying, of course, although one could argue that his dissipa-

---

5. Horace's giving Buddy and Molly each a nickel recalls the ironic ending of *Roots*, when Mr. Tyler gives Horace a dime.

tion contributes to his early demise. Before he dies he does ask his two best friends, George Tyler and John Howard, his law partner, to take care of Horace and Lily Dale, and at first it appears that his friends will step into the void he leaves behind. John Howard says, shortly after his death, "I'm going to be as close to that boy [Horace] as I can, for Paul Horace's sake," and George Tyler responds, "We all will want to look out for him" (*Four Plays* 58–59). They pay for the funeral expenses and encourage Horace to follow in his father's footsteps and study law. Even Terrence, Horace's uncle, offers to help Horace in his studies.

These good intentions come to naught, however. Act 2 begins with a discussion between Horace and his Grandfather Thornton about the fact that Horace has missed school and is behind in his studies. Horace mentions the offers for help he has received, but then adds, "Uncle Terrence hasn't been feeling so well lately himself, so he can't help me. Mr. George Tyler is never home, and Mr. John Howard helped me twice . . . but lately he has been too busy. I wonder if you or Uncle Albert could maybe help me sometime?" to which his grandfather replies, "I can't son. I know nothing about all that. You'll have to do that on your own. Your Uncle Albert knows nothing about it either. He quit in the fourth grade, you know" (*Four Plays* 62–63). Shortly thereafter, John Howard dies in his sleep.

Ideally, Pete Davenport, who becomes Horace's stepfather before the end of his play, would have filled the role of father to Horace, but as we have seen, that does not happen. Thus the conversation between George Tyler and Horace that concludes the play becomes even more ironic, given the string of fathers and father-substitutes who have failed Horace at this critical juncture in his life. Mr. Tyler is now living in what was the Robedaux house, Horace's grandmother, aunt, and uncle having moved away. He comes out of the house and sees Horace, who says he has decided to "give up law" and become a "merchant"—that is, to accompany his uncle Albert to the Gautier plantation and clerk in the store. Mr. Tyler replies, "I think it's a wise decision for a boy in your circumstances. Of course, being the good friend of your daddy's I was, I would have done all in my power to help you, but I think you are doing the right thing." With his usual insensitivity, he adds, "There's been some changes, haven't there? Your daddy's dead, the Robedauxs moved, your mama married again—a lot of changes." When Horace, turning away, begins to cry, he says, "Now you mustn't cry. You've been mighty brave up till now," inviting him into the house to see how he's changed it: "You wouldn't know it now" (*Four Plays* 87). When Horace declines politely, he gives him a dime and says, "Buy yourself something," salving his conscience, one assumes, and the play ends.

The subsequent play, *Convicts*, revisits and extends the theme of abandonment. When they arrive at the Gautier plantation, Uncle Albert drinks and gambles his days away, incapable of providing any guidance or support to Horace; if anything, it's Horace who supports him. This point is driven home by Billy Vaughn, Henry Vaughn's alcoholic, ne'er-do-well brother, who stops by the plantation store on Christmas Eve day with his drunken wife, Asa, to bring Horace to town. "My God," Billy says, "I don't know what Horace's people are thinking of, letting him work out here in this Godforsaken place" (*Four Plays* 94). "It sickens me," he continues. "It sickens me to see a boy abandoned this way," saying that he wishes he and Asa could raise him. Well-intentioned as he may be, this is just drunken talk. In the end, Horace spends Christmas Eve at the sickbed of the besotted Soll Gautier, the plantation owner, hoping to get Mr. Soll to pay him the $11.50 he owes him for the past six months' work so he can buy a tombstone for his father's grave. He doesn't get paid, of course. In yet another role reversal, Soll turns to Horace for help instead of providing it. Hallucinating that one of the black convicts is trying to kill him, he makes Horace promise not to leave him, and, should he die, to stay by his body until it's buried, which he does. When the caretaker Ben points out that Mr. Soll didn't keep any of his promises to Horace, he quietly replies, "I'd feel better if I kept mine" (*Four Plays* 161).[6]

The source of Horace's steadiness and integrity is ultimately mysterious, given the string of adults who have egregiously failed him. He has had virtually no positive male models, no father or father substitutes to teach him how to live. The same is true of his decision to stop drinking and gambling, remarked upon in Chapter 2, especially

6. Mr. Soll's refusal to pay Horace after promising to do so functions as a metaphor for all the adults who fail Horace as a child: Corella, his grandparents, Pete Davenport, Uncle Albert, John Howard, George Tyler—the list is extensive.

in the face of the many alcoholics who populate this community—another recurring character type. In the *Cycle* as a whole, at least nine figure prominently: Paul Horace, Uncle Albert, Billy Vaughn, and Brother in the Thornton-Robedaux-Vaughn clan; Mr. Coons in *Lily Dale;* Mr. Ritter; Soll Gautier; Bobby Pate; and Cousin Lewis. While to a large extent the behavior of these men is tolerated by their families and the community at large, it is clear what a toll drinking takes on the lives of both these individuals and those who love them. Thus the fact that Horace could just stop, mysteriously, while others like Mr. Coons and Bobby Pate take "the cure" again and again to no avail testifies to the depth of his love for Elizabeth, whom he credits as his reason for quitting.

The portrait Foote paints of alcoholism in this community is clear-eyed and unsentimental, reflecting accurately what was a pressing problem in communities such as Harrison during this era, especially since alcoholism was not yet recognized as a disease and there was no recourse except "will power." Marian Burkhart, pointing to this phenomenon and Foote's skillful handling of it, sees it as an example of his deromanticization of Southern myths:

> The mythic figure particularly subject to debunking in the Cycle is the southern "good old boy," rough and ready, governed more by a sort of frontier chivalry than by the law, a free spirit who finds his strength in whiskey, the good, clear liquor from the old brown jug, central—as in Faulkner's "The Bear"—to the male ritual of telling hunting tales and finding therein the courage to hunt again. Around Harrison, Texas, the center of Foote's personal Yoknapatawpha County, such men are unmitigated disasters who ruin their families, waste their fortunes, kill others, and addle their brains, and there is no solution for this rampant alcoholism other than the Keeley Cure, the inefficacy of which is a thread running wryly through Foote's tapestry.[7]

The fact that both Brother and Cousin Lewis become murderers under the influence of alcohol is an index of its destructive potential.

Along with orphans, fathers and father figures, and alcoholics, Foote gives us an overabundance of pairs of brothers in the *Cycle,* using them to comment upon family relationships, both positive and

---

7. Burkhart, "Horton Foote's Many Roads Home," 112.

negative. In *Convicts* alone there are five pairs. In some cases, enmity is the salient feature of the relationship. Soll Gautier is driven by hatred of his brother Tyre, who owns the plantation next door. He calls Tyre a "mean, no-good bastard" and "a liar, a thief, a killer," adding, "I hope his soul will rot in hell forever" (*Four Plays* 125). "Thank God you've got no brother," he says to Horace. "They steal everything you've got, cut your heart out, and smile all the while" (*Four Plays* 126). Other brothers are intensely loyal to one another. In three different cases—that of the Brodler brothers; the convict Jessie Wilkes and his half-brother, Sherman Edwards; and Ben Jackson, Soll's convict-turned-overseer—men kill their brothers' murderers in revenge, even when it leads to their own deaths. Mr. Soll mentions a fifth pair of brothers, black convicts he shot as they were trying to escape his plantation. While each of these seemingly desultory stories, woven into various conversations, is characterized by violence of some sort, Horace is more concerned with matters of lineage: who is related to whom, and how Jessie Wilkes and Sherman Edwards can be brothers and have different last names. It is important to him to keep such things straight. He asks Martha, the black servant (who, along with her gentle husband, Ben, serves as his substitute parent), "What happens if you're not divorced, but your first wife dies and you marry again. When you die and go to heaven, which one of the women do you claim as your wife? . . . And take Sherman Edwards . . . he's got a white daddy and a colored mother. Now, when they all go to heaven together, what's going to happen?" (*Four Plays* 118). It is a world structured by families, by brothers and sisters, mothers and fathers. When these units are shattered, chaos ensues. Horace's obsession about buying a tombstone for his father's grave comes from this matrix: his need for order demands that even if only in death, his father's life must be recognized and honored if his own lineage is to be intact.

Foote's duplication of stock character types, then, functions both to make connections between plays and to create resonances which extend the implications of any individual type beyond a single instance. He uses image patterns and symbols in a similar fashion. The title of the first play, *Roots in a Parched Ground,* suggests two sources of imagery, that of flowers and vegetation (roots) and the need for fructifying water (parched ground), which he employs to depict the social and cultural changes brought about by the Civil War. The stage directions that open *Roots,* set in 1902, state simply, "This was not an affluent time in the lives of these people" (*Four Plays* 5), an understated reference to the fact that both the Robedauxs' and the Thorntons' family fortunes were lost in the Civil War, leaving them poor if not destitute. In these plays Foote, like Faulkner, traces the decline of aristocratic Southern families who were unable to adapt to changed conditions or cope with the loss of their fortunes after the war. In conveying this seachange, he uses imagery of flowers and lush vegetation associated with the past to contrast with images of drought and dryness linked with their present life.

The Robedaux patriarch, Horace's grandfather, owned a vast fleet of ships, as Mrs. Robedaux explains to her grandson: "Your grandfather's ships sailed around the world. And we were educated people: ministers, lawyers, and doctors, and scholars—Latin scholars and Greek scholars. We lived then in a world that valued those things" (*Four Plays* 69). Two of Paul Horace's brothers founded a newspaper, and the Robedauxs had a beautiful home in Galveston, surrounded by "cape jasmines and camellias and oleanders" (*Four Plays* 68). But the classical learning associated with the Robedauxs and the aristocratic life they led does not prepare them for the hurly-burly of the marketplace or life without money. When their fleet is destroyed in the war, they are unable to adapt to the changed conditions which confront them.

As Corella Thornton, obviously biased, puts it to Horace, Jr., years later, "They couldn't take care of themselves." When he asks why not, she replies flatly, "Because they were all too educated. You see, before the war they owned a shipping fleet in Galveston and they were very rich, but then the Yankees destroyed their fleet and they lost all their money and they were all so educated they couldn't do anything" (*Two Plays* 124). But even Sally Robedaux, Paul Horace's sister, concedes that her brother Terrence couldn't run the newspaper after their brother Carl died. She says to her mother, "No one could understand the editorials when he wrote them. If you don't know Latin and Greek, you're lost trying to read what he writes. People just laughed at his editorials, Mama—you know that" (*Four Plays* 12). As commentator Carter Martin points out, "Paul Horace and his brother . . . have classical libraries and read both Latin and Greek, but, like Faulkner's Compsons, they have become dissipated, lost their family's money and position, and are almost completely ineffectual in any practical sense."[8]

The Thorntons' fortune was invested in land. Corella's Grandfather Thornton, the family patriarch, was the governor of Texas, and "his plantation ran from here to the coast," according to John Howard, who adds, "The Thorntons shouldn't have lost their land. They were cheated out of it" (*Four Plays* 28). Young Horace in *The Death of Papa* tells Gertrude that his great-great-grandfather had "two big plantations and one hundred twenty slaves" (*Two Plays* 117).[9] Yet within two generations, Corella is reduced to sewing men's shirts for a living.

Both families, then, have rapidly descended the social scale, and their members live with the memories of a past of ease and comfort in sharp contrast with their present struggles. The images associated with the past, the Cape jasmines and camellias and oleanders of the Robedauxs' Galveston home, for instance, convey a sense of lushness and delicate beauty. It is a telling detail that Paul Horace loved these flowers, and, according to Terrence, "wanted one day to live near a sandy soil on the coast so he could have Cape jasmines growing again." His mother responds, "Well then, he'll have to go without. The soil here is too rich for Cape jasmines. I've tried many a time to grow them" (*Four Plays* 68). Their past life cannot be transplanted to the present soil.

Their present life is described in images that connote dryness and drought. While the exact nature of Paul Horace's illness is never explained, for instance, his last days are characterized by his dry, raspy breaths. Years later both Lily Dale and Horace recall the deathbed

8. Carter Martin, "Horton Foote's Southern Family in *Roots in a Parched Ground*," *Texas Review* 12, nos. 1–2 (1991): 78. For further discussion of the Robedaux and Thornton families' precipitous decline in the context of Southern literary themes, see pp. 78–80.

9. These fictional details correspond to events in Foote's family history, which he discussed in an interview he gave to Robert Flynn and Susan Russell. A sidebar on Albert Clinton Horton, Foote's great-great-grandfather, after providing further historical details, notes, "He served as acting governor of Texas while Governor James Pinckney Henderson commanded troops during the Mexican War. He was considered one of the wealthiest men in the state but the Civil War wrecked his fortune." Robert Flynn and Susan Russell, "Horton Foote," *When I Was Just Your Age* (Denton, Texas: University of North Texas Press, 1992), 19.

vigil in terms of his coughing and struggling to breathe (*Four Plays* 233 and *Two Plays* 163). In *Roots in a Parched Ground,* Horace spends his spare time looking for empty whiskey bottles to sell; indeed, the final scene of the play sees him doing just that. The empty bottles become an ironic symbol of Horace's situation at this point. There is to be no communal wine, no sustenance for Horace. This implication is confirmed by the full quotation from which the play's title derives, taken from William Carlos Williams's "Raleigh Was Right": "Love itself a flower / with roots in a parched ground." Though love can and often does grow in inhospitable soil, if the environment is completely parched, it will eventually die.

These images of drought and dryness occur in a different form in the later plays, especially *Cousins* and *The Death of Papa,* where the economy's dependence on cotton and therefore rain is a paramount factor in the town's survival. In *Cousins,* Horace has to renegotiate his bank loan because business is bad; cotton crops have failed and the farmers have no money to spend in his store. Foote himself recalls as a very young child being aware of the critical need for rain: "My father had a bit of a struggle because our whole economy depended on cotton, which I learned early. It was the first thing I learned to ask. 'How's the cotton?' My earliest memory of my father was walking out with him and looking at the skies to see if it was going to rain or not."[10] The images of dry, parched land, raspy breaths, and empty whiskey bottles combine to suggest an emotional and spiritual aridity that works against sinking roots, making permanent human connections.

Variations on the flower imagery introduced in *Roots* also appear in later plays, associated, significantly, with weddings, new homes, and deaths. The final scene of *Valentine's Day,* for instance, which is composed of several cross-cutting conversations, is laced with references to roses. Elizabeth is describing her wedding day to her father, while Bobby Lee and Miss Ruth, two other boarders where Horace and Elizabeth live, interject with only tangentially related comments. The connecting thread running through this meandering conversation, shaped by associative rather than linear logic, is roses: those that Elizabeth carried on her wedding day, the sweetheart roses that Mrs.

10. Foote, quoted in Flynn and Russell, "Horton Foote," 18.

Vaughn planted the previous fall on the graves of Elizabeth's two infant sisters, and the roses she plans to plant in the new house her parents are building for her and Horace: "Red roses, yellow roses, pink roses, sweetheart roses, and climbing roses" (*Three Plays* 107).[11] Here flower imagery is used as a kind of leveler, juxtaposing marriage and a new family with the tragedy of infant deaths, while moments before references are made to the recent suicide of George Tyler. To emphasize this irony, Foote closes the play by having Miss Ruth, hopelessly in love with the alcoholic Bobby Pate, sing quietly "Oh Promise Me."

A similar conjunction occurs in the final scene of the subsequent play, *1918*. World War I has just ended; Brother, drunk and irresponsible, never makes it to the war or even to a potential new job in Galveston; and Horace and Elizabeth, still mourning the death of their infant daughter Jenny in the 1918 flu epidemic, welcome a new son into the world. Amidst references to these events, Horace mentions that a neighbor, Mrs. Boone, placed flowers on Jenny's grave, and Elizabeth asks what kind. Sweet peas, cosmos, periwinkles, snapdragons, and verbenas, Horace tells her, and Elizabeth keeps repeating these words, mantra-like, as she drifts off to sleep. It is all of a piece, in Foote's world; death cannot be separated from life.

The seamless meshing of life and death is nowhere more apparent than in the many references to the graveyard, perhaps the most prominent single unifying motif of the *Cycle*. The chief instance of this, of course, is Horace's determination to purchase a tombstone for his

11. These words, interestingly, conclude the play. In a narrative including such dramatic events as Horace and Elizabeth's elopement, estrangement, and reconciliation with the Vaughns; the poignant failed relationship between Miss Ruth Amos and the drunken Bobby Pate; and the violent suicide of Mr. George Tyler, this might seem an anticlimactic conclusion. It is, however, typical of Foote's mature work, as Gerald Wood points out in "The Nature of Mystery in *The Young Man from Atlanta*": "As Horton Foote develops as a writer, his characters become less assured about their own motives and goals; consequently, there are fewer passages where they explain their feelings, mistakes, and conclusions. His mature dramas have little closure; explanations, if any, are tenuous, the endings acting more as lulls than resolutions." Wood, "Nature of Mystery," 180. Ted Mann, cofounder of the Circle in the Square Theatre and colleague of Foote's, made a similar comment about the ending of his 1986 production of *The Widow Claire*: "At first the audience just sat there," he said, "not knowing what to do. It was like a sentence ending before the final punctuation mark." Ted Mann, interview with the author, January 8, 1999.

father's grave, a theme which informs several plays and finally culmi-
nates in *1918,* the seventh *Cycle* play. It is first established in *Roots in
a Parched Ground* in a conversation Horace has with his friend Lloyd
shortly after his father's death. Having just told Lloyd that he'll be
working at the Gautier plantation for "four bits a week," Horace asks
how much tombstones cost. When Lloyd says about a hundred dollars, adding, "Take you a long time to save a hundred dollars," Horace remains silent, but his determination is clear.

It is his overriding concern in *Convicts,* the second *Cycle* play. Although he is intimidated by Mr. Soll, the plantation owner, Horace
screws up his courage and insists that he be paid the $11.50 he is
owed for six months' labor so that he can buy a tombstone for his
father's grave. Indeed, the discussion of graves and gravestones forms
a leitmotif which appears in a variety of contexts throughout this play,
which in many ways can be read as a sustained reflection on death and
dying. Early in the play Horace tells Martha that he's just seen the
fresh grave of a convict who has been killed, and he's worried that it
has no marker on it. "If we knew his name we could put his name on
a board and put it over his grave," he says. "I wonder if anybody said
a prayer over him when they buried him" (*Four Plays* 97). It is a concern that will punctuate other conversations in the course of the play.
One's death must be marked, ritualized in some fashion to make
sense of one's life, Horace feels, just as in life, genealogies must be
kept straight and family histories preserved.

A bit later, as he talks to Horace about his father's death, Mr. Soll
reminisces on the elaborate, $5,000 tombstone he bought for his
own father, bringing it by boat from New Orleans, though when
Horace later looks for it in the graveyard he can't find it. "He was
lying," Ben says. "Didn't have nothing on it—just a slab of marble
sticking up with his name on it. If the convicts didn't keep it weeded
over there, you wouldn't be able to find it for the brush in a week"
(*Four Plays* 162). This theme of impermanence extending even after
death is reiterated in Soll's comment about his mother's grave on Sa-
lurie Island being washed away by a tidal wave and Ben's final comment over Soll's grave in the play's closing scene. Asa, Soll's niece,
has inherited all his property in spite of his contempt for his brother
and his express wish that this not happen. As they stand over his

grave, Ben says of Asa, "She's gonna let the weeds and trees and the cane get this land. Six months from now you won't know where anybody's buried out here. Not my people, not the convicts, not Mr. Soll. The trees and the weeds, and the cane, will take everything. . . . The house will go, the store will go, the graves will go, those with tombstones and those without" (*Four Plays* 162–63).

This ironic image of the cane obliterating socially constructed categories—the members of Ben's family, who remained on the plantation as paid laborers after the Civil War; the black convicts; and the whites all have separate burial grounds—speaks to the destructiveness of society's racial and economic divisions. Soll's last words illustrate the ultimate futility of this mind-set: "Don't let them bury me with my own family," he says to Horace, "because my brother and his daughters are going to be buried there and I don't want to be buried by them or near them. I'd rather have convicts near me than that stinkin'—" (*Four Plays* 160). These are his final words. Death cuts him off in midsentence, as if to insist upon the ludicrousness of people's petty feuds and prejudices. We all come to dust in the end; nature reclaims its own.

The motif of death, dying, and burial rituals, in fact, dominates the entire play, one of the bleakest in the *Cycle*. We hear of several murders and witness one on stage (the sheriff kills a convict, trying to escape), along with Mr. Soll's simulated death and his actual one. Ironically, Horace, whose primary reason for staying at the plantation is to earn enough money to purchase his father's tombstone, is drawn reluctantly into Soll's death. The old man has taken a liking to Horace and asks him to spend the night with him, and he is alone with Soll when he dies. In fact, Mr. Soll is holding on to the boy so tightly that his hand has to be pried from Horace so they can put him in his coffin. The play ends with Soll's funeral, the circumstances of which are as ironic as the death itself. Since he had insisted that he wanted no preacher, prayers, or hymns at his funeral, the convict-overseer Jackson sings the only song he knows, "Oh, dem golden slippers," as Horace and Ben, the only other mourners, look on.

All of the remaining plays feature either a death or a near-death. In *Lily Dale*, as we have seen, Horace becomes ill with malaria and nearly dies. The play's title and Lily Dale's name derive from a ballad Paul Horace used to sing about the untimely death of the beautiful

Lily Dale and her "little green grave" in the "flow'ry vale." The Widow Claire in the play by that name has lost her husband to typhoid; in *Courtship,* both Syd Joplin and Sybil Thomas die in the flower of youth. The climax of *Valentine's Day* is punctuated by the suicide of Mr. George Tyler (recalling the suicide/disappearance of Mr. George Ritter in *Roots*), and *1918* is replete with deaths from both World War I and the flu epidemic.

It is in this play that Horace's obsession with placing a tombstone on his father's grave surfaces for the last time. Ironically, by this point, some sixteen years after his death, no one is certain which grave is Paul Horace's, and Horace, coming down with the flu and very nearly dying himself, attempts to write Cousin Minnie to find out. The play's first and penultimate scenes take place in the graveyard, with Horace speaking to Sam, the black gravedigger. In the latter scene, the tombstone is finally in place and Horace is visiting it when Mr. Vaughn arrives with the news that Elizabeth has just had their baby; once again, birth and death are interwoven. The last two plays, *Cousins* and *The Death of Papa,* are structured around the near-death of Corella Thornton and the actual death of Henry Vaughn.

In this third motif, then, that of deaths, funerals, and cemeteries, nature and family intersect. On the one hand, the graveyard is seen as an extension of the town. Families are buried together as if social units function even after death; hence Horace's concern that his paternal lineage be literally set in stone. These social paradigms cut both ways. On the one hand, the value of family as a civilizing agent is apparent, as well as its perhaps even more important function of conferring identity upon individual members. On the other hand, the categories society constructs, reflected in the segregated cemeteries in Harrison and on the Gautier plantation, testify to the destructiveness of the racism that informs this world. While the flowers planted on the graves reflect society's potential for bringing grace and beauty to life experience, the image of the cane in *Convicts* obliterating the tombstones suggests symbolically that these socially constructed divisions are unnatural.

The third technique that Foote employs to unify the *Cycle* and magnify meaning is that of parallel and inverted events which function both within and among the plays. We have already noted the parallel between Corella Thornton's marriage of convenience to Pete

Davenport and the Widow Claire's decision to marry Ned in order to provide a secure home for her children. In *Courtship* we learn in passing that Mr. Vaughn's sister Lucy evidently made a similar choice, marrying a man twenty years her senior, although ironically he died an untimely death, leaving her with four children to support; security, it turns out, can never be guaranteed. While this scenario is duplicated in three different plays, *Roots, Courtship,* and *The Widow Claire,* subtly reinforcing women's vulnerable position in this society, the same point is made from a slightly different perspective using parallelism within a single play. *Courtship,* whose title signals the paramount importance of this social ritual in early-twentieth-century society, presents us with three variations on the theme of the "wild" young man and the dire consequences of making the wrong marital choice. The fate of Syd Joplin and Sybil Thomas, Elizabeth's parents imply, could be hers if she chooses to marry Horace, who is also known to drink and gamble. The *Cycle* is also saturated with the deaths of parents or parental figures, the most obvious being the two which begin and end the narrative: the death of Horace's father in the first play and that of Elizabeth's in the last. When one includes the death of Mr. Soll, whose passing can be viewed as a parody of the tragic death of Paul Horace in the previous play, and the near-death of Corella in *Cousins,* the list expands to four within a nine-play span. The parallels between Horace's two brushes with death in *Lily Dale* and *1918,* the one from malaria and the other from influenza, link those two plays in our mind.

Perhaps the most striking plot parallel, however, and one I would like to explore at greater length, is that of the death of Horace and Elizabeth's first child and that of Elizabeth's two sisters, who also died as infants. References to the deaths of Elizabeth's two baby sisters, which appear in four of the nine plays, first occur in *Courtship,* when Laura says to Elizabeth, "I wonder why did the two little girls die and not us? Why are they out in the graveyard and we are here?" (*Three Plays* 38). At this point, the parallel, drawn between the two sisters who lived, Laura and Elizabeth, and the two who didn't, is used to comment on the vagaries of fate. The story is expanded in *Valentine's Day,* when Elizabeth tells about the time when as a five-year-old she tried to take Laura, then two, to the cemetery to look for the grave of their dead sister, and Mr. Billy Lee found them and helped them locate the grave: "He put us both on his horse and took us out to the graveyard, and we found her grave with the little lamb on it. He said she's not there, she's in heaven, and I said who is there then, and he said no one. Well, I said, how did she get out of there, and he said God took her home with him" (*Three Plays* 97). Upon the death of Elizabeth and Horace's own daughter Jenny, named after the dead sister, the parallel shifts from that of Elizabeth and Laura as sisters contemplating their own experience to that of Elizabeth as mother, now understanding the deep pain her mother went through in the same situation. As she tells Horace, now safely out of danger from the flu, that their child has died and she buried her next to his father's grave (the tombstone has a little lamb on it, she says, "like my little sister's"), they both turn in their grief to Mrs. Vaughn. "Mama, help us," Elizabeth cries. "How did you stand it when you lost your children?" In typical Foote understatement, Mrs. Vaughn simply says, "You just stand it. You keep going" (*Three Plays* 150).

The death of baby Jenny and the birth of Horace, Jr., coinciding with the end of World War I, bring *1918* to a close. Foote does not dwell on their pain. We are allowed only the brief glimpse in the scene mentioned above and a conversation Elizabeth has with the neighbor girl, Bessie, right before she goes into labor, when she confesses that she "worried for the longest time [that] that's why my Jenny was taken, because I named her after a dead baby" (*Three Plays* 166), pondering perhaps life's most perplexing mystery: the death of innocent children. She has spoken to her minister, who assured her that Jenny's death was God's will, but that only makes it harder for her to deal with. "Do you believe that, Bessie?" she asks. "Do you believe it was His will that Jenny died?" (*Three Plays* 166–67).

The depth of Elizabeth and Horace's loss is quietly indicated once more, in *Cousins,* when in the midst of a quiet conversation about nothing of consequence, Elizabeth says to Horace, about to go buy hamburgers for their dinner, "I love you," and he responds with the same words, holding her in his arms. Then, "Today is Jenny's birthday," and Horace: "I know." They don't need to speak about it. Elizabeth says she plans to take a flowering plant to the cemetery later, then adds, "It's like Mama says, you think of her differently than the others, but you think of her" (*Two Plays* 90). That's all, but it tells us all we need to know.

This quiet scene with its deep undercurrents of pain, loss, and ac-
ceptance, contrasts strikingly with the last time the connection is
made between these infant deaths in *The Death of Papa*. Young Horace, now ten, in visiting the cemetery with his Grandmother Vaughn
comes across the graves of both his mother's infant sister and his own.
Like his father, curious about genealogies, he asks, "Was my sister
that's dead named for this Jenny that's dead?" When Mrs. Vaughn
responds that that is the case, he says, thoughtfully, "This Jenny is my
aunt. I'm older than she is. I'm older than my own aunt, and my
daddy is older now than his father," then adds, "I'm hungry" (*Two
Plays* 135). What was a wrenching experience for his mother and her
mother before her becomes to young Horace just a piece of history.

These parallel and connecting episodes function on several levels.
Structurally, they weave the plays into a seamless whole while they
deepen and enrich our experience of individual plays. We do not need
to know Horace and Elizabeth's history to understand the scenes in
Cousins and *The Death of Papa*, but if we do, we are much more
aware of the depth of feeling that underlies their exchange in *Cousins*
and the irony of young Horace's matter-of-fact comment to his
grandmother in the sequel play. A kind of dialogue between the plays
sets up ripples of significance that extend beyond a single instance to
create patterns of meaning. Like the plays' recurring character types
and interlocking image patterns, these plot parallels and inversions
are instances of Foote's remarkable economy of means and technical
virtuosity. On a thematic level, they reinforce the notion of life as a
cyclic experience as well as an individual one. Each generation has
circumstances to face which are unique to its own moment in history,
the flu epidemic and World War I being prime examples, while some
experiences, like the death of a child, are common to all generations.

To illustrate how all these techniques work together within a single
play, I turn to *Valentine's Day,* whose dramatic structure is perhaps
the most polyphonic of all nine plays. At first glance it appears to be
a straightforward narrative of love and reconciliation; upon closer inspection, however, its complex construction becomes evident. It is
not, in fact, one story, but several, woven together like the contra-
puntal melodies of a musical composition.

The play takes up Horace's tale less than a year after his marriage
to Elizabeth, showing us the young couple just embarking on their

life together. A brief play, just one act and a little over fifty pages in length, it covers two weeks in their life. We learn in the opening scene, set on Christmas Eve, 1917, that Horace and Elizabeth had eloped the previous Valentine's Day and that the Vaughns have refused to speak with either of them in the ten months since then. It is clearly a painful situation, one of which the whole town is aware. Mr. George Tyler says to Elizabeth, for instance, "I've heard tell . . . when they [the Vaughns] meet you uptown by accident they turn their heads and look the other way," to which she simply responds, "Yes Sir" (*Three Plays* 58). Before the play is over, Elizabeth will be reconciled with her parents, and she and Horace, currently living in a boardinghouse, will be making plans to move into a home of their own, a gift from Mr. Vaughn. This would seem to be the spine of the action: a movement from estrangement through reconciliation to harmony. In fact, the reconciliation takes place in scene two, less than a third of the way into the play; the real climax of the action is the suicide of Mr. Tyler, who in any other play would be considered a minor character.

This, in a nutshell, illustrates the unorthodox way in which Foote shapes his plots. Rather than the linear, conflict-driven structures that we are accustomed to, he presents us with dramas whose organizing principle seems to be associative rather than logical, with characters drifting on and off stage, woven into the action and then disappearing and reappearing later on. This has a kind of disorienting effect, defying our usual analytical strategies and categories. We would expect to focus on the Vaughns' change of heart, ostensibly with some explanation of their transformation—they come to appreciate Horace's fine qualities, they learn of something laudable that he has done, they succumb to pressure from other family members, or the like. But not only do we never learn why they decide to rescind their disapproval of Elizabeth's marriage; we aren't even allowed to see it take place. Their re-establishment of contact with Elizabeth takes place in a phone call off-stage, which Elizabeth relates to Horace, as quoted in the previous chapter, with Mrs. Vaughn calling to ask if they can bring over some Christmas presents. When they arrive, no one says a word about the painful months just past; it's as if they never occurred. Foote does not villainize the Vaughns or focus on the conflicts one might expect to dominate the relationship of Horace with his in-laws.

Eschewing conflict-driven plots for subtler fare, he keeps us at a distance from emotion, passing over potentially melodramatic scenes for the inner drama of ordinary lives. Events that dramatists might make the high point of the action—Elizabeth and Horace's wedding and the death of their infant daughter provide two more examples— take place either between the plays (the former) or off-stage (the latter).

What, then, shapes the action of this play? If one looks closely, there is, in fact, a movement from estrangement to harmony. The first scene takes place on Christmas Eve, but it contains references to Horace and Elizabeth's elopement the previous Valentine's Day.[12] Elizabeth, waiting for Horace to return from work, is describing the anguish of the day before she eloped to Bessie Stillman, the strange young neighbor girl who visits her in the boardinghouse, when Mr. Tyler knocks on the door. It is his second appearance of the evening; he's "off" again, as Bessie puts it, describing his eccentric behavior. In a conversation which begins with "They tell me you and Horace eloped," Mr. Tyler recounts the facts of that day: the Methodist preacher refusing to marry them, the Baptist preacher insisting that they call Elizabeth's parents first, the fact that the Vaughns haven't forgiven them. The combination of Elizabeth's and Mr. Tyler's accounts of the wedding not only establishes for the audience the circumstances of Elizabeth and Horace's marriage and present status; it communicates the small town ambiance, with the townspeople, privy to Elizabeth and Horace's affairs, functioning as a kind of Greek chorus. Very much in the Southern oral tradition, it's a kind of communal storytelling.

A similar atmosphere pervades the play's closing scene. Those present include Horace and Elizabeth; Mr. Vaughn; Bobby Pate, the landlady's alcoholic son who lives upstairs; and another boarder, Miss Ruth Amos, in love with Bobby. Their desultory, intercutting conversations cover a range of topics, including Horace and Elizabeth's wedding. Mr. Vaughn's presence and his interest in what happened—he asks what kind of flowers they had and inquires about

12. In naming this play *Valentine's Day* in spite of the fact that the action takes place on Christmas Eve (as well as a closing scene a few weeks later), Foote emphasizes the importance of both Elizabeth and Horace's wedding, which will change the course of their lives forever, and the transformative power of love.

their wedding gifts—reframes what was a bittersweet story in scene 1, its joy overshadowed by the Vaughns' disapproval. A second topic of conversation, the new house Mr. Vaughn is building in back of his own for Horace and Elizabeth, seals their reunion and removes any lingering doubts as to the Vaughns' feelings (not coincidentally, these topics are linked with flower imagery, as noted earlier in this chapter).

Placing the opening and closing scenes side by side reveals that the play's action does, on one level, trace the movement from estrangement to reconciliation. However, equally important are the stories of the townspeople that Foote weaves into the action: George Tyler's unhappy marriage and failure as a father to both his son Steve and Horace, to whom he feels obligated; Bobby Tate's alcoholism and gambling and Miss Ruth's futile dreams that he will reform; Brother's dissipation and failure to take hold of life; and even the story of strange Bessie, who floats in and out of the action like a ghost.[13] In this play, perhaps more than any other in the *Cycle*, the town itself is the protagonist, a fact which the dramatic structure emphasizes.

In weaving these disparate stories together, Foote utilizes the stylistic strategies described in this chapter, creating parallel characters and events, repeating key motifs, and returning to imagery used in previous plays. In reintroducing George Tyler, for instance, a character who hasn't appeared since the *Cycle*'s first play, *Roots in a Parched Ground*, Foote reiterates a motif as well as a character type: the failed father. The picture of Mr. Tyler presented in the earlier play is that of a capable but insensitive man, unable to see that he is failing to live up to his promise to Paul Horace to take care of his orphaned son. In *Valentine's Day*, fifteen years later, we see the changes that time has wrought. His life has been ruined, it appears, by the fact that he mar-

13. Bessie, who insists on calling Elizabeth "Mary" for reasons which are never explained, is an intriguing character. Foote said in an interview with Ronald L. Davis, regarding this character, "A lot of people are puzzled by Bessie, and they talk about her a lot. Their first assumption is she's retarded, but she's not. . . . I took her from someone my mother told me about who insisted on calling her Mary. My mother's name was Hallie. My mother, that first year of her marriage, was alone a lot, since her parents were not speaking to her. And this girl spent a great deal of time with her and talked to her. My mother was very fond of her, but the girl was eccentric." Davis, "Roots Interview," 314.

ried the wrong woman. Although he was in love with Horace's Aunt Mary, for reasons he never explains he married her cousin Sarah instead. Now, obsessed with this fact, he suffers from delusions that his wife is trying to poison him; the previous Christmas he tried to stab her with a butcher knife. "I've had a difficult life, you know," he says to Horace, "since I betrayed Mary. I've had no happiness. I've been punished unmercifully for what I've done" (*Three Plays* 90). He also feels he's betrayed Horace. In the same scene Mr. Tyler says, quoting Paul Horace's last words to him, " 'George, I'm going to die. Promise me you'll look after my children. Promise me you'll never let them go hungry.' *(Pause)* I didn't keep my promise. And I'm sorry; I didn't keep my promise about a lot of things" (*Three Plays* 90). Apparently in an effort to make amends, he gives Horace ten $100 bills for Christmas.

While it's true that Mr. Tyler did fail Horace, his fixation on past failures prevents him from seeing the needs of his own son, Steve, in the present. Steve patiently follows after his father, trying to keep him from getting lost or coming to harm, retrieving the money he is lavishly giving away not just to Horace but to all his "colored friends." Thus it's ironic that at the moment of his death, it is not Steve he calls for, but Horace, still mumbling something about promising Paul Horace he'd look out for his son. This vignette about a tragically misspent life returns to the motif of abandoned sons introduced in *Roots*, expanding it to include Steve as well as Horace. Mr. Tyler's gift of $1,000, later retrieved, works in a similar fashion, subtly recalling the dime he gives Horace at the end of the first play.

The parallels between Bobby Pate and Brother function in much the same way. Bobby takes his place in the long line of alcoholics who populate Harrison. Self-pitying and irresponsible, he is frozen in the past, telling Elizabeth and Bessie about his former wife, who left him, breaking his heart: "Mama says that's what I get for marrying beneath myself. She says it never works out. Mama says being born common is like a curse, you can't do nothing about it. 'Well, common or not,' I said, 'I loved her' " (*Three Plays* 59). Sounding much like the bums in O'Neill's *The Iceman Cometh,* who use their litany of past pain, long forgotten, to excuse their drinking in the present, Bobby wallows in self-pity. He says at one point that he was a baby when his father died, in response to a discussion about Horace's being an orphan, and Miss Ruth says, "You weren't a baby. You were a grown man," to which Bobby simply replies, "I was?" and changes the subject. Perhaps the most telling line is his comment that he told his mother that they should get a family plot in the graveyard (a motif which surfaces in this play, as well), adding, "We have to get one. I want us together even in death" (*Three Plays* 104). His unhealthy dependency upon his mother, whom he quotes at every turn, helps account for his childlike, immature behavior, along with the fact that everyone in town, including his mother, Miss Ruth, and the doctor who comes to sedate him when he becomes violent, in accommodating his behavior makes it possible for him to continue. Although they didn't have access to our contemporary concept of *enabling,* the phenomenon is clearly in evidence here.

Thus when we see Brother following in Bobby's footsteps, with the Vaughns coming behind to clean up his messes and pay his gambling debts, it is not difficult to predict what will become of him. The thematic connection between these two characters is subtly reinforced by several references Bobby makes to Brother. Ironically, he accuses Brother of "drink[ing] like a fish" (*Three Plays* 60), and we learn that Bobby and Brother have a $40 wager (though Brother insists it is only $2) on the outcome of a local trial. Bobby has taken the Keeley Cure many times, to no avail (recalling Mrs. Coons' husband in *Lily Dale*), and during the course of the play he escapes his mother's watchful eye on a trip to Galveston, which was being made for yet another attempt at rehabilitation. This detail, too, reminds us of Brother, who will be guilty of a similar stunt in *1918,* when he is supposed to go to Galveston to work on a cotton boat. Brother's protestations that he is giving up drinking and his promises that he will "straighten out" are as worthless as Bobby's. The parallels between these characters and the interweaving of their stories, which reverberate with echoes of those of other alcoholics throughout the *Cycle,* work together to create the texture of the town as a whole, expanding the significance of their individual stories beyond their own boundaries.

References to four different murder trials in the course of the *Cycle,* all having to do with crimes of passion in which the murderer goes free, have a similar effect. We're familiar with the case of Cousin Lewis killing his cousin, Jamie, and the murder Brother commits in a barroom brawl in the *Cycle*'s final play. These violent deaths, both of which are tolerated by the law as well as society, are foreshadowed by two references in *Valentine's Day*. Bobby tells the story of Raymond Happ, who walked into the local saloon and shot the bartender: "He said, 'I told you if you sold my daddy another bottle of whiskey, I'd kill you.' And he took out a gun and killed him. Let him go free, too, because they said Mr. Briggs had made a drunkard of his daddy by selling him whiskey" (*Three Plays* 78). This anecdote is related in reference to the trial of a Mr. Galbraith, who shot Mr. Mason in broad daylight over a dispute, a trial which is providing much of the town's excitement at the time of the play. Brother bets Bobby $40 that Mr. Galbraith will be convicted and sent to prison, but we are not surprised when he is released, given Harrison's penchant for tolerating this kind of violence. These separate incidents, spread out across the span of nine plays, serve both to unify the plays and create a sense of familiarity in the audience: these are events and people we begin to feel we know firsthand.

In a similar fashion, George Tyler's tragic suicide at the climax of the play brings to mind the untimely death of George Ritter, his contemporary in *Roots in a Parched Ground*. At the time of their deaths, both men had reached an impasse in their lives which seems to have been overwhelming. Mr. Ritter finds he no longer has a place to live, because Mr. Tyler buys the house he's been boarding in and plans to rent it as a whole house at a price Mr. Ritter can't afford. With a single, seemingly inconsequential conversation, his life is changed, though at the time he turns down Mr. Tyler's offer to rent he only says quietly that he's decided to leave Harrison in a week or two. Shortly thereafter, he has disappeared, and as *Roots* closes, the townsfolk are searching for his body in the river bottoms. Mr. Tyler's death is just as sudden. After seeking refuge in the bottoms and being recovered, he admits to Horace that he needs help and seems ready to accept it, but at the last minute he runs from the sheriff, who has taken him into custody, and stabs himself in the heart with a butcher knife.

The association of both deaths with the river brings to mind still another motif, that of the treacherous bottoms. Gertrude, the black maid in *The Death of Papa*, drowns in the river, and as a young boy, Horace was stranded by flooding water and ended up staying a month with the drunken Brodler brothers, a story which is related in *Convicts* (and one which gave the title, *The Night of the Storm,* to the original text of *Roots*). These and other references to the river establish it as a source of danger, creating tension between this use of water imagery and the images of dryness and drought that bespeak another kind of destruction.

Other familiar motifs that surface in this play are those of the orphan and the graveyard. We have encountered the graveyard motif already in Bobby Pate's comment to his mother about buying a family plot. In that same scene Mr. Vaughn mentions the story of Mr. Billy Lee finding Laura Elizabeth and Jenny as young children looking for the cemetery where their baby sister was buried, and earlier Elizabeth tells Bessie the same story, though in more detail (*Three Plays* 97 and 104). Foote uses Bobby Pate once again to introduce the theme of being orphaned. Near the end of the first scene, in a conversation in Horace and Elizabeth's room in the boardinghouse, Bobby comments, relative to the many different houses Horace has lived in, "Horace, Mama used to worry about you growing up. 'Bobby, what is to become of that boy? He lives like an orphan,' she'd say. 'He's got no home.' 'Hell, Mama,' I said, 'He's no orphan. He's got a mama.' 'Where is she?' Mama asked. 'Why isn't she here taking care of him?' " (*Three Plays* 61–62). While Horace doesn't respond to Bobby and this strand of the conversation is dropped, Foote reintroduces the motif of abandonment that we have encountered throughout the *Cycle:* in *Roots*, for instance, when Horace tells his friends that he's on his own now; in *Convicts,* when Billy exclaims with incredulity at the fact that Horace's "people" let him stay at the godforsaken Gautier plantation; when Corella can't allow Horace to stay with them once Pete returns from Atlanta in *Lily Dale.* All of the plays, in one way or another, take up the burden of this song. In *Valentine's Day,* Horace at last has found a home. Although it's only one room in a boardinghouse, the love that he and Elizabeth share transform this space into a haven of peace and tranquillity. Even Mr. Vaughn comments on this fact. Near the end of the play he says to Horace, whom he is clearly beginning to regard with affection, "There's peace in this room and contentment. That's why I like to come here, I think. I said to Mrs. Vaughn, 'They don't have much but they're contented. You feel that' " (*Three Plays* 103). Others seem to respond in a similar fashion. It's as if Horace and Elizabeth's room is a magnet for all the people who drift in and out: the Vaughns, Bessie, Bobby Pate and Miss Ruth, George Tyler and Steve.

Interestingly, in the same speech quoted above, Mr. Vaughn also says to Horace, "Everyone says to me . . . Poor Horace . . . never had a father. Well, like I told Elizabeth, I never had a father either. (*Pause*) And now I have no son. I'll hate myself for saying this tomorrow, but God forgive me I feel it; I have no son at all. He's a stranger to me" (*Three Plays* 102–103). Linking father, son, and son-in-law to the orphan motif, this comment foreshadows the close of the *Cycle,* when after Mr. Vaughn's death and Brother's precipitous decline, he and Horace change places, with Brother symbolically becoming the orphan.

This theme and that of the graveyard are masterfully interwoven with the use of plant imagery in two key scenes: one between Horace and Elizabeth, directly after their reconciliation with the Vaughns, and the closing scene. In the former, Horace speaks of the pain he felt in being abandoned by his mother and his determination to someday have a home of his own. He says to Elizabeth, "I am no orphan, but I think of myself as an orphan, belonging to no one but you. I intend to have everything I didn't have before. A house of my own, some land, a yard, and in that yard I will plant growing things, fruitful things, fig trees, pecan trees, pear trees, peach trees . . . And I will have a garden and chickens" (*Three Plays* 83).[14] In the closing scene, this dream is on the verge of coming true. Mr. Vaughn is building a house for Horace and Elizabeth to bring their new baby home to, and although Horace insists that it be in Elizabeth's name only, too proud to accept this gesture as a gift to himself as well, he will, indeed, have his home at last. As mentioned earlier in this chap-

14. Horace's speech is reminiscent of the well-known passage in Steinbeck's *Of Mice and Men* in which George articulates their mutually shared dream to Lennie, his companion. This vision, a version of Jung's "green earth" archetype, is rooted in nature: George and Lennie will have a little place of their own with "a big vegetable patch and a rabbit hutch and chickens," and they'll "live off the fat of the land." The components of the dream are similar to those which inform Horace's ideal: harmony with nature, financial independence, and a community with which to share the experience, even if that consists of only one other person. See John Steinbeck, *Of Mice and Men/Cannery Row* (New York: Viking Press, 1945), 14.

ter, flower imagery is used to link references to Elizabeth and Horace's wedding, where the flower girl carried roses; the two small graves of Elizabeth's infant sisters, where Mrs. Vaughn planted sweetheart roses; and the flowers Elizabeth plans to plant in the yard of their new home: "Red roses, yellow roses, pink roses, sweetheart roses, and climbing roses" (*Three Plays* 107).

This flower imagery, the last visual icon of the play, symbolically suggests the fulfillment of Horace's dream, the search ended at last. We know, aware of the pain that awaits Horace and Elizabeth in the death of their own infant daughter (another episode linking the graveyard with flowers), that this ending is no "happily ever after"; Foote's vision of life is never that naive. Should we have any doubt, the final sounds we hear in *Valentine's Day* are those of Miss Ruth singing "Oh Promise Me" quietly as the curtain rings down, with Elizabeth joining in. In terms of plot and character, we are amply prepared for this song, since Miss Ruth, who frequently performs at church and soldiers' benefits and fancies herself "the songbird of the South," is heard practicing throughout *Valentine's Day* and *1918,* with her voice heard floating over the action from backstage. Foote uses her songs to good effect, sometimes to punctuate certain themes, like the patriotism of the war effort with "The Star-Spangled Banner," and sometimes ironically, as when we hear her sing "After the Ball" immediately upon the Vaughns' departure, having reconciled with Horace and Elizabeth. In this scene, her singing of "Oh Promise Me," a romantic song which she performed at Horace and Elizabeth's wedding, simultaneously underlines their deep and ongoing love and recalls ironically the many unkept promises that Bobby Pate has made, as well as Miss Ruth's knowledge that there will be no wedding for her.

In music, polyphony (or *counterpoint*) is defined as the art of combining melodies and the texture that results from this combination of individual melodic lines. It seems an apt term for the structure of this play, which consists of a rich blend of the lives of all these characters, who function not just as minor characters in the lives of Horace and Elizabeth but also as major characters in their own dramas. Though George Tyler's tragic death is the occasion for Elizabeth's "I don't want to get old" speech, for example, the emotional high point of the play, it is equally important in its own right as the culmination of his life as we have come to know it throughout this play. Likewise, Bobby Pate and Brother, while serving as foils for Horace and illustrating what might have been his life story, are also the center of their own dramas of loss.

In a letter he wrote me once concerning his writing style, Foote quoted at length from an Ezra Pound passage regarding aesthetics that he felt characterized his own style as well. In describing the act of writing poetry, Pound says, "Objectivity and again objectivity, and expression: no hindside-beforeness, no straddled adjectives (as 'addled mosses dank'), no Tennysonianness of speech; nothing— nothing that you couldn't, in some circumstance, in the stress of some emotion, actually say." And later: "Language is made out of concrete things. General expressions in nonconcrete terms are a laziness; they are talk, not art, not creation. They are the reaction of things on the writer, not a creative act by the writer."[15] It is no surprise to me that Foote quotes this particular passage, since it so succinctly reflects his own aesthetic. His characters certainly speak in words that ordinary people could "actually say"; it is what gives his language its vibrancy and life. As for the concreteness that Pound refers to, Foote achieves this in his own work by weaving individual stories together like the threads of a tapestry, each a unique and fascinating drama in its own right, yet at the same time serving as a subplot in the stories of the other townspeople. To link them, he utilizes the repetition of stock character types, motifs, and imagery, revealing both their parallels and their contrasts. In so doing, he connects plays which both stand alone and work together to tell Horace's story.

This interconnectedness of Horace's story with those of the other townspeople, revealed in the structure of individual plays and the *Cycle* as a whole, speaks to the issue of identity raised in the previous chapters. Both the dramatic structure and the content of these plays argue that identity is the function of both individual and collective experiences. Horace is shaped by both his experience of family and the town as extended family; by the fact that he is born into the Thornton-Robedaux clan and this particular small town, which in turn reflects the values of its larger cultural contexts (Texas, the South, the United States) and its historical moment. At the same

15. Foote, letter to the author, April 25, 1994.

time, he is an individual unlike any other, in Harrison or the world at large.

Foote's blending of individual stories into a seamless whole becomes in the last analysis, then, a comment not just upon the nature of small-town life but on the composite nature of individual identity. Horace as an individual makes certain choices which change the course of his life: he stops drinking, he marries Elizabeth instead of Claire, he doesn't invest $500 with Cousin Monty. At the same time, he is who he is by virtue of his membership in this family, this town. Similarly, he is both the principal character in his life drama and a minor character in those of others; as he is subsumed in their life stories, they are subsumed in his in an elaborate network of causality and interdependence.

Foote's setting the action of *Valentine's Day* in Elizabeth and Horace's boardinghouse is a masterful stroke in that regard. While it provides a plausible rationale for the many visitors who come and go (Bobby and Miss Ruth, for instance, live upstairs), it also serves as an appropriate icon for the complicated web of relationships that constitute Horace and Elizabeth's life in particular and identity in general. They exist as a couple, deeply in love and absorbed in one another yet in the midst of and affected by the actions of countless others who flow around them.

Foote, then, uses both structural and stylistic strategies to reinforce his themes and explore the central mysteries of life: Why do people turn out as they do? How free are we to determine our own destinies? What is the relationship between the individual and the society from which he or she emerges? These questions will be examined from a different perspective in Chapter 5, which explores yet another of Foote's structural innovations: the pairing of entire plays.

5

POINT-COUNTERPOINT

Paired Plays, Multiple Perspectives

When asked by film critic Sheila Benson in a 1996 interview, "What is a Horton Foote story?" Foote replied, "I'm attempting an ongoing saga, a moral and social history of a certain section of the country, specifically this part of Texas." All of Foote's plays can be seen as a part of this "ongoing saga," drawn from material he absorbed as a child, listening to the stories of his parents and grandparents, aunts and uncles. It would be hard to overemphasize the importance of these stories to Foote's work. The following comment by the playwright is typical of the many instances where this comes up in interviews: "I spent a lot of my life listening. All kinds of stories. Constantly told, retold. So the days when I wasn't on this earth were as real to me as the days that I was."[1]

It is not surprising, then, that these materials get worked and reworked, sometimes showing up in more than one play. In *Courtship,* for example, Elizabeth tells Laura a story about their Aunt Lucy, who fell in love with her first cousin but was forbidden to marry him. "Neither of them ever loved anyone else," she says, "and every day at four o'clock Cousin Irvin would pass Aunt Lucy's house on his way home and rain or shine she would be sitting on the gallery waiting for him to pass by and they would bow to each other" (*Three Plays* 8–9). In *A Trip to Bountiful,* the protagonist Carrie Watts tells this same story about herself.

1. Sheila Benson, "MM Interview," *Modern Maturity,* Nov.–Dec. 1996, p. 53; Flynn and Russell, "Horton Foote," 22.

At times, Foote takes this process one step further, playing out different endings to the same story. In an interview with Terry Barr and Gerald Wood, speaking of his writing methods, Foote remarks, in this regard,

> This might interest you, as work patterns. *Flight* and *Courtship* are about the same story, only done differently. And actually it is my mother's story, and Mr. Vaughn uses that in *Courtship* by saying "If you'd married that man [Syd Joplin], you know, see what would've happened." Now in *Flight* I had her marry the man. But she never married the man.
>
> QUESTION: I see that, I see this doubling in your work. I see *Tender Mercies* as a reworking of *The Traveling Lady* and *Baby, the Rain Must Fall* [the film version of *Traveling Lady*].
>
> FOOTE: Very likely.
>
> QUESTION: It's the same story, with the dark side, as *Tender Mercies*.
>
> FOOTE: Yes, yes.[2]

It is a strategy he adopts in *The Orphans' Home Cycle,* as well. In addition to the multiple voices he blends within individual plays and the incremental repetition of character, theme, and image across the nine-play spectrum, Foote employs the strategy of pairing three sets of dramas, playing off one against the other to add yet another layer of meaning. The first and second plays of the *Cycle, Roots in a Parched Ground* and *Convicts,* treat Horace's childhood, each revolving around the death of a father or a father figure. Plays four and five, *The Widow Claire* and *Courtship,* take up Horace's story as a young man on the brink of marriage. Both of these plays are shaped by a young woman's choice of a lifemate, a crucial decision for any woman of that era; as Horace courts both of them, we see the path not taken (Claire) and the one he eventually adopts (Elizabeth). The *Cycle*'s closing plays, numbers eight and nine, show Horace as a mature man, now husband, father, and proprietor of his own business. Both plays again explore a similar topic: the critical illness and near-death of Corella, Horace's mother, and the unexpected, actual death of Henry Vaughn, his father-in-law. *Cousins* situates this serious matter in a

---

2. Gerald C. Wood and Terry Barr, " 'A Certain Kind of Writer': An Interview with Horton Foote," *Literature/Film Quarterly* 14, no. 4 (1986): 235.

semi-comic context, as we have seen in Chapter 2; *The Death of Papa* is much more somber in its overtones. Yet both present moments when Horace and Elizabeth must confront the death or possible death of a parent and the implications this has for their future.

This structural doubling performs several different though related functions. The first and third pairings take a similar topic and examine it from multiple perspectives, while the second actually plays out two different endings to the same scenario, Horace's choice of a wife. All of them invite the audience to reflect on the questions posed by the *Cycle* at large: How free are we to shape our life journeys? What factors influence our choices and change our lives at critical junctures, and how much control do we have over them? How do individual, familial, and cultural components contribute to the fate we choose, if indeed, we "choose" at all?

In regard to this last matter, the interaction of individual agency with received familial and cultural codes and conditioned responses, it is important to note once again that while *The Orphans' Home Cycle* tells the story of an individual, Horace Robedaux, it simultaneously chronicles a culture at large, contributing to the "ongoing saga" Foote referred to in his conversation with Benson. An examination of this element, then, the *Cycle* as cultural history, will be an important part of our consideration in this chapter as we reflect on the multiple perspectives present in these paired plays.

The first set of plays, as we have said, introduces us to Horace as a boy. As *Roots* opens, Corella, separated from her husband, has come home from Houston, where she lives with Lily Dale, working as a seamstress; she has left Horace in her parents' care. By the end of the play, Horace's father will have died, his mother will have remarried and moved permanently to Houston with Lily Dale and Pete, and his paternal grandmother and extended family will have moved away, leaving him alone, if not orphaned. As detailed in the previous chapter, this play tracks the abandonment of Horace not just by his father, mother, and grandmother, but also by the father-substitutes who vowed to watch over him. Its emotional climax, quiet as it is, occurs with Horace's matter-of-fact statement to his friend Lloyd, "I'm on my own" (*Four Plays* 84), this at the tender age of twelve. He plans to accompany his Uncle Albert to the Gautier plantation on the Gulf

Coast to clerk in the store there for fifty cents a week; his days as a self-sufficient "adult" have begun.

In addition to marking this turning point in Horace's life, *Roots* establishes several themes that will recur throughout the *Cycle*, most notably the search for a family and the commitment to buying a tombstone for his father's grave. We also observe from the outset character traits that will serve Horace well, traits that are not evident in either Corella or Lily Dale, so far as we can tell. He is, we note, a very sensitive boy, responding deeply to the events he observes taking place around him, though he doesn't show his emotions. When Albert tells Corella that "Big Horace is very low," for instance, Corella merely says "Oh?" and goes on sewing; moments later, Horace quietly gets up and leaves. This will be his pattern throughout this play and as he grows older. He tends to avoid emotional scenes or direct confrontations, preferring to keep his own counsel. Thus when he begins to cry in the final scene with George Tyler, it reveals the depth of the pain he is feeling at this point.

We also see signs of his ability to read situations accurately and respond accordingly, taking whatever steps are called for. When he learns that Corella is coming to Harrison with his new stepfather, thinking that they are planning to "educate [him] in law and Lily Dale in music" (*Four Plays* 70), he starts going to school every day and catches up with his studies, even though he had fallen far behind. He also gives up chewing tobacco when he learns that Pete doesn't use tobacco. He tells his friend Larry he gave it up "because my stepfather doesn't [chew]. He doesn't chew, he doesn't drink, he doesn't smoke. As a matter of fact, he doesn't have any bad habits at all." When Larry asks him what he calls his stepdaddy, Horace responds, "I don't know. I'll call him what he wants me to call him" (*Four Plays* 74–75). He is eager for a new father and will gladly do whatever it takes to please him. Sadly, as we know, Pete rejects Horace and crushes any hopes that he cherished of becoming a part of their family unit. Typically, when that becomes clear to him, he simply leaves, going down to the river, where he smokes a pipe and tells his friend that it's "too noisy" at his house, referring to his new stepfather simply as "Mr. Davenport."

The theme of abandonment, established by the death of his father and the failure of various father-substitutes—Pete Davenport,

George Tyler, and John Howard—to step into the breach, is continued in the sequel play, *Convicts,* set on the Gautier plantation in
1904, two years later. As the play opens, we are introduced to a scene
of desolation. For reasons that are never explained, Billy Vaughn has
decided to come to the plantation and bring Horace back to Harrison
for Christmas. It is Christmas Eve day when he enters the Spartan
plantation store with his drunken wife, Asa, looking for Horace. The
opening dialogue emphasizes the cold, lonely, and isolated atmosphere. Billy, calling the plantation a "Godforsaken place," says,
"What are his people thinking about, letting him stay out here surrounded by convicts? There's only two white families between here
and Harrison" (*Four Plays* 94). We learn from Martha, the black servant, that a convict who has murdered a fellow prisoner has been
caught and chained to a tree while Mr. Soll goes to Harrison to fetch
the sheriff; the other convicts are locked up in their quarters to prevent further violence. When Billy asks where Horace stays, Martha
replies that he didn't like it up at the "big house," so he sleeps on the
floor of the store. Albert, Horace's uncle and in theory if not in practice his protector and guide, has left him to go gambling.

In this short scene, we are quickly made aware of the desperation
of Horace's circumstances. He is essentially cut off from civilization,
left to fend for himself in a setting where violence seethes just below
the surface. The plantation is worked by black convicts, who might as
well be slaves. When Billy mistakenly thinks that the fields are empty
because it's Christmas, Martha replies, "You know Mr. Soll don't give
nobody any time off. He'll work them Christmas Day too. Always
has. Only reason he don't have them out in the fields now is so trouble won't spread" (*Four Plays* 94). They are treated callously and cru-
elly, and as becomes increasingly evident as the action unfolds,
violent outbreaks are not uncommon. That Billy Vaughn, himself no
paragon of virtue, is appalled by Horace's situation and even ex-
presses a desire to raise him underlines the theme of abandonment
established in *Roots.* Billy, in fact, uses that very word: "It sickens me
to see a boy abandoned this way," he says (*Four Plays* 95).

Yet Horace's first appearance dispels any suggestion that he feels
sorry for himself. He has been down at the field where they found the
dead convict, he tells Martha, and shortly thereafter he goes to talk
with the murderer, still chained to the tree, sharing his tobacco and

matter-of-factly striking up a conversation. This scene, as well as the earlier one with Martha, reveals that Horace does not see himself as isolated, racially or otherwise. Though as a boy raised in the South he is aware that race is a social category, he doesn't make judgments based on race as Billy and Mr. Soll do. The degree of his affection and respect for Ben and Martha, who function as surrogate parents while he is here, is clear. As in the earlier play, Horace is also sensitive, observant, and finely attuned to his surroundings. He is very concerned about the convict, Leroy (it is significant that Horace is the only one who bothers to ask his name), as well as the man he murdered. It is also a matter of some importance to Horace that the murdered convict's grave be marked, and when Leroy is killed by the sheriff, *his* grave, as well.

Convicts, then, reinforces the character traits we observed in *Roots in a Parched Ground,* portraying Horace as a mixture of vulnerability and strength. It also extends the theme of Horace's need for a place to belong, a need which is revealed in his obsession with families and family relationships as well as his desire to buy a tombstone for his father's grave. When Martha tells him that Billy wants to take him to Harrison for Christmas, for instance, he replies without hesitation, "I don't want to go until I get my money. There's no tombstone on my daddy's grave and I want to make a down payment on one. It worries me to death there is still no tombstone on my daddy's grave" (*Four Plays* 96). It's one of the first things he tells Leroy about himself, as well: "I came out to help out my uncle, but I ended up doing all the work because he spent all his time up at Mr. Soll's house gambling. I hope to earn enough money out here to put a tombstone on my daddy's grave" (*Four Plays* 99–100). This mission defines his life and determines his choices.

Horace's relationship with Mr. Soll, in fact, revolves around this commitment. Confronting Soll with the fact that he hasn't been paid requires courage on Horace's part, given the old man's eccentric ways, violent outbursts, and present drunken state, but he does so immediately upon Soll's return with the sheriff: "You told me yesterday you'd pay me my wages today, Sir. I been working here six months, Sir, and I'd sure appreciate being paid. You see, I may be going into Harrison, and I want to pay down on a tombstone for my daddy's grave" (*Four Plays* 109–10). Soll promises to pay him and tells him to "come up to the house" later. This becomes the spine of the action: Soll's vow to pay Horace (he variously promises him a hundred dollars, "maybe even a thousand," and "the biggest god-damned tombstone in Texas") and his continual failure to honor his promises. The old planter seems to draw comfort from Horace's presence and insists that he stay with him through the course of the day and throughout the night, which ends up being his last.

Soll's gradual disintegration and eventual death is played off against the innocence of Horace, drawn into this drama against his will. It is one which would terrify any young boy. Soll, hallucinating as a result of hours of drinking and, we assume, a lifetime of accumulated guilt, sees things that are not there, including convicts he is convinced are trying to kill him, and shoots randomly at invisible targets. Throughout the ordeal, however, Horace stays at Soll's side, honoring his promise not to leave him. The contrast between the steadfastness of the young boy and the faithlessness of the old man informs the entire play, establishing its central irony.

These two strands of the action, Horace's determination to secure a tombstone for his father and his vigil at Mr. Soll's deathbed, link *Convicts* with *Roots in a Parched Ground*. The vigil, in particular, provides an ironic counterpoint to the death of Paul Horace in the earlier play. If Horace's father is a flawed, ultimately weak man, he is at least kind, gentle, and concerned about his son. If he has a failing, it is that he cannot stand up to his mother—hardly a criminal offense. His death is experienced as a tragedy, at least to Horace and his own mother and siblings, and the deathbed vigil is portrayed with gravity.

The death of Mr. Soll, on the other hand, can be regarded as almost a parody of its *Roots* counterpart, and Soll himself, unlike the distinguished if disappointing Paul Horace, representative of the very attitudes that led to the South's demise. He is, to begin with, a flagrant racist. More than any other character in the play, he thinks in racial terms. He says to Horace, "You're white, aren't you?" When Horace replies that he is, Soll continues, "We're the only two white people between here and Harrison except for the overseer and the two guards" (*Four Plays* 145). When Soll learns that his black trustee, Jackson, a paroled convict, had killed a man years earlier, his first response is, "Wasn't a white man, I hope?" Jackson replies, "No Sir," to which Soll adds, "Was it a colored man?" (*Four Plays* 141). The life itself is of no meaning; in Soll's scheme of things whether the man was white or black is definitive.

Similar examples abound. Thus we are not surprised when Soll is incredibly casual about killing the black convicts. A few examples will suffice here. Jackson informs Soll that a convict has died after being forced to work when ill:

JACKSON: Sherman Edwards is dead.

SOLL: Who the hell is Sherman Edwards?

JACKSON: Brother of that convict that had his throat cut.

SOLL: Somebody kill him?

JACKSON: No Sir. He just died. He told you he was too sick to work, but you didn't believe him.

SOLL: Who's burying him?

JACKSON: I am. I bury them all.

(*Four Plays* 157)

Soll takes no cognizance of the fact that he is responsible for Edwards's death, forcing him to work when he is sick. He shows no remorse and is equally casual about the death of Edwards's brother; his only concern is their burial. Jackson's "I bury them all" speaks volumes.

Soll's description of killing four convicts who were attempting to escape is if anything even more chillingly nonchalant. "I shot one as he was trying to run," he tells Horace. "I seen him start and I hollered to him to stop and he wouldn't, but kept on running and I shot him. Killed him with the first shot. I shot two brothers that ran away together and I found hiding in a shack down near the river. . . . The more you kill the more they are," he says (*Four Plays* 131), like he's describing some sort of perverted carnival game. The fourth escapee hid in the closet of Soll's bedroom, his cane-cutting knife in hand, apparently waiting to ambush him. Hearing noises in the closet, Soll shot him through the door: "And Will or Philip or whoever the hell his name was [the overseer] opened the goddamn closet door and the goddamn convict bastard fell out of the closet riddled with bullets. I think every shot I fired in there hit the bastard, and he was still holding the goddamn knife he used for cutting brush and cane in his hand" (*Four Plays* 130). This murder, at least, seems to penetrate

Soll's conscience at some level. During the action of the play, as he stays awake all night with Horace at his side, he is paranoid about a convict in the closet waiting to kill him and sporadically shoots at the closet door, even when Ben searches it and assures him it's empty.

Soll's total disregard of the humanity of the black convicts carries over to his attitude concerning the black women he's appropriated sexually over the years. Throughout this day, as he rambles over the grounds with Horace, he asks about women long dead, whose names he can't keep straight. He asks Ben where Nancy is, and Ben informs him that she's been dead over fifteen years; likewise Julia and Sarah. The past and the present merge in confusing fashion in Soll's mind; "Who the hell is out here?" he asks. The blacks on his plantation, men and women alike, are there solely for his pleasure and profit. Sexist as well as racist, his comment to Horace is telling: "A lot of good-looking women out here, you know. We'll find one you like. I had my first woman by the time I was eleven. What the hell was her name? Carrie or Bernice" (*Four Plays* 127). As we observe him at the end of his life, disoriented by years of drinking, debauchery, and a deadened conscience, he represents the moral bankruptcy that results when one race is given total power over another.[3] Soll also represents the antithesis of positive Southern values, particularly those of family, religion, and civilized living. We have already mentioned Soll's antipathy toward his brother Tyre and Tyre's two daughters, whom he calls "whores" (*Four Plays* 136). His last words are instructions that he not be buried with his family. He also doesn't want a preacher or any

---

3. In the Barr-Wood interview quoted above, Foote says of writing about African Americans: "It's a terrible thing about the Blacks and me. And I feel badly about it because actually I owe them a great debt. They really sustained me in many ways as I was growing up. . . . but I've gotten so conscious of the fact I almost sense in myself and don't write about them because I really think maybe only a Black person can really write about them. And I'm afraid I'll write about them in a naive point of view and not a real point of view. So I avoid writing about them, and it's a real loss to me." I would argue that in *Convicts,* the *Cycle* play which deals most directly with black history and has the most black characters, Foote's portrayal is anything but naive. In his portraits of the lives of Ben and Martha, Jackson, and especially the convict Leroy, who can't even do the math to figure out how long it will take him to pay off his $500 fine at $7 per month, we see the desperation and sense of futility of their lives as well as the complex social and political mechanisms that keep them in bondage. Wood and Barr, "A Certain Kind," 236.

hymns sung at his funeral; he "can't bear" them, he says (*Four Plays* 151). His lack of education and any semblance of manners, combined with his primitive living conditions, make a mockery of the time-honored Southern tradition of gracious living and the love of learning.

Finally, the Southern culture's reverence for honor and the sanctity of one's word is satirized in Soll's flagrant breaking of promises. He promises huge sums to Horace. "I'm gonna give you a hundred dollars. Maybe even a thousand" (*Four Plays* 145–46), he says, and later, opening a suitcase purportedly full of money—over ten thousand dollars—he vows to give Horace half. The suitcase, of course, is as empty as his promise, just like his resolution to leave Jackson everything he has (*Four Plays* 142). Soll's failure to pay Horace for his labor and his continued false promises as the play unfolds function as an icon of the debt Horace is owed by his biological father and all the father-substitutes who have reneged on their obligations.

In a brilliant stroke on Foote's part, this moral bankruptcy is linked explicitly with Southern values in a scene in the film version of *Convicts*, when Soll gives Ben and Martha a Confederate bill for a Christmas gift. When Martha protests that the bill is worthless, he responds, "Hang on to it. You never know." To further emphasize Soll's thematic connection with the Old South, the film has Soll, played by Robert Duvall, dressed in an old Confederate army jacket. In the play, Soll's identification with the Confederate cause is indicated in the dialogue, when he asks Horace if his father was a veteran, then says, "I was a veteran. I fought in every goddamned battle they'd let me," after which he vows to buy "the biggest goddamned tombstone in Texas" for Horace's father with angels and two Confederate veterans on it (*Four Plays* 134). Late that night, unable to sleep, he asks Horace to read him an old newspaper he spots. It turns out to be dated 1865 and is about the fact that Texas has not been allowed to re-enter the Union. When Soll asks why, Horace responds, "Because she was in the Confederacy" (*Four Plays* 160). Moments later, Soll dies.[4]

I point to these details because in addition to providing texture,

4. This scene is expanded in the film version of *Convicts*. Horace begins reading the article, which is about the decisive Civil War battle which Texas lost, and as he reads, Soll dies.

they make explicit the Civil War backdrop that informs not just this play, but also its prequel, *Roots in a Parched Ground*. In *Roots,* we are introduced to two prosperous families, the Thorntons and the Robe-dauxs, who have been financially destroyed by the war, their history indicated only in the retelling of family stories. In *Convicts,* both in the plantation setting and the character of Soll Gautier, we see drama-tized before our eyes the conditions that led to the decline of the Southern aristocracy, both the issues and the attitudes that led to the war and ultimately spelled the doom of a way of life. Although *Convicts* is set in 1904, some forty years after the Civil War, in terms of the quality of life for the blacks, essentially nothing has changed. The convicts might as well be slaves, for all the freedom they have. Their very lives are subject to the whim of Soll, the plantation owner, and the sheriff, who as a representative of the law, should be their protec-tor. It is telling that when Leroy, the convict-murderer, tries to es-cape, the sheriff shoots him, and afterwards is nonchalant about it. There is no mention of an inquest or other legal proceeding; Soll sim-ply offhandedly tells Ben to bury him. In the case of Ben and Martha, though they are not legally bound to stay on the plantation, they have no other viable options. Ben tells Horace, "I was born out here. Right at the end of slavery time. My mama and daddy are buried out here. Our cabin was right over yonder. Mama and Papa worked on here for wages after slavery time—a lot of the old folks did. When they began to die off, Mr. Soll brought in convicts to work the place" (*Four Plays* 98). Tragically, Ben and Martha will have no place to go upon Soll's death; this is the only life they have known.

In a final irony, it is an appropriate touch that Soll, who lied about everything else, was also lying about the elaborate tombstone he brought from New Orleans for his father's grave. In the final scene, as they prepare to bury Soll, Horace says that he looked for the tomb-stone in the Gautier family plot and couldn't find it, to which Ben replies, "He was lying. Didn't have nothing on it—just a slab of mar-ble sticking up with his name on it. If the convicts didn't keep it weeded over there, you wouldn't be able to find it for the brush in a week" (*Four Plays* 162). Not only does Soll's lack of integrity carry over to the matter of his father's tombstone (providing a telling con-trast with Horace's commitment to honor his father, which we know he will fulfill), but the convicts must keep the plot weeded to prevent it from disappearing. Throughout the play the ineptitude of the ruling white culture, including Soll, Billy, and Asa, is redeemed by the constancy and competence of the blacks, without whom the plantation would cease to function. This final scene once again drives that truth home.[5]

Thus as cultural history, *Convicts* provides the broader context that is only implied in *Roots* in briefly sketched anecdotes. In terms of plot, the two deaths around which the action resolves, that of Horace's real father and that of Soll, a father figure manqué, both connect the plays in our minds and provide an instructive contrast. In *Roots,* Paul Horace's last days take place in the proverbial bosom of his family, attended by his mother, siblings, and loved ones; it is regarded with the greatest solemnity. Young Horace's access to his father in these last crucial days is controlled by his Grandmother Robedaux, as we observed in Chapter 3, though he is deeply invested in the event; he is not allowed to go to the funeral, being thought too young.

The death of Soll Gautier couldn't provide more of a contrast. Having cut himself off from his family, Soll's last hours are spent in the company of Ben and Jackson, his employees, and Horace, whose name he has a hard time remembering. Horace attends Soll against his will, afraid both of the old man's violent unpredictability and of death itself. He was, we recall, a near-witness to the death of Leroy just hours earlier. In his conversation with Leroy, Horace asks him if he is afraid to die and, with his usual honesty, says that he himself is. A short while later, Leroy is dead, joining the convict he murdered;

5. This point is effectively underlined in the film version in a scene which doesn't appear in the play. We see an exterior shot of Tyre's plantation house, complete with the requisite front gallery, white columns, and imposing oaks; a drunken Billy and Asa are inside being served Christmas dinner by a black maid. Both Billy and Asa, dressed in formal attire—tuxedo for Billy and elegant gown for Asa—are seated at a beautifully appointed table. Before the meal's conclusion, however, Billy passes out, his head falling into his plate, while Asa looks on contemptuously; throughout the scene, the maid stands by quietly, waiting to be of service. Later, Billy must be helped up to bed by a black servant. It is a telling scene, damning in its implications.

Along similar lines, it is ironically appropriate that at one point Soll is convinced that he buried his money in one of the convict's graves (though he can't remember which one). His treasure, which depends on convict labor, rightfully belongs more to them than to him.

soon thereafter, a third convict, Sherman Edwards, dies as well. Surrounded thus by death, we understand his trepidation when Jackson says to Horace at the beginning of act 2, as he enters Soll's bedroom that night, "He's about driving me crazy asking for you to come up here. He says he wants a white person with him when he dies" (*Four Plays* 138). Horace's duty is to be the requisite "white person," ushering Soll into the next world. Thus this death-watch contrasts with that of Paul Horace in its sadly impersonal context, Horace's feelings about the dying person, and the key role he is forced to play in the event itself.

Perhaps even more telling, however, is the contrast in tone in the depiction of the two events. While Horace's father's death is portrayed as a tragedy, for himself as well as for his children, the rendering of Soll Gautier's death is almost comic in nature. It isn't even clear that Mr. Soll will really die. As he orders Jackson to have the convicts build his coffin, predicting his imminent death, we expect this to be one more broken promise. Although he is seventy-eight years old and has shown signs of disorientation throughout the preceding day, there is no clear indication that he is on the point of death. Thus when he says, "One minute I think I'm gonna live and the next minute I think I'm gonna die. Right now I think I'm gonna die," we find it hard to credit (*Four Plays* 158).

The play, in fact, presents us with a mock death and resurrection. Soll climbs into his coffin and appears to be asleep, but then Jackson and Ben declare that he is dead. Some conversation ensues about the details of his funeral when they hear a knock from the coffin (significantly, at first Jackson thinks the noise is caused by a rat). Ben says, going over to the coffin, "My God! He's risen from the dead!" reaching into the coffin to help Soll out. The religious language Foote employs is heavily ironic. This, to be sure, is no savior come back from the dead. In fact, Soll's first words are, "Hand me my gun" (*Four Plays* 156). Shortly afterwards he says that he's decided he "ain't never gonna die," and orders them to remove his coffin. His actual death occurs minutes later, as Horace, now alone with Soll, reads to him from the 1865 newspaper mentioned earlier. Soll's grip on Horace's hand is so tight, Ben has to pry it loose.

That detail, the tight grip, is, I think, an important one. This death, like his father's and that of the convicts, has taken hold of Horace. Part of Horace's coming of age as depicted in these two plays is his coming to terms with death. "Is that all there is to dying?" he asks Ben. "Your breath just stops?" When Ben allows that to be the case, for peaceful deaths, at any rate, Horace makes the connection with his father's death: "That's all that happened to my daddy, my grandmother said. One minute he was breathing and the next minute he stopped. That's not so bad" (*Four Plays* 160). He speculates on whether Soll and his father "minded dying," a question he raised earlier in regards to Leroy. Ben thinks Soll "minded it the worst way," and Horace, agreeing, adds, "And I think my daddy did. That's what worries me" (*Four Plays* 161). It is not so much the physical pain associated with death as it is the pain that comes from the termination of a life that is either flawed or unfinished. Death removes the possibility of change, whether that means making amends or taking a new direction.

Though Paul Horace's death is treated seriously and has enormous implications for Horace and Soll's is framed satirically, even grotesquely as a kind of black humor, and is of little moment in terms of Horace's external circumstances, both represent a loss of innocence for the youth. Given his sensitive and reflective nature, it is safe to assume that the impact of both experiences will contribute significantly to the way he sees the world from this point forward. One last comment in this regard. We have said that though each of us is shaped to a large extent by our familial and cultural contexts, individual experiences and temperaments are also a critical part of the mix. As Horace, who has stayed the night with Soll in spite of his own fears, honors his promise to stay with the body until it is buried and then participates in the makeshift funeral service, we observe with wonder his strength and integrity. When Ben points out that Soll didn't keep any of his promises to Horace, the boy simply responds, "I'd feel better if I kept mine" (*Four Plays* 161). Where that steadfastness comes from, given that he had no father or father-substitutes to model such behavior, remains in the last analysis a mystery. Somewhere in the blend of family and culture and individual response, Horace has chosen the path of integrity. It is a decision that will serve him well.

The Widow Claire and *Courtship,* the fourth and fifth plays of the *Cycle,* take up Horace's story as a young man. *Claire* is set in 1912 when Horace is twenty-two; *Courtship* takes place three years later. Both deal with the critical decision of choosing a wife, a decision which will change forever the course his life will take. While *Courtship* dramatizes Horace's courting of Elizabeth, which will eventually lead to their marriage, *The Widow Claire* presents us with the path not taken. It may seem a strange subject for a play. It is, in fact, the only one of the nine that focuses not on something that happens to Horace but on something that *doesn't*. This fact is particularly interesting in light of the fact that it was the last of the nine to be written. As Foote explained to me, when he shared the other eight plays with a colleague, the producer of PBS's *American Short Story* series, he suggested that Foote write one more play to provide additional background on Horace as a young man; the resulting play was *The Widow Claire.*[6]

These two plays, like *Roots* and *Convicts,* occurring side-by-side, profit from being considered in tandem and, for a variety of reasons, invite such an approach. Their structures, in the first instance, are strikingly similar. Although they tell us a great deal about Horace at this stage in his life, both plays, in fact, are focused on the women being courted: Claire and Elizabeth. The external action of each play is minimal. Horace calls on Claire, competing for her affections with Val, who appears on stage, and Ned, who doesn't, just as in *Courtship* he calls upon Elizabeth, whose parents disapprove of the match. If the plot-lines seem somewhat flat, it's because the essential action is interior. Before each play ends, Claire and Elizabeth have chosen their life-mates. Claire will marry the safe if unexciting Ned, and Elizabeth will marry Horace, if he asks her. In understanding the significance of these choices in the lives of Claire and Elizabeth, as well as the lives of the men they will marry, we come to know as much about the culture in general as we do about Horace as an individual. Once again the chronicle of an individual life is inextricably interwoven with that of the culture at large.

The title of *The Widow Claire,* like all the *Cycle* titles, is carefully chosen. It alerts us to the fact that in some ways this play is more about Claire than Horace. It also insists on the fact that for a woman of this era, marital status is the defining element of one's identity:

6. Laurin Porter, "An Interview with Horton Foote," 181–82.

Claire is a *widow*. Because she is young—only twenty-eight years old, with two children, ages nine and ten—she is something of an oddity in Harrison society. Married at sixteen, she was a mother at seventeen. This in itself was not unusual for the time; indeed, we learn that her own mother married at fifteen and her older sister Sissy, at fourteen. But as the only widow in town under fifty, Claire does not fit neatly into Harrison's social categories. She is still young enough to want to go dancing and pretty enough to be asked, but such behavior is frowned upon by the town matrons.

Claire's situation points to the vulnerable social and economic position of women of this period. Claire had done nothing out of the ordinary in marrying when she did; in fact, she was following the cultural prescription for young women of that time. She also loved her husband. According to Horace, he was a good man, handsome and well-liked, and he seems to have been a devoted husband and father. He provided well for Claire, leaving her the house she lives in and two rental houses; in the days before Social Security, life insurance, and retirement pensions, this was all that could be expected. His sudden death from typhoid fever, however, leaves Claire with no means of support beyond the rental houses, with two young children to care for, in addition to the fact that she is without companionship for the rest of her life unless she marries again. That, of course, is the double bind Claire finds herself in. She is too young to want to remain single, but as a mother with two children, she is no longer prime "marriage material."

This point is made clear by the opening dialogue. Horace is in his furnished room getting ready for a date while four of his friends are playing poker. When it comes out that Horace has a date with "the Widow Claire," Felix says, "I had a date with her a month ago, but her kids wouldn't leave us alone." Ed adds, "I'd keep away from her. Who wants those kids around your neck? Whoever gets her is gonna get it" (*Four Plays* 257). The discussion turns to whether or not she is pretty, and Felix comments, "I think she's losing her looks. She used to be a beauty." Spence adds, "They tell me widows can be dangerous. You be careful over there, Horace" (*Four Plays* 257–58).

It is a very economical scene. In addition to the expository information it relays, Horace's impending date (as well as his refusal to join the poker game) and the fact that others have dated Claire, also, it reveals in a nutshell the dilemma of the young widow. As a married woman, she is obviously sexually experienced and therefore considered both "fair game" and "dangerous." The children are seen as an obstacle, presumably interfering with the possibility of sexual activity of some kind, and viewed as a long-term burden, should marriage become an option.

The plot itself, as mentioned earlier, is less than dramatic by conventional standards. Horace calls on Claire the night before he is scheduled to leave for a six weeks' business course in Houston. He has had dates with her on two previous occasions and seems quite fond of her, a feeling which Claire reciprocates. In the course of the evening we meet Claire's two children, Buddy and Molly, from whom we learn that she is also being courted by Ned, a traveling salesman who is approaching forty and who, though steady and reliable, may (or may not) dye his hair to look younger, and Val, who drinks, can't hold a job, and has in the past hit Claire. While Horace is at Claire's, Val arrives with a friend, then leaves; after Horace leaves he returns, and Buddy, alleging violence, runs to Horace's boardinghouse and begs him to come back, which he does.

Throughout all these comings and goings, Claire is trying to decide what to do with her life. It's clear that she likes Horace, though he is six years younger than she, and she asks him if he's ever found a girl he'd like to marry. In the early morning hours, Claire finally says, "It's come to me just as clear what to do. I'm not going to marry anybody," vowing to move to Houston with her children, buy a duplex, live downstairs and rent the upstairs. "I'm so relieved," she says, "now it's come to me what to do. The kids almost had a fit when I told them I wasn't going to marry Ned. But I said, 'Shoot, I'm not getting married just to please you.' I have a right to lead my own life, don't you think?" (*Four Plays* 321). But in the end, she opts for security, deciding to marry Ned after all. It's interesting that she sends for Horace to tell him herself before he leaves town. She clearly cares deeply for him and, if circumstances were different, they might have married, a possibility both are aware of. They part reluctantly, as Horace leaves to catch the train to Houston. The stage directions, which end the play, state that Claire "waves a last farewell as the lights fade, and we never know if he sees her or not" (*Four Plays* 330).

As in *Courtship*, the central action is interior, and revolves around the woman being courted more than around Horace. At the same time, we learn a good deal about Horace as he interacts with first Claire, then Elizabeth. In the first play, we see him to good advantage in the context of his male counterparts, both his poker-playing friends and later, Val and Val's sidekick Roger. While Horace is no saint—he drinks, has gambled his share, and is provoked into a "savage" fight with Val—he has a sense of direction that is beginning to give shape to his life. He can't loan Ed any money or get into the poker game because he needs all his money for business school; relative to the card game he says, "No, thank you. I tried that before" (*Four Plays* 256). Capable of learning from his experience, he overcomes any temptation he might have to double his money, as Archie suggests. Later in the play in a scene between Felix and Archie, as they talk about their hopes for the future, Felix says, "Maybe we should go to business school in Houston like Horace" (*Four Plays* 301). Archie just wants to have a good time, he says, while Spence wants to become a professional gambler. In a milieu which seems to hold forth limited opportunities to young men, Horace, at least, has ambition and a sense of direction. He tells Claire he doesn't want to marry until he has a job and some money set aside, and explaining that he doesn't like to gamble, having observed his Uncle Albert, he adds, "I'm a pretty serious person, I guess, Claire" (*Four Plays* 296). He is, indeed, "serious," what we might call steadfast, a man of integrity. All of this information, in addition to filling in some gaps in Horace's characterization, prepares us to see him as a good choice for Elizabeth in the following play, in spite of Mr. Vaughn's insistence that he is wild.

While it does provide information about Horace as well as Claire, this play also paints a richly textured portrait of a small Southern town in the early twentieth century, enabling us to understand, among other things, the vulnerable position of its women. Like their counterparts throughout the country at this time, women in Harrison had very circumscribed career opportunities; indeed, "career" is not a word that would even occur to them. Unable to support themselves, they are dependent upon their fathers and husbands not just for emotional and social definition, but for their very lives. The *Cycle* provides us with several examples of women's limited choices in this regard. When Corella is forced to support herself upon her separation from

Paul Horace, for instance, she first tries to run a boardinghouse with her sister, and when that fails, she moves to Houston and works as a seamstress in a department store. Both are acceptable "feminine" pursuits. The boardinghouse is an extension of a woman's role as homemaker and hostess more than a business venture; it fails, in fact, because Corella is unable to collect the rent from the boarders. Sewing, of course, is an acceptable female occupation—one of the arts of the accomplished Southern woman. Unfortunately, it is hardly a sufficient source of income. Ultimately, Corella turns to marriage as a more practical long-term means of providing for herself and Lily Dale. Remarriage, then, is one option for the widow, often prompted more by financial exigency than love.

Another choice is the role of the respectable widow, depending upon the largess of extended family and what little resources one's husband may have left and devoting the remainder of one's life to one's children—the option Claire at first tells Horace she has chosen. Although this would leave her lonely and personally unfulfilled, it at least would guarantee her a place in society. We note, in this regard, that Claire's reputation is already beginning to suffer. Val has been seen leaving her house in the early morning hours, and the neighbors, she tells us, watch her every move. Horace's Aunt Inez, once Claire's best friend, has abruptly ended their relationship. "Sissy says it's because I'm receiving company again," Claire tells Horace. "She says she [Inez] doesn't approve of that. 'Sissy, what does she want me to do?' I said" (*Four Plays* 282). She is torn between her understandable youthful desire for male companionship and the need to be a respected member of society.

Ultimately, as we know, she opts to remarry, choosing Ned because he will be a good provider. This is evidently seen as a better option than being a spinster, the lowest rung on the female social scale. Claire's three younger sisters, reported to be "plain," have gone to stay with an aunt in Galveston, we're told, because none of the men of Harrison will date them. It is their last-ditch effort to find someone to marry them and thus avoid being "old maids," a fate which terrifies Elizabeth's sister Laura in *Courtship*. "I'm not going to be an old maid," she vows, to which her Aunt Sarah quietly responds, "I'm an old maid, honey. There are worse things in this world" (*Three Plays* 16). But for Laura and her peers, nothing could be worse. In this culture, for a woman marriage represents the crowning glory of her maidenhood. It is her access to adult society, defining her role and conferring both purpose and respectability. It is also, not insignificantly, her sole means of financial support.

In his portrayal of women characters and the ways in which they are defined by gender roles and expectations, Foote demonstrates considerable understanding and sensitivity. His women encompass the full range of ages and types: from the youthful Laura and Elizabeth in *Courtship,* on the brink of marriage; to happily married women like the older Elizabeth and Mrs. Vaughn and the unhappily wed—Corella and Cousin Monty's wife Lola; to lonely spinsters like Miss Ruth Amos and widows like Claire. The degree to which they lead happy and satisfying lives depends largely, if not exclusively, on their marital status and, if married, the quality of the match, a cultural reality of this period which Foote clearly appreciates. This understanding, along with his ability to create strong, independent women who thrive in spite of these cultural limitations, is no doubt related to the close relationships he had with his own mother, grandmother, and wife, a fact which Foote himself acknowledges. In the Barr-Wood interview, for instance, when asked to comment on his "wonderful female characters," Foote replies, "Well, I had a very close relationship with my mother—and my grandmother. I think that's where it all started because they were very influential in my life. . . . Alan Pakula, who knows my work, I guess, as well as anybody . . . thinks all my women are based on my wife. And I would suspect he's not too far wrong. I'm not conscious of that, either, you know. And it's interesting that since Kim Stanley is older now, my daughter [actress Hallie Foote]—she plays my women better than anyone that I know. And she has a lot of her mother in her, I suppose."[7]

7. Wood and Barr, "A Certain Kind," 232. In *Horton Foote and the Theater of Intimacy,* Wood writes of Foote's strong women characters that their power comes from "their closeness to the primary patterns of life. Whatever the style of their lives, they are inspired by their attachments—to others (like Rosa Lee [in *Tender Mercies*]), to the rituals of daily living (like Mrs. Thornton in *The Oil Well*), and to the cycles of nature (like Carrie Watts in *The Trip to Bountiful*)." He argues that Foote's presentation of women is influenced by his religious background as a Christian Scientist and the writings of Mary Baker Eddy, the founder, who conceives of God as more "feminine" than "masculine." Wood, *Theater of Intimacy,* 24–25, 27–29.

Both *The Widow Claire* and *Courtship,* then, while they add a chapter to Horace's life story, foreground their female protagonists and add another level to our understanding of the culture. One final observation. When we consider *The Widow Claire* from Horace's perspective, we observe that just as Horace is set off to advantage in contrast with his peers, Elizabeth fares well when compared to Claire. The differences are subtle, but significant. Claire drinks, smokes cigarettes, and swears, and she seems to be sexually permissive for that time, especially in regard to Val. Though by today's standards her behavior may seem tame, the standards of her own era would find otherwise. Horace's circumspect courtship of Elizabeth and the deep respect which he accords her, when viewed in the context of *The Widow Claire,* are more clearly etched.

The linking of these two works thus provides a kind of intertextuality, creating a conversation between the plays. While each play is self-contained, not needing the other to be clear, both are enriched when one considers them together. The same is true of the final two plays of the *Cycle*—*Cousins* and *The Death of Papa*—both of which deal with the death (or potential death) of a parent. Structurally, these two plays interact with one another in a concentrated, more focused manner than with the other plays in the *Cycle.* Because we have examined these plays in some detail in Chapter 2, I will only comment on them briefly here in order to point out their structural parallels and the ways in which they are linked.

Cousins, the eighth play, takes place in 1925, seven years after *1918;* the action of *The Death of Papa* occurs three years later, in 1928. Both take up Horace's story as he and Elizabeth are solidly in the middle years of their marriage, the "sandwich" generation as we would call it today, concerned about their aging parents and their own young children. *Cousins* focuses on the Thorntons, while *Papa* is centered around the Robedaux clan. The former deals with the near-death of Corella, Horace's mother, and is set within a semi-comic context, while the latter begins with the actual death of Henry Vaughn, Elizabeth's father, treated as a tragedy for both the family and the town—two different treatments of the same life experience.

As with both of the other sets of paired plays, upon close inspection *Cousins* and *Papa* reveal striking parallels in the way in which their action is structured. On one level, at least, *Cousins'* action seems to be shaped by the serious illness of Corella Thornton. Horace and Elizabeth, alerted to her condition and imminent surgery, immediately set out for Houston to be at her side for what may be her last moments of life. Neither Corella's near-encounter with death nor Horace's confrontation with her, if one could even call it that, proves to be the climax of the play, however. Corella comes through the surgery successfully about two-thirds of the way through the play, and the action switches back to Horace's store in Harrison two months later. The real emotional climax of the play is Minnie's "a family is a remarkable thing" speech, in which she lets go of the anger toward Corella which she has nursed all these years and admits that she actually envied the Thorntons. This strand of the action, Minnie's need to have her version of reality validated by "placing a few facts" before Horace, along with Cousin Lewis's pathetic retelling of his murder of his cousin Jamie, is as compelling as Corella's experience; as we have seen so often in Foote's dramas, the subtext becomes the text.

The same is true in *The Death of Papa*. While the title suggests that this play will tell the story of Mr. Vaughn's death, that event has taken place before the curtain rises. The play is actually structured by various characters' reactions to the death and the implications it has for the family as a whole. Brother's futile attempt to assume his father's position as family patriarch and business manager; young Horace's efforts to understand the nature of racism, poverty, and death in his encounters with Gertrude and his trips to the cemetery with his grandmother; and Horace, Sr.'s struggle to provide for his family financially and emotionally constitute the action and shape the issues of the play. Henry Vaughn's death merely sets these events in motion. Thus the death or impending death of a parent, while a critical element in both plays, is not in itself the central action.

Both plays also bring to closure strands of the narrative that were introduced in the opening play. Minnie's bitterness toward Corella, seen in *Roots in a Parched Ground,* doesn't resurface until *Cousins,* where it is resolved. We know from *Lily Dale* that Horace has ambitions to go to business school, and in *The Widow Claire* he is about to leave for Houston, where he will stay with his cousin, but Minnie as a character doesn't reappear until this penultimate play. It is typical of Foote to assign such important lines to a minor character. Her speech about family not only resolves at last the division in the

Thornton-Robedaux clan regarding the unhappy end of Corella and Paul Horace's marriage, as Minnie realizes the futility of holding on to old anger; it also comments on the nature of families in general and sets the scene for what will take place in the final play. "A family is a remarkable thing, isn't it?" she says. "You belong. And then you don't. It passes you by. Unless you start a family of your own" (*Two Plays* 92). Because she hasn't started her own family, Minnie discovers that she is alone as the next generation is born and takes her place. In *The Death of Papa,* we will observe this phenomenon in the dissolution of the Vaughn family. Henry Vaughn, seemingly impervious to time and change, is suddenly gone without warning. Within a few short months, Brother has dissipated much of the family fortune and is forced to leave town in disgrace, and Mary, who has decided to travel for a while, is considering selling her house and moving to Dallas or Houston. Elizabeth and Horace are the only members of the family left in Harrison, as one generation gives way to the next; the impending arrival of their baby seals their status as the new standard-bearers.

Another minor character, Lily Dale, also reappears in *Cousins* for the final time. The traits we observed in her as a young woman, especially her selfishness and materialism, have hardened and become, if anything, more pronounced. She defines herself in terms of her wealth—her new home, new piano, and new Packard, and a stubborn insistence upon her musical talent, in spite of all the evidence to the contrary.[8]

Even more importantly, Horace's quest for a family, introduced in *Roots,* is in both *Cousins* and *The Death of Papa* clearly seen to have come to a successful conclusion. *Cousins* treats this theme in a semi-comic fashion, as we saw in Chapter 2, with Horace's relatives seeming to stretch out into infinity. Nearly half the town appears to be a cousin or a cousin once removed, putting to rest any question of Horace's being an orphan. *The Death of Papa* returns to this theme in a much more somber mood, with Mary turning to Horace for advice now that her husband has died, and Brother saying to Horace

8. Several "rags" composed by Foote's paternal aunt, Lilyan Dale Coffee, the real-life counterpart of Lily Dale, can be found in the Horton Foote archives: Box 117, Horton Foote Collection, DeGolyer Library, Southern Methodist University.

that now he (Horace) has a home while he himself doesn't. The orphan and the son have traded places.

In addition to the structural parallels and thematic connections between these last two plays, Foote employs the strategy of playing out two different endings to the same situation that we saw in *The Widow Claire* and *Courtship*. In this case, the scene is a confrontation between Horace and Corella over the issue of her abandonment of him as a young boy. In *Cousins,* Corella is sufficiently upset by Minnie's attack on her in the ladies' room of Foley's to try to explain her position to Horace. She says to Horace in the hospital, "Cousin Minnie said she despised me and that you hated me. She said when you were here at the business school and living in the same house with her that you would never have gotten through business school if it hadn't been for her helping you. She said she was the only one in your whole life that had ever taken any interest in you. (*Pause.*) Do you hate me, Son?" (*Two Plays* 40). Horace, of course, replies that he doesn't hate her and he never said that to Minnie, but she persists: "And did you tell her she was the only member of your family that ever took any interest in you?" The irony of Horace's gentle answer is lost on her, however. "No Ma'am. I couldn't have," he says; "That wouldn't be true," going on to cite his aunts and grandparents as encouraging and helpful. "And I was always interested," Corella adds (*Two Plays* 40). What could have been an opportunity for Horace to unleash his resentment, or at least unburden his soul, passes unremarked, and this scene, potentially a moment of high drama, moves quietly on.

In *The Death of Papa,* Foote revisits this moment, playing out a different ending. At various points throughout the play, Corella, visiting Horace and Elizabeth, has commented that she thinks Horace, Jr., reads too much. Near the play's end, her concern surfaces once again. "I think overeducation is a curse," she says. "I can name you boy after boy that were [*sic*] overeducated like Terrence Robedaux and weren't worth killing" (*Two Plays* 189). Horace's impassioned response in defense of his son, as mentioned in Chapter 2, is also an articulation of his own bitterness at her abandonment of him as a young boy: "And I can name you boy after boy whose family had no interest at all in them or what they learned. Who no one cared if they went to school or if they didn't. What they had to bear, what they had . . . I could tell you heart-breaking stories . . . about those boys"

(*Two Plays* 189). This is as close as Horace comes to telling his mother directly about the pain she has caused him. It is much more emotional than the corresponding scene in *Cousins*, as if for whatever reason—perhaps because he is defending his son—he finally feels free to speak his mind and heart. And although Corella is unable or unwilling to acknowledge what she has done, at least Horace has at last confronted her about it, bringing a sense of closure to an issue raised in the *Cycle*'s opening play.

Finally, *The Death of Papa* serves as an effective coda to the *Cycle* as a whole in that in addition to bringing to a conclusion Horace's individual and familial history, at least insofar as something ongoing can be said to conclude, it also paints the picture of a culture at the end of its tether. The death of Elizabeth's father marks both the end of an era in the Vaughn family and the end of a way of life in the town.[9] Mr. Vaughn's tendency was to conduct business with a promise and a handshake, keeping his word and assuming that others would keep theirs. Mrs. Vaughn indicates this to Elizabeth late in the play, having gone through her husband's books: "He had so little in writing. Half the money owed him he has only the notation in his ledger book and he never bothered to get people to sign notes. That's always how he did business. His word and their word" (*Two Plays* 179). In the same spirit, he often made decisions based more on compassion and loyalty than profit, which accounts for the universal affection in which he is held in Harrison. Horace's Aunt Inez's comment to Corella shortly after Henry's death is typical: "He did a lot of good to a lot of people. I have my farm today because of him. After T. [her husband] died I just couldn't face the debt he had left on our

---

9. Charles S. Watson comments in this regard, "*The Death of Papa* concludes this saga of the South with the passing of Horace's grandfather, a New South businessman of civic spirit; the commercial south that will begin the next year, in 1927 [*sic*], is heralded by the coming of talking pictures—the announcement of modern times in Harrison, Texas." Although there are several inaccuracies here (the year is 192*8*, and Henry Vaughn is Horace, *Jr.'s* grandfather), his point about the coming of a new era is on target. Davis makes a similar point in his interview with Foote when he says of the *Cycle*, "You really have two themes in those plays: the personal theme, and the bigger theme of the breakdown of a whole social system," an interpretation to which Foote assents. Charles S. Watson, *The History of Southern Drama* (Lexington, Ky.: University Press of Kentucky, 1997), 200; Davis, "Roots Interview," 313.

farm and I went to Mr. Vaughn and I said, 'Mr. Vaughn, I'm going to have to turn this farm back to you.' 'No such thing,' he said. 'You'll pay it out any way you want to, any amount, as long as you want, but you are going to keep it.' And I did. Thank God!" (*Two Plays* 109). The operative paradigm here is the town as extended family, where those who are blessed with more resources help out those with less; where all are treated with dignity and considered of equal worth.

Brother's cold, profit-driven approach to business represents a sharp contrast to his father's benevolence. One of his first decisions, for instance, is to "get rid of Leon," the caretaker of the farm Mary entrusts to his keeping, because he's too old. When his mother protests that "Leon has been on that place as long as your papa has owned it," adding that "it would kill him [Henry] if you took him off there," Brother simply says, "I'm sorry, but if I'm going to run it, I'm going to run it" (*Two Plays* 129). He also decides to put half of the cotton into pecan trees, insisting that pecans are the "coming" money crop.

Brother represents the new generation's no-nonsense approach. That this lack of concern for others is problematic is suggested by the extent to which it fails, both morally and financially. Brother's pecan trees fail, as do his schemes to get rich quick by investing heavily in cattle. In fact, in purchasing cattle he is fleeced by Mr. Will Borden, a man whom Henry Vaughn had saved from financial ruin years earlier.

Mr. Borden's willingness to exploit Brother's lack of experience points to the fact that Brother isn't the only one who is changing. The town as a whole seems to have lost what cohesiveness it once had. Mary's attempts to collect on the debts owed her husband meet with lies and resistance. "Most of them pretend they don't remember," she tells Elizabeth. "They ask where is the note they signed? Or they tell a worse lie. They say, 'We paid him back' and if you ask for the receipt they say, 'Since there was no note I naturally asked for no receipt'" (*Two Plays* 179). Foote does not sentimentalize about the transition the town is undergoing. While the Brothers of the world are certainly shown unblinkingly, the dangers of Mr. Vaughn's approach also become apparent.

This is perhaps most clearly indicated in the anecdote of the pecan tree, an episode Foote bases on actual biographical experience.[10] Mr. Vaughn extracted a promise from the city fathers that they would not cut down a favorite pecan tree on land he donated for a new road, but after his death, they chop it down anyway. The times have changed; one's word is no longer sufficient, nor the memory of past good deeds. Brother complains bitterly that though his father saved the bank from ruin fifteen years earlier with a $50,000 no-interest loan, they now treat him "like anybody else." Ironically, Brother wants to treat others dispassionately but complains when he is treated that way. This, however, is the new order.

Henry Vaughn's death, then, marks the passing of an era. As such, it is a fitting close to the *Cycle,* which, as we have said, chronicles not just an individual but a cultural history. The final two plays, both in their interactions with one another and their tying up of loose ends, work effectively to bring the *Cycle* to a close. They also focus our attention on another critical matter, one we encounter in virtually all Southern literature, the relationship of past to present, which we turn to in Chapter 6.

10. Freedman, introduction to *Two Plays,* xix.

6

THE PRESENCE OF THE PAST

The Orphans' Home Cycle and the Nature of Time

The matters we have discussed thus far regarding *The Orphans' Home Cycle,* the role of family in shaping individual identity versus the influence of culturally embedded codes and mores, the relationship of the individual to society, the extent to which one is or is not free to choose one's destiny, all contribute to and are subsumed in the question of time. To what extent, these plays ask, are our fates already sealed when we draw our first breath? How autonomous is the individual in the present moment when seen in the larger context of past experiences and influences?

We are not surprised that Foote, a Southerner, is sensitive to the complex relationship of past to present. It is a commonplace of literary criticism that Southern writers are obsessed with the past. Until Vietnam, the South was the only area of the country to have lost a war and thus to experience its history as a decline, a fall from grace. The glorification of the antebellum era as a golden age of grace and beauty is a thread which runs through literature by Southerners and about the South well into the twentieth century, culminating, perhaps, with *Gone with the Wind,* the quintessential popularization of the plantation myth. Serious and popular Southern literature alike are informed by a vague sense of loss and longing, of being expelled from Eden. You can't go home again, Thomas Wolfe mourns; the past can't be recaptured. Yet its presence is always felt; it is never truly past.

To understand Foote fully, I would argue, one must come to terms with his take on this issue, both because it is so fundamental to the

Southern Weltanschauung and because it undergirds the central questions about identity and free will with which the *Cycle* deals. What is the precise nature of time, according to these plays? Is the past enemy or friend, the source of truth or falsehood, bondage or blessing? Can one—should one—ever be free of the past?

The extent to which Foote grounds the *Cycle* plays in actual historical events—the Civil War backdrop, the flu epidemic of 1918, World War I—argues persuasively for his sensitivity to the power of history to change individual lives. Indeed, the *Cycle* is itself a history, both of an individual life, that of Horace Robedaux, and of the larger units, rippling outward like concentric circles, of which Horace is a part: his family (consisting of two intersecting circles, the Thorntons and the Robedauxs), the boardinghouse, the town, the country, and ultimately, the world. All the world's an orphans' home, the title tells us, implying that somehow Horace's story is everyone's story; his history is our history.

One way to approach Foote's apprehension of the nature of time and its impact on individual human lives is to contrast his plays with the fiction of William Faulkner, indisputably the greatest writer of the South, and the work of Eugene O'Neill, widely recognized as the greatest American dramatist, thus positioning Foote at the intersection of two traditions, Southern literature and American drama. Though of course other Southerners have struggled with the vexed relationship of past to present (indeed, virtually *all* Southern writers, in one way or another) and O'Neill is hardly the only American dramatist whose plays are informed by this concern, the positions of these two artists provide an instructive contrast to that of Horton Foote which will, I think, allow us to understand more clearly his cultural and philosophical orientation in regard to this issue.

Much has been written about the role of time in Faulkner's fiction. Over the years critics have attempted to articulate the ways in which time functions in a given work as well as Faulkner's philosophy of time in general. One of the earliest examples, a classic essay which is often anthologized, is Jean-Paul Sartre's "Time in Faulkner: *The Sound and the Fury*," first published in 1939 in *La Nouvelle Revue Française*. In this essay Sartre argues that time is the real subject of Faulkner's famous novel. "If the technique adopted by Faulkner seems at first to be a negation of time," he writes, "that is because we confuse time with chronology." Unlike other novels whose actions lead up to a climax, an event which gives shape and meaning to the episodes which precede it, *The Sound and the Fury* does not privilege any one event as more significant than any other. It would be impossible to choose, for instance, among Caddy's marriage, Benjy's castration, Quentin's suicide, or Jason's pursuit of young Quentin. They all exist in a kind of simultaneous suspension, with one episode invoking and sending us back (or forward) to another. Faulkner's concept of the present, according to Sartre, is "not a circumscribed or sharply defined point between past and future. His present is irrational in its essence; it is an event, monstrous and incomprehensible, which comes upon us like a thief—comes upon us and disappears."[1]

In explaining how this works, arguing that only the past in a Faulkner novel seems real, Sartre employs the brilliant analogy of a man sitting in a moving convertible looking back over the terrain he has just traversed. The countryside immediately outside the car is seen in his peripheral vision as shadows and points of light; only when it recedes into the distance can it be clearly apprehended. So with Faulkner's characters who, always looking backwards, seem to move through the present as if impelled by forces they only dimly understand, if at all. Comparing Faulkner to Proust, for whom "salvation lies in time itself," the past for Faulkner, Sartre argues, "is unfortunately never lost; it is always there, almost as an obsession."[2]

Another article on the same novel written thirty-five years later, Arthur Geffen's "Profane Time, Sacred Time, and Confederate Time in *The Sound and the Fury*," argues persuasively that an analysis of these three modalities of time helps explain the decline of the Compson family. Faulkner makes certain critical choices, Geffen argues, like the June 2 date of Quentin's suicide and the April 8 of Easter Sunday, based on a "day-before" pattern. June 2 is the day before the anniversary of Jefferson Davis's birthday, which in many Southern states at the time of the novel's action was celebrated as a holiday; April 8 is

1. Jean-Paul Sartre, "Time in Faulkner: *The Sound and the Fury*," trans. Martine Darmon, in *William Faulkner: Three Decades of Criticism,* ed. Frederick J. Hoffman and Olga W. Vickery (East Lansing: Michigan State University Press, 1960), 226.

2. Ibid., 229.

the day before Lee's surrender to Grant at Appomattox, marking the end of the Civil War. Geffen contrasts this historical backdrop, which he terms "Confederate time," with profane and sacred time, using Mircea Eliade's definitions in *The Sacred and the Profane,* to explain why Quentin, Mr. Compson, and Jason are all defeated by time while Benjy and Dilsey, in transcending profane time, experience the redemption available in sacred time and ultimately endure. He concludes his analysis by arguing that for Southern whites who have rejected Christianity, the substitute civil religion of commemorating the past holds out false hope. The use of the day-before pattern suggests this by pointing to events which hold forth the promise of fulfillment, but fail to deliver. "For the Compsons," Geffen argues, "any possibility of communal or individual transcendence is gone. Faulkner has powerfully underscored this latter point by linking—via the anniversary and the day-before patterns—the dates and critical events of each section of the novel to the Confederate experience of defeat, surrender, and ineradicable remembrance of failure."[3]

It would be hard to overestimate the importance of time in Faulkner's work. Generally, though not always, it is conceived of in historical terms. Characters are impelled by events from their individual pasts as well as—and often, more compellingly by—events from the shared past of all Southerners, the watershed event being, of course, the Civil War. The present moment always takes place in the shadow of the past, which for the white Southerner means the war and all its repercussions. This position is effectively summed up in a well-known passage by Gavin Stevens in *Intruder in the Dust,* which is worth quoting at some length:

> For every Southern boy fourteen years old, not once but whenever he wants it, there is the instant when it's still not yet two oclock on that July afternoon in 1863, the brigades are in position behind the rail fence, the guns are laid and ready in the woods and the furled flags are already loosened to break out and Pickett himself with his long oiled ringlets and his hat in one hand probably and his sword in the other looking up the hill waiting for Longstreet to give the word and it's all

---

3. Arthur Geffen, "Profane Time, Sacred Time, and Confederate Time in *The Sound and the Fury,*" *Studies in American Fiction* 2, no. 2 (1974): 194.

in the balance, it hasn't happened yet, it hasn't even begun yet, it not only hasn't begun yet but there is still time for it not to begin against that position and those circumstances which made more men than Garnett and Kemper and Armistead and Wilcox look grave yet it's going to begin, we all know that, we have come too far with too much at stake and that moment doesn't need a fourteen-year-old boy to think *This time. Maybe this time* with all this much to lose and all this much to gain.[4]

If the war is the defining moment in Southern history, that point at which the fall from grace begins, Stevens argues, one can always return in one's memory to that point where the outcome was still hanging in the balance as if to change the ending by sheer force of will and come forward to a different present.

Clearly Faulkner's characters' consciousness of the past, specifically here the historical past, permeates their experience of the present. The above passage is preceded by the line, also said by Stevens, "Yesterday wont [*sic*] be over until tomorrow and tomorrow began ten thousand years ago."[5] This line, especially the phrase "ten thousand years ago," shades over into another manifestation of time frequently encountered in Faulkner, that of a mythic past not unlike Jung's concept of the collective unconscious, though embedded specifically in Southern culture. Characters like Lena Grove, Joe Christmas, Gail Hightower, and Doc Hines in *Light in August,* for instance, are impelled by memory, but of things they can't necessarily recollect. Witness the passage which begins the chapter where the five-year-old Joe Christmas accidentally sees the dietitian at his orphanage having sex, an episode which will change his life forever: "Memory believes before knowing remembers. Believes longer than recollects, longer than knowing even wonders."[6] When the enraged and frightened dietitian is caught in the act and calls Joe a "little nigger bastard" though his skin is "parchment colored," this epithet becomes part of his identity. Though the specific memory eludes him, the experience will shape his life and ultimately contribute to (one might even say "cause") his

---

4. William Faulkner, *Intruder in the Dust* (New York: Random House, 1948), 194–95.

5. Ibid., 194.

6. William Faulkner, *Light in August* (New York: Random House, 1932), 111.

murder of Joanna Burden. Many of Faulkner's other characters, in this novel and elsewhere, seem to move through life with a kind of clairvoyance, as if compelled by a memory larger than themselves. Whether the memory is individual, historical, or mythic, the presence of the past is palpable and determinative. And always what is critical is the history of the South as a whole rather than any single, individual experience of it.

Eugene O'Neill, too, is obsessed with time, particularly in his later plays, both those of his unfinished historical cycle, *A Touch of the Poet, More Stately Mansions,* and *The Calms of Capricorn,* and the autobiographically derived *The Iceman Cometh, Hughie, Long Day's Journey,* and *A Moon for the Misbegotten.* The predominant mode of time in these plays is linear time, time of the clock and calendar. In one way or another, each of these plays is structured around an ideal which is located in the past, whether a moment of past glory or hopes realized, or the obverse, the loss of a dream.[7] As the characters move forward upon a linear continuum into the future, the distance between themselves and their ideal inexorably increases. Thus time becomes the enemy, a measure of ever-greater loss.

The characters' present is saturated by memory, a second crucial modality of time as it functions in these dramas. Haunted by the ticking clock and the loss it brings, they alternately seek forgetfulness and oblivion, often in alcohol, or live in memories of glory gone a-glimmering. One thinks of the bums who live at Harry Hope's saloon in *The Iceman Cometh,* for instance, forever repeating their "pipe dreams" in a collective litany, or Con Melody in *A Touch of the Poet,* who ritualistically re-enacts the high point of his life on the yearly anniversary of the Battle of Talavera, when the Duke of Wellington singled him out for praise. In *Long Day's Journey into Night,* the endless arguments among the four Tyrones, an effort to escape their shared sense of guilt, have been repeated so many times the characters anticipate each other's lines; they, too, are drenched in memory, trying to make sense of a past gone awry.

---

7. An exception here is the unfinished play, "The Calms of Capricorn," in which the protagonist, Ethan Harford, is obsessed with setting a new clipper ship record for sailing around Cape Horn from New York to San Francisco. Although his goal lies in the future, not the past, time—the ticking clock—is still the enemy and ultimately defeats him.

That the past casts a shadow over the present and determines the future is perhaps most succinctly summed up by Mary Tyrone's well-known line, "The past is the present. It's the future, too. We all try to lie out of that but life won't let us." This vision results in a fatalistic philosophy, a sense of resignation and despair. Earlier in the play, for instance, Mary, having resumed her morphine habit though still trying to hide that fact, says to her son Edmund, "None of us can help the things life has done to us. They're done before you realize it, and once they're done they make you do other things until at last everything comes between you and what you'd like to be, and you've lost your true self forever."[8] Espousing this position, while it is hardly comforting, allows Mary and her counterparts in O'Neill's world to escape responsibility for their present actions. Thus in *The Iceman Cometh,* when the drummer Hickey returns to Harry Hope's saloon for his yearly binge but this time tries to entice the bums out of their drunken oblivion and into the world of the present, he becomes the enemy, the *iceman.*

The nature of time, that is, the relationship of past to present and the function of memory, is different in O'Neill and Faulkner. While it is true that in both cases the present moment is always responding in some way to the pressure of the past, so much so that one might say with Mary Tyrone that the past isn't really past at all, in Faulkner the past is a collective one, whether historically or mythically construed. While characters of course act out of their awareness of their own individual pasts, behind that history, whatever it is, always looms the backdrop of the South's collective history: slavery, the rape of the land and the Native Americans from whom it was stolen, the Civil War. Ike McCaslin's discoveries about his grandfather, old Carothers McCaslin, in section 4 of *The Bear* is both an excursion into his individual history and a coming to terms with the ills of slavery. In *The Sound and the Fury,* as Quentin contemplates his personal history on the last day of his life, several times specifically recalling his grandfather, the last important Compson, we are aware that he was a brigadier general in the Confederate army and that his greatest defeat occurred at the Battle of Shiloh on April 6 and 7, 1862. These dates, of course, are the days of the action of the first and third section of

8. O'Neill, *Long Day's Journey,* 87, 61.

the novel.[9] Thus again, behind individual history stands Southern history. In O'Neill, on the other hand, characters' memories are limited to their own individual pasts: Con Melody's moment of glory in the Battle of Talavera (*A Touch of the Poet*), Simon Harford's idyllic memories of his childhood experiences in his mother's garden (*More Stately Mansions*), Erie Smith's fond memories of his dead friend Hughie (*Hughie*).

Memory also functions differently in the two artists' work. Faulkner's characters either are compelled by a kind of collective unconscious they don't even recognize as such ("Memory believes before knowing remembers") or they live with a vague sense of longing for a past they themselves have never experienced: the Edenic myth of the South before the "fall." Here there is some overlap with O'Neill's characters, who lull themselves with memories of a lost ideal, though those moments are located in their own individual histories, somewhere on a linear continuum.

This notion of an ideal is key in both cases. As I argue in *The Banished Prince: Time, Memory, and Ritual in the Late Plays of Eugene O'Neill,* the need to recapture the ideal moment and the failure of memory to do so precipitates moments of confession in O'Neill's late plays, all of which in various ways are structured upon the Catholic ritual. Invoking ritual calls upon a third modality of time operative in these plays, what Eliade calls "mythic" or "ritual" time. Because rituals embody the shared ideals of a believing community, ideals which exist outside time, by participating in religious rituals believers are able to suspend time and its eroding powers, existing, however briefly, simultaneously in and outside of time. This "redemption" from time has restorative powers, returning the individual to linear time refreshed and renewed.[10] Occasionally Faulkner's characters participate in sacred or mythic time; we referred earlier to the examples of Dilsey and Benjy in *The Sound and the Fury*. But for the most part, they remain locked in linear or "profane" time. While O'Neill's late plays invoke mythic time more frequently, their dramatic structure leading to a confession which serves as the climax, only in *A Moon for the Misbegotten* does the confession prove efficacious. My point,

9. Geffen, "Profane Time," 178.
10. See Laurin Porter, *Banished Prince,* chapter 1.

which will become clearer when we contrast O'Neill and Faulkner with Foote, is the fact that O'Neill calls upon religion, however symbolically represented, as an antidote to history and that this is key to his philosophy of time.

Given his Southern background, it is no surprise that Foote, like Faulkner, is acutely attuned to the impact of the past upon the present. Growing up in Wharton, Texas, especially in his particular family, he could hardly escape this influence. We have noted elsewhere that as a young boy, for instance, he fell asleep each night listening to his parents on the porch outside his bedroom exchanging gossip and stories about days gone by; as he absorbed the talk of family members around him, according to his own report, the lives of people long dead often became more real to him than those of people he encountered every day. His daily visits to the cemetery with his grandmother after his grandfather's death also made an indelible impression on him. In an interview with Samuel G. Freedman, he says, "My grandmother was in mourning for two years. . . . Every afternoon we'd go out for a drive with her chauffeur. First, we'd go and see how the cotton crop was. Then we'd come here [the cemetery]. She'd bring flowers and sometimes she'd sit and cry. I always felt at home here."[11]

It is appropriate, then, that the graveyard looms as such an important symbol in *The Orphans' Home Cycle*. Rather than just a final destination, the end of time, as it were, it serves as an icon for the meeting of past and present. The living continue to visit their dead, as Sam, the gravedigger, tells Horace in *1918*: "You know Mrs. Stewart? She comes here every day rain or shine at four o'clock, summer and winter, and visits the grave of her boy that was drowned in the river. That's been four years now. Lots of ladies come out twice a week and visits their husbands' or their children's graves. Mrs. Goody, Mrs. Merriwether, Mrs. Bolton, Mrs. Jessie" (*Three Plays* 115). Like Mary Vaughn, who visits her dead husband's grave daily, these women keep their loved ones alive in their hearts. By the same token, animosities and unresolved issues also find their way into the cemetery. Sam says, "After Mr. Willis and Mr. Hayhurst shot and kilt each other, both their widows would come out, sometimes be here at the same time, but they wouldn't speak" (*Three Plays* 115). Horace's

11. Freedman, introduction to *Two Plays,* xi.

anxiety about placing a tombstone on his father's grave; Elizabeth's anguish over where to bury baby Jenny, in the Robedaux or Vaughn plot; interest in what kind of flowers Mrs. Boone placed on Jenny's grave—all these subtly reinforce the notion that the graveyard is a continuation of Harrison society. It is more a resting place than a final destination.

Foote also uses the cemetery to introduce metaphysical questions about the nature of time. When Horace, Jr., visits the graveyard with his grandmother and sees the graves of Paul Horace and his infant sister Jenny, he says, "If my sister had lived she would be twelve years old next month. . . . My Grandfather Robedaux would have been sixty-five. He was thirty-two years old when he died. Daddy is thirty-six. He is four years older than his own father" (*Three Plays* 132). Death, the cessation of time, allows for the impossible: the son is older than the father. On another occasion, when Elizabeth tells young Horace she is pregnant and says that she'd like to have a girl, since she already has two boys, he replies, "You have a girl, too. She is dead, but you have her," then asks, "What happens to you when you die?" (*Three Plays* 151). The lived experience takes place within the stream of time, as these questions imply, begging the question of what happens when time stops.

The graveyard, then, functions symbolically to focus our attention on the intersection of past and present and the vexing question of the nature of time. The *Cycle* plays also explore the concept of memory, which, as we have seen in both Faulkner and O'Neill, flows inevitably from considerations of the past-present nexus. In general, memory is portrayed as faulty, or at least highly subjective. At issue, for instance, is the question of where Paul Horace is buried and whether Horace has placed his tombstone on the right grave. The opening scene of *1918*, set in the cemetery, strikes this note of uncertainty, as Horace, who is finally able to afford the tombstone, doesn't know where to put it and asks Sam, who serves as an unofficial historian in these matters. "Wasn't there no marker on the grave?" Sam asks, to which Horace replies, "Must have been at one time. See there are three unmarked graves. My father is buried in one, my Uncle Cal and my Uncle Steve are buried in the others. I haven't been out here in a long time. My memory was that there was a board on each grave, but when Mr. Deitrick [the merchant from whom Horace purchased the gravestone] came out to look it over he said there were none" (*Three Plays* 111). Sam finally suggests that Horace consult some of the "old-timers," the repository of local history. It is an issue of such importance to Horace that even as he is coming down with the flu, he attempts to write his cousin Minnie about it. Her opinion will later be contested by Mrs. Boone, a Harrison resident who insists that Horace had the tombstone placed on the wrong grave: "Minnie is wrong. I came to all their funerals and I remember," she tells him (*Three Plays* 171).

Our principal access to the past, memory can be—often *is*—unreliable, a fact which Foote emphasizes in a seemingly insignificant bit of dialogue between Horace and Horace, Jr., in *The Death of Papa*. Looking at a photograph of his father which his uncle sent him to show young Horace, Horace, Sr., says, "To tell you the truth, I don't remember his looking like this at all. He looks like he's in his early twenties. He looks younger than I do, doesn't he?" Then he adds, "My memory of him was that he had a mustache and he had reddish hair. He was a small, thin man. To tell you the truth, whenever I think of him, I think of him like he was when he was so sick. He was so thin and he coughed a lot. I wanted to go visit him, but I was almost afraid to go, because I knew how sick he was" (*Two Plays* 163). Horace's comment suggests that his memories of his father are colored by his final contact with him as he lay dying, a memory so tinged with fear that it blots out earlier images of his father as healthy and vigorous. Interestingly, this comment is immediately followed by his telling young Horace that he is keeping his father's broken watch in a safe at the store and that when his son turns twenty-one, he intends to repair it and give it to him. It is significant both that the watch is broken—time has literally stopped for Paul Horace—and that Horace has chosen this keepsake, the symbol of time's passing, to bequeath to his son.

Indeed, one could argue that on the deepest level, the entire *Cycle* is informed by questions of time. The fact that it is structured as a history, both of an individual life and a family, immediately introduces issues of chronology, of past and present. Each play, with the exception of *Valentine's Day,* begins by specifically stating the place and time of the action: for example, Harrison, Texas, 1902–1903 (*Roots*) or Floyd's Lane, Texas, 1904 (*Convicts*). *Valentine's Day* simply states "Christmas Eve 1917." Like beads on a string, each drama adds another chapter to Horace's story, emphasizing the linear nature of individual experience. This chronological record is reinforced throughout the nine plays by various characters' referring to events that happened in previous dramas, circling back via memory to an earlier point in time. Foote's use of historical events like World War I and the flu epidemic as a backdrop to the narrative further reinforces the notion of historicity. Our understanding of these particular lives must begin with an awareness of the specific space-time continuum in which they take place.

Perhaps the play which most clearly demonstrates this fact is *1918,* the only play to actually take its title from a date. When one thinks of the momentous events that occur in the course of this play, both private and public—Horace's near death and the loss of baby Jenny, the world's first global war, an epidemic that wipes out fifteen people in this tiny town in a single day—it is interesting, given all the possible choices available to him, that Foote selects as his title the year of the action. It seems to insist that human experience takes place in time, that none of us can escape the historical moment into which we're born and during which we live.

It follows that of all the *Cycle* plays, *1918* is the one where the action is most closely identified with historical events. Certainly Foote takes great care to situate the other plays in specific historical contexts, as we have noted, with the texture of mores and manners, conversation and casual references reflecting the particular era of the play in question; *Convicts,* for instance, with its post–Civil War ambiance, is literally drenched in history. But in *1918,* the action of the play is propelled by historical events, specifically, World War I and the flu epidemic of 1918. Horace's pledge of $4,000 in war bonds prompts Mr. Vaughn to offer to support Elizabeth and Jenny so that Horace can join the army, much to Horace's chagrin. Brother wants desperately to enlist and asks Elizabeth to play "Over There" on the piano; his talk is of battles and generals and Mr. Dietrick's being a German spy. Interspersed with comments about the war and reports of Harrison boys who have been killed or wounded in battle are references to friends and neighbors who have come down with the flu, followed quickly by Horace himself becoming desperately ill. This intersection of global and local concerns, particularly the flu epidemic, which brings the war to the homefront in a way distant battles never could, focuses our attention on the fact that history is not something that happens *out there*. To paraphrase Tip O'Neill's famous line "All politics is local," this play insists that all history is local.

Foote reinforces this notion by deftly interweaving reports of war deaths with those caused by the flu, until the two seem almost interchangeable. Early in act 1, which establishes the historical context of the action, all conversations seem to end with references to new deaths, either from the war or the flu. We learn that Elizabeth's friend Allie's husband was badly gassed and is in a hospital in France and that Leland Harris is shellshocked, then that T. Abell, the husband of Horace's Aunt Inez, is ill, as is Clay Boone, Horace's friend. Horace reports that Clay has "been out of his head for two days. He thinks he's in Germany fighting the Germans" (*Three Plays* 121), making the war-flu connection explicit. Shortly afterwards, word arrives that both T. and Clay are dead.

Or another example: Elizabeth tells her mother that she's thinking of hiring a nurse to watch Jenny so she can resume teaching piano lessons, and Mrs. Vaughn replies, "I don't know where you'll find one. All the help I know are busy nursing people with the flu," listing the families on their street who have been stricken: the Cookenboos, the Taylors, the Outlars, the Boultons. "Mrs. Cookenboo thinks the Germans brought the germs over here," she adds. "She says it's part of what they call germ warfare" (*Three Plays* 131), a rumor which is later espoused by Brother, as well. Further linking these two phenomena, Horace reports his Uncle Albert as saying pointedly, in response to Horace's reluctance to enlist, that T. Abell might've been safer on the battlefield in France than dealing with the "pestilence" at home. Indeed, when Horace himself becomes ill he, like Clay Boone, hallucinates that he's in France fighting.

All of these examples insist that far from being an abstract, impersonal force, global events like wars and epidemics impinge upon the lives of individuals in concrete, personal fashion. We live out our lives within a context defined by events, movements, and cultural phenomena larger than ourselves, even if we are unaware of their influence on our day-to-day affairs. What is crucial about Foote's historical sense, setting him apart from both O'Neill and Faulkner, is his interest in the impact of history on individual lives within the context of family.

In Faulkner, as we have noted, history, specifically the fall of the South, looms larger than any individual character's experience of it, frequently, if not always, subsuming individual will and volition. The reverse is true in O'Neill, where history simply serves as a backdrop to individual action. When Con Melody, the would-be Irish aristocrat who has fallen on hard times in *A Touch of the Poet*, prefers John Quincy Adams to Andrew Jackson, whom he calls "that idol of the riffraff," we know it is because he desperately needs to insist upon his own former wealth and status.[12] In *The Calms of Capricorn*, Ethan Harford's attempt to set a new clipper ship record from New York to San Francisco takes place as the steamship is just beginning to replace sailing vessels. O'Neill's concern in these cases, as in the autobiographical dramas, is always the individual and his dream (I say "his" because the dreamer is nearly always male). Time becomes the enemy as the dream recedes ever further into the past. In Foote's plays, on the other hand, the critical question is how the individual responds to the march of time and the historical-cultural conditions with which he or she is presented, a response which is played out within the context of family. For in Foote, as opposed to O'Neill, where the ideal is associated with individual aspirations, or Faulkner, where the ideal is associated, however vaguely, with the lost Eden of the past, the ideal is located within relationships, and specifically, familial ones. History for Foote is embedded in *family* history. Though he's clearly aware of and concerned about historical events and cultural movements, and though these factors impact his characters both as individuals and within social units, the history that really matters in the plays of Horton Foote is that of the individual within a family.

Thus as we have said, the entire *Cycle* is structured by Horace's desire for a family, beginning with the opening play when he is orphaned and the subsequent play, *Convicts,* which portrays his lonely childhood; *Lily Dale,* which tracks his final effort to be incorporated into Corella and Pete's family; an aborted (*Widow Claire*) and finally successful choice of a wife (*Courtship* and *Valentine's Day*); and the

12. Eugene O'Neill, *A Touch of the Poet* (New Haven: Yale University Press, 1957), 37.

gradual establishment of his own family (*1918*). By the last two plays, Horace is solidly at the center of a family which seems to include, as *Cousins* humorously suggests, the entire town. *The Death of Papa,* a more serious treatment, ends appropriately with Brother's comment that now Horace is the patriarch and he the orphan.

Several motifs run throughout the nine plays, providing continuity and context, as we noted in Chapter 4, one of them being Horace's dream of placing a tombstone on his father's grave. It is appropriate, then, that *1918,* the seventh play, opens with a scene in the graveyard where Horace, finally financially able, is making arrangements to do so at last. It has taken sixteen years from the time he made his vow as a twelve-year-old boy; he is now twenty-eight and the father of a baby girl. Before the play ends, he will have lost his daughter, his Uncle T., and countless friends and neighbors, nearly dying himself. The penultimate scene in this play filled with death is also set in the grave-yard. Bracketing the action with this memento mori, Foote invites us to contemplate the nature of life, death, and time.

As I see it, the *Cycle* presents two different, if overlapping, perspectives on time as it is experienced by the individual and the family unit. The most obvious of these is historical or linear time, implicit in the chronological structure of the *Cycle* as a whole as well as within individual plays. The World War I setting of *1918,* which embeds the action in specific historical events, for example, insists on the linear nature of time. This is further emphasized by lines that, as so frequently happens with Foote, seem to be throw-away—what Foote calls "texture." They do not advance the plot or provide key information and seem, in fact, inconsequential. When Horace comes to Elizabeth's bedside immediately after the birth of their new son, the first thing he says to her is that he has been out at the cemetery, and that Mrs. Boone was there, putting flowers on her son Clay's grave. It was his birthday, Horace adds, then says that she placed some flowers on baby Jenny's grave, as well. He asks Elizabeth what time the baby was born, then comments that he himself was born between four and five in the morning and asks if she was born "exactly" at 7 A.M. "I guess so," Elizabeth responds. This thought of time and its precise measurement prompts Horace to comment that he knew a boy born on the 29th of February and says, "I wouldn't care to be born then. Would you?" (*Three Plays* 174). This seemingly desultory talk is not really what's on either of their minds, of course, as is clear when Horace's next words are, "Elizabeth . . . I love you." Their deep emotions on the birth of their new son, following so soon upon the death of their daughter, can't be approached directly; they are contained, as it were, in inconsequential talk. At the same time Foote uses this small conversation to focus attention on the linear nature of time, which we track in carefully calibrated units, marking off the passing of hours, days, and years in an attempt to control it by imposing a paradigm that measures its flow. Horace's comment about being born on February 29, for instance, brings to mind the fact that to keep calendars accurate, each fourth year we add an extra day to February. Setting the action of act 2, scene 1, on Armistice Day, November 11, 1918, a date of such historical importance that it has become a national holiday, has a similar effect, reminding us once again of clock and calendar.

Time is the medium in which we live. The concept of eternity, of timelessness, eludes us precisely because we can't imagine existence outside its boundaries. Aristotle's definition, time as the measure of motion, points to the fact that all nature is in constant flux, and time measures its passage. The most graphic example of this phenomenon in *1918* is perhaps Elizabeth's pregnancy, which becomes increasingly obvious as the play progresses until "her time has come" and she delivers a baby boy.

Time is also integral to the construction of identity. We commonly accept the fact that for the individual, time begins with birth, as it ends with death. Thus the concept of an identity outside time defies our imagination. Young Horace tries to come to grips with this when he asks Martha in *Convicts* who a man's wife would be in heaven if he was married twice on earth, or what Lily Dale will say to her real father when she meets him in heaven, since she calls Mr. Davenport "Daddy." "The way it looks to me now," Horace says, "is that everything is going to be real mixed up in heaven" (*Four Plays* 118). Twenty-four years later Horace, Jr., asks similar questions of his mother: "If I see Daddy's papa in heaven, how am I going to know him? I have never seen a picture of him" (*Two Plays* 151). These questions assume that heaven is simply a continuation of life on earth, maintaining its physical characteristics and social categories, a natural assumption for a child to make. As adults, we smile at this naïveté, but are hard-pressed to offer alternative descriptions, since we, too, are trapped in time and cannot conceive of being as other than a continuation of what *is*.

It is noteworthy, in this regard, that Foote consistently overlaps references to birth and death in *1918*, as if to challenge our thinking about this division. Moments after Elizabeth tells Horace that while he was ill with influenza their baby died, the bells ring out announcing Germany's surrender, and Brother and Mrs. Vaughn burst into the room joyfully with the good news. Horace and Elizabeth must deal with what is probably the greatest pain any couple can endure, the death of a child, in the midst of universal rejoicing about the end of deaths from the war. Shortly after that, Elizabeth tells Horace that she's pregnant and will have their second child in six months.

When Elizabeth goes into labor, Bessie, the strange girl who insists on calling Elizabeth "Mary," is with her as, coincidentally, she had been during her labor with Jenny. As they talk, waiting for the doctor to come, Elizabeth confesses to Bessie, in one of the play's most poignant speeches, "I'm ashamed but I'm not so happy about having this baby, I don't want this baby. I want my other baby back. I want Jenny back. I don't want this baby at all" (*Three Plays* 166). Again, birth and death are interwoven. This connection is further reinforced by the fact that Horace learns of his son's birth while he is in the cemetery, visiting his father's grave, and that while there, Mrs. Boone has come to place flowers on her son Clay's grave in honor of his birthday.

This blurring of the division between life and death, time and timelessness, suggests a second modality of time in these plays. We have said that for the individual, time is experienced as linear. Thus as he travels through time, Horace becomes the repository of thousands of individual experiences—a walking history, as it were. This linearity turns on itself in *1918*, however, when Horace, coming down with the flu, hallucinates that he is back in Houston taking a business class and living with his cousin Minnie. He asks Elizabeth where his mother is and has forgotten that their former physician, Dr. Andrews, is dead. His high fever blurs the distinction between past and present, bringing moments from a previous stage of his life into his immediate consciousness. It is not that he is remembering the past, but that he experiences past and present simultaneously. While this is obviously explicable in terms of his illness, on a thematic level it points to Foote's vision of the relationship of past to present. In one way or another, we bring the past with us as we go. Key experiences from Horace's past, Corella's abandoning him, for instance, leaving him behind and taking Lily Dale to Houston when she marries Pete, will always exert pressure on the present moment to a greater or lesser extent. It is not insignificant that when he hallucinates, the scene that Horace most vividly describes is one where he comes to Corella's house for his breakfast, as was his custom while in Houston, and she meets him at the door with "terror in her eyes." Mr. Davenport, he quickly realizes, had not gone to work that morning, and Corella had to hide the fact that she had been feeding Horace every morning. "I never felt comfortable or welcome in my mother's house from the day she married him," he says (*Three Plays* 141). Interestingly, this is immediately followed by his thinking that he's in France and Mr. Vaughn is the general, pinning a medal on him. Both scenes reflect Horace's feeling of vulnerability in the face of male authority figures who would put him in harm's way.

Thus while each individual play emphasizes the linear nature of time, as does, from one perspective, the *Cycle* as a whole, *The Orphans' Home* also brings into focus a second quality of time that allows the present to contain the past, allowing for the simultaneous experience of multiple points on the linear continuum. Elizabeth's speech to Bessie as she goes into labor with her second child, which we spoke of earlier in this chapter, for instance, reveals that her feelings about her new baby and indeed the very experience of labor itself are overlaid with her memory of her labor with Jenny and Jenny's subsequent death. More than simply a function of memory, however, which involves looking back on an incident which is "dead and gone," Elizabeth's experience of her present moment in some mysterious fashion exists simultaneously on two planes; it is as if she lives in the present and the past at the same time. Foote's decision to have Bessie present for both labors locks in this connection. He even has Elizabeth comment on this fact. "You waited with me last time while Horace went for the doctor, remember?" she says to Bessie. "Only that time we weren't living in our own home, and my mother and father were out of town" (*Three Plays* 164).

Bessie's presence and her role as listener to Elizabeth's confession about her fears and sorrow brings to mind a third moment for the reader who is familiar with the entire *Cycle:* Elizabeth's "mortality speech" in *Valentine's Day* immediately after she receives news of George Tyler's suicide. She is once again alone with Bessie, Horace having just gone to offer his condolences at the Tyler home. Trying to take in the fact of Mr. Tyler's death, she says, almost to herself, "I can't believe he was just here and now . . ." (*Three Plays* 99). Bessie, not the most perceptive of conversationalists, changes the subject, commenting that in two and a half weeks it will be Valentine's Day, marking Horace and Elizabeth's first anniversary, and asks Elizabeth if she's glad she's married Horace, then if she thinks she'll love him as much in twenty-five years, then in fifty. "How old will you be when you've been married fifty years?" she asks. Elizabeth says that she'll be seventy-four, Horace will be seventy-seven, and adds that her baby will be forty-nine, then bursts out crying. The speech which follows, simple but poignant, serves as the emotional climax of the play: "I don't want to get old, Bessie, and I don't want Horace to get old. I want everything to stay as it is. When I'm seventy-two Mama and Papa will be dead unless they live to be a hundred. I don't want anybody I love to die, Bessie, ever, not Horace, not Mama, not Papa. Not Brother, not my sisters, not my baby I'm going to have" (*Three Plays* 100).

Both Bessie's questions and Elizabeth's speech emphasize the apprehension of time as chronological, historical—the linear paradigm. It is essentially a rational construct, wherein time is regarded as an absolute, measurable property of experience. These passages, however, also suggest an arational way of apprehending time. As Elizabeth goes into labor with her second child, the memory of her first labor is in some ways more real to her than her current situation, and it colors, one might even say *determines,* what she experiences in the present moment. Though somewhat akin to O'Neill's depiction of characters like the Tyrones or Con Melody, whose present awareness is tinged with regrets from the past, Foote's characters aren't consciously reacting to a lost ideal or trying to escape into memory; rather, at specific junctures their experience seems to contain both past and present simultaneously.

Art adds still another layer to this already complicated phenomenon, allowing us to "read" forwards as well as backwards in time. For instance, audience members familiar with the entire *Cycle* will bring to Elizabeth's mortality speech in *Valentine's Day* the knowledge that her daughter-to-be, the infant Jenny, will not live to be forty-nine, just as we know that her father, like George Tyler, will die on the street, away from his loved ones. As we read forwards and backwards, individual moments on the linear continuum are charged with added significance.

The audience's ability to see double, to superimpose moments from the past on the present and vice versa, while not, strictly speaking, a modality of time, since fiction takes place outside "real" time and space, allows for a simultaneity of experience and understanding which we cannot access elsewhere. Foote's skillful employment of structure in the *Cycle* makes this possible. While each play stands alone, replicating the linear dimension of experience, events unfolding minute by minute, the *Cycle* as a whole allows us to see characters simultaneously at different points of their lives: Elizabeth before her first child is born, not wanting to die, and Elizabeth anticipating the birth of her second child, having lost her first; Horace the twelve-year-old orphan and Horace, father and patriarch.

The example of Horace, the most developed *Cycle* character, provides the clearest instance of this simultaneity. In the scene between Horace and Corella in *The Death of Papa,* for instance, where Horace finally speaks his heart to his mother about being neglected as a child in reference to her comments about Horace, Jr.'s reading too much, we see him as both child and man, orphan and father. When he says, "I could tell you heartbreaking stories, too, about those boys [neglected children]" and "what they had to bear," we know though he speaks in generalities that he is speaking of himself (*Two Plays* 189). This exchange also brings to mind his visit with Corella in the hospital in *Cousins,* in which he sidesteps the confrontation he ultimately has in *Papa.* When Corella, in the play, asks him about the charges Minnie made, that Horace didn't love her and that she [Minnie] was the only one in the family who took an interest in Horace, he says that wasn't true: his aunts and grandparents were concerned about him; Corella quickly adds, "And I was always interested" (*Two Plays* 40). Both of these scenes, which make reference to Horace's childhood, bring the image of Horace from *Roots* to bear in the present moment, allowing us to "see" two Horaces simultaneously. Similarly, when Mrs. Vaughn says to Horace near the end of *Papa*, "You used to drink and gamble as a young man. You were wild and you got into trouble" (*Two Plays* 191), remarking on how he's changed, we hold in our consciousness both the sober, responsible Horace of the present moment and the alter egos of Horace in *The Widow Claire*—his roommates and cronies who dramatize the path which Horace at some point opted not to take.

This doubling technique, examined in detail in Chapter 4, contributes to our ability to achieve dual levels of awareness throughout the *Cycle*. The orphans and adopted sons that crop up, for example— Buddy in *The Widow Claire* and the boy Mrs. Boone adopts in *1918*, as well as all the references to being orphaned made by Will, Mr. Vaughn, Pete, and others—create a double vision, a simultaneity of experience. Like the mother who looks at her grown son and sees both the face of the adult he has become and that of the infant, toddler, and little boy he used to be, as audience we "see" simultaneously Horace as child and man, son and father. While this is perhaps true of any fictional character who is sufficiently developed, it is especially pertinent in this case, both because as drama it presents, without comment or mediation, a sequence of events, and because as a cycle, it gives us not one portrait of Horace but nine, which we superimpose one on the other.

Perhaps the best way to explain this property of time, both the past-in-the-present that the characters experience and the reader's aesthetic experience of multiple perspectives, is to borrow the language that Minnie uses in the climactic scene of *Cousins* when she talks about the nature of families. It is the moment when she has given up the grudge against Corella which has dominated her thinking for over twenty years, finally relinquishing her bitterness and acknowledging that she is essentially alone in the world. Noting that many of her cousins are dead and she doesn't know the new ones who have taken their place, she makes the "a family is a remarkable thing" speech quoted earlier. "You belong," she says, "and then you don't. It passes you by. Unless you start a family of your own" (*Two Plays* 92). Her description of family is similar to that of a wave, which while it seems palpable and static at any given moment is constantly in motion. As particles of water accumulate ever greater mass and move toward shore, the wave crests, shattering into thousands of individual droplets like broken glass, and a new wave begins to build. To a child the family seems permanent, unchanging just as any given moment of time seems static and immutable, while in reality both are in constant flux. Time as it is manifest in these plays captures something of this paradoxical tension between stasis and dynamism. The *Cycle* argues that experientially, if not logically, we can simultaneously encompass our present and past selves, adult and child. It's not that we switch back and forth in time via memory but that in certain emotionally heightened moments we experience both past and present at the same time.

We have said that for Foote's characters, unlike those of Faulkner and O'Neill, the ideal, the "good," is not located in the past, whether individual or mythic, and also that it is associated in some essential way with family. These two facts go a long way toward finally explaining the difference between the essentially tragic vision of Faulkner and O'Neill and the more optimistic philosophy of Horton Foote.

Faulkner's characters live and move and have their being, to paraphrase St. Paul, in a world characterized by a sense of loss. In *Go Down, Moses,* for instance, the image of the vast and pristine wilderness before old Ikkemotubbe, the Chickasaw chief, sold it to Thomas Sutpen, the white man, looms like a lost Eden, casting its shadow forward into the present and tingeing all with darkness. Thus we read in the opening passage of section 4 of *The Bear,* where Ike McCaslin learns the truth about his past as he reads through the ledgers in the old commissary:

> He could say it [i.e., repudiate his inheritance], himself and his cousin [Cass] juxtaposed not against the wilderness but against the tamed land which was to have been his heritage, the land which old Carothers McCaslin his grandfather had bought with white man's money from the wild men whose grandfathers without guns hunted it, and tamed and ordered or believed he had tamed and ordered it for the reason that the human beings he held in bondage and in the power of life and death had removed the forest from it and in their sweat scratched the surface of it to a depth of perhaps fourteen inches in order to grow something out of it which had not been there before and which could be translated back into the money he who believed he had bought it had had to pay to get it and hold it and a reasonable profit too.[13]

13. William Faulkner, *The Bear,* in *Go Down, Moses* (New York: Random House, 1940), 254.

The original sins of the rape of the land and the exploitation of both the red and the black race have led to the post-lapsarian state in which Ike finds himself. Although in this section of the novella, set in 1888, Ike is twenty-one, in a sense his life is already over, determined by events which took place long before he was born. Faulkner's vision of the South's decline goes beyond the loss of the Civil War and the erasure of a way of life which inevitably followed (however romanticized in its conception) to the original rape of the land and the people, black and red, who were subjugated to support it. Thus Ike, in discovering his grandfather's perfidy in committing both miscegenation and incest, fathering his own grandchild, feels he has no choice but to repudiate his inheritance, which he sees as fatally tainted.

Likewise Quentin Compson in *The Sound and the Fury* cannot simply live out his life between the years of 1891 and 1910, his actual lifespan, making autonomous choices in the present moment, since the sins of the fathers, both literally (i.e., his Compson forebears) and figuratively (the white, Southern, aristocratic males who have preceded him) have to a large extent already determined his fate. In the Old Testament sense, the sins of the fathers are visited upon the sons "unto the third and fourth generation." The opening of Quentin's section of the novel, like that of Ike McCaslin above, establishes this fact from the outset: "When the shadow of the sash appeared on the curtains it was between seven and eight oclock and then I was in time again, hearing the watch. It was Grandfather's and when Father gave it to me he said I give you the mausoleum of all hope and desire."[14] Linear time, the ticking watch, is indeed the death of hope in this novel. Though the Southerner can return in his imagination (and it is primarily a *male* imagination in Faulkner) to the moment Gavin Stevens describes right before Pickett's charge, the end of the war and the events that followed can't be changed any more than those that precipitated the war in the first place.

Thus Faulkner's is essentially a tragic vision, shaped by a sense of human limitation rather than potential; he tells tales of lives lived out in the shadow of loss, both personal and communal. It is a post-lapsarian view of experience; life "after the fall." I choose these theological terms—*Eden, sin, fall*—deliberately, since I think that Faulk-

14. William Faulkner, *The Sound and the Fury,* ed. David Minter, 2nd ed. (New York: W. W. Norton, 1994), 48.

ner's essential concerns are not so much with political or social realities as they are with mythical ones. His is a world without a redeemer. Except for individuals who experience or dispense grace (one thinks of Dilsey and Lena, for instance), Faulkner's characters live out their lives in a fallen world, burdened by time. It is crucial to keep in mind, however, that anterior to this sense of loss hovers the Eden of the wilderness, the "before" to this "after."[15]

Many of O'Neill's characters, too, especially those of his late plays, live under the shadow of loss. Unlike Faulkner's characters, however, it is not a cultural or historical loss but an individual one. Time becomes the enemy, since it moves them ever further away from a moment in their pasts when ideals seemed within reach. Act 4 of *Long Day's Journey into Night,* for instance, is structured around a series of confessions which articulate these lost ideals. For James Tyrone, it was the moment when he reached the pinnacle of his acting career, and Edwin Boothe, the premier Shakespearean actor of his day, claimed that Tyrone was doing Shakespeare better than he was. This moment is coupled with Mary's love, which for the moment hangs in the balance with his ambitions. Jamie, their elder son, confesses an ideal lost to his brother Edmund: the moment he first caught his mother "in the act with a hypo," taking morphine. His life from that moment has been a falling off, a downward spiral. Mary's ideal is dramatized in her final midnight entrance, deep in a morphine trance, trailing her wedding dress and talking of wanting to become a nun. Her wedding represents an ideal moment when she could be both virginal and pure (the nun image) and on the brink of marriage and motherhood.

Other examples follow this same pattern, with variations: Erie Smith remembers his dead friend Hughie (*Hughie*), Con Melody recalls his days of former glory (*A Touch of the Poet*), Simon Harford longs for his childhood hours in the garden with his mother Deborah (*More Stately Mansions*), and the bums at Harry Hope's saloon dream

15. In "Horton Foote and Mythic Realism," Wood discusses the works of Faulkner, Katherine Anne Porter, and Flannery O'Connor in terms of this narrative, arguing that "for each of these Southern mythic realists the fall from Eden is the central mythic reality, the story before all others." Gerald C. Wood, "Old Beginnings and Roads to Home: Horton Foote and Mythic Realism," *Christianity and Literature* 45, nos. 3–4 (1996): 365.

about real or imagined past triumphs (*The Iceman Cometh*). In each case a sense of goodness and integration is associated with the past, located for individual characters somewhere along the linear continuum of their lives. A second important feature of many of these ideals is the fact that they reconcile tensions which in the ordinary course of their lives cancel each other out. For James Tyrone, for instance, his ambitions as an actor, which require an itinerant lifestyle, preclude a settled family life. His desire for personal achievement and his need for a family pull in opposite directions. Thus also Jamie's need to be an autonomous adult and his desire to remain a dependent child, like Simon Harford's conflicting feelings about his wife and his mother, cannot be reconciled in "real"—that is, linear—time.

This, of course, is the lure of the ideal, which beckons precisely because it seems to hold forth the promise of opposites reconciled, differences canceled out. The ideal of democracy, for example, rests on the notion that all people are equal and yet each individual is supreme—an irreconcilable opposition. O'Neill understands, as does F. Scott Fitzgerald, another Irishman, that once the ideal enters the stream of time and hence the world of reality, it is tainted. Only as it hovers somewhere out of time and space can it exist as ideal. Like the green breast of the New World beckoning to the Dutch sailors in the closing passage of *The Great Gatsby,* it alone is "commensurate to [our] capacity for wonder."[16]

The concept of the ideal, then, functions differently in O'Neill and Faulkner. Though both are in the past, casting a long shadow over the present, in Faulkner the ideal is communal rather than individual. It is not so much a specific moment in the past as it is a vague, mythologized state that precedes the history of the South's decline. Imaged variously as the pristine wilderness, the moment before Pickett's charge, or a state of harmony with nature, we are aware of it primarily by its absence. It is a lack, a void. In O'Neill's plays, individuals believe (or have convinced themselves) that at some point in their past the ideal was within reach, a conviction which casts a pall over their present experience.

Foote's characters' experience of time and their relationship to

16. F. Scott Fitzgerald, *The Great Gatsby* (New York: Charles Scribner's Sons, 1925), 182.

their dreams presents a decided contrast to the vision which informs the works of Faulkner and O'Neill. It is significant, in the first instance, that in the *Cycle* plays there is no paradise that antecedes the fall from grace. Horace's saga begins with his father's death and the subsequent dissolution of his nuclear family. Although we can imagine his life before this turn of events, perhaps, it is not dramatized for us; indeed, it's barely mentioned. What little we know about Paul Horace and Corella's marriage we have to piece together from passing comments, and other than the description of the night Corella and the children left the Robedaux homestead, we have no descriptions of the family as a whole. Indeed, that episode only describes Corella and the two children. Thus there is no sense of a lost ideal which Horace seeks to regain, no image from the past that he seeks to replicate—only a goal to find or create a new family somewhere in the future.

Contrast this with the vision which informs *More Stately Mansions,* the sixth play in O'Neill's projected eleven-play cycle, *A Tale of Possessors, Self-Dispossessed.* In that play the protagonist, Simon Harford, speaking with Deborah, his mother, recalls a fairy tale she told him years ago as they sat together in her garden retreat. In the tale, a young prince is banished from his kingdom by a beautiful enchantress who tells him he must search the world over for a magic door, the entrance to his old realm. He will know it when he finds it, she tells him, as indeed he does. But at the last minute he hears the enchantress speaking from the other side, warning him that if he opens the door, he may find a barren desert "where it is always night, haunted by terrible ghosts and ruled over by a hideous old witch" who will devour him. The prince, unable to decide if she is lying or telling the truth, can neither bring himself to open the door or to leave. "So he remained for the rest of his life standing before the door, and became a beggar, whining for alms from all who passed by,"[17] the story ends. This tale, with its obviously symbolic overtones, becomes a metaphor for Simon's life. As he searches the world over for a sense of fulfillment and peace that eludes him, he is cursed with the memory of idyllic days in the garden with his mother when all his needs were

17. Eugene O'Neill, *More Stately Mansions,* ed. Martha Gilman Bower (New York: Oxford University Press, 1988), 193.

met. Whether or not this memory is accurate is beside the point; its very existence casts into the shade any happiness he experiences in the present. Nothing can measure up to his sense of an ideal lost, one left behind him somewhere in the past.

This theme recurs with striking regularity in all of O'Neill's late plays, as we have noted earlier in this chapter. It's not just that the various personae have experienced the loss of something or someone they hold dear; it's that this loss takes on the nature of an ideal which can neither be recaptured nor forgotten. They are all, like the banished prince, cast into outer darkness by their conviction that goodness resides "back there" somewhere in time.

A second and related point is that for Horace "the good" is not so much an ideal as a goal, an aspiration. Ideals, we have said, do not exist in the time-space continuum, the flux of experience. They hover over the horizon like the green breast beckoning the Dutch sailors precisely because by definition, in reconciling opposites, they cannot ever be fully realized. They are, that is to say, *ideals,* not reality. That they inform reality, give our lives shape and meaning, is undeniable, but they are available only via memory or dreams and are impervious to change.

When O'Neill's characters look longingly back, they are creating a confluence of conditions that never existed, except in their memories. The bums at Harry Hope's, for example, delude themselves and one another as they maintain their pipe dreams of hopes realized (the name of the saloon's proprietor is no accident). Faulkner's characters, likewise, live in the shadow of a vaguely defined but powerful image of a lost Eden. Horace, on the other hand, commits himself to aspirations that are within reach. While his goal of placing a tombstone on his father's grave, for instance, seems nearly impossible on his salary of 50 cents per week, he ultimately achieves his objective, as we know, though it takes him sixteen years. His dream of belonging to a family seems equally unlikely at the outset, but that, too, is finally realized.

One can point to several reasons for this. First, his aspirations are associated with the future, not the past. Not looking backwards to a memory which has taken on the aura of a golden age, Horace is bound to no ideal, so that he can look to the future and the creation of something new. It is also significant, I would argue, that in the process, his willingness to acknowledge the moral ambiguity of the world around him precludes the ideal. He does not delude himself about the limitations of those he loves—Corella, for instance. At the same time, he does not dwell on past injustices, as we saw in his comments to his clerk and cousin Gordon in *Cousins.* Like Minnie in that same play, he is able to let go of past pain and move on.

Another fundamental contrast between a character like Horace and those of O'Neill's plays are that for Horace, happiness, if it is to be achieved, will come within the context of relationships.[18] O'Neill's dreamers, for the most part, are individualists for whom marriage and family are perceived as limiting. From Ruth, who prevents the dreamer and poet Robert Mayo from wandering *Beyond the Horizon* (1918) to Abbie Putnam of *Desire under the Elms* (1924), Nina Leeds of *Strange Interlude* and Lavinia and Christine Mannon of *Mourning Becomes Electra,* women are the agents of death, literally or figuratively. Women in O'Neill's cycle plays are also dream-destroyers, entrapping their men in the snares of love and domesticity, as we see in the example of Sara Melody and Nora, her mother (*Touch of the Poet*); Sara and Deborah Harford, Simon Harford's mother, in *More Stately Mansions;* and Nancy, Ethan's wife in *The Calms of Capricorn.* The same is true of the off-stage women in *Iceman:* Rosa Parritt, the antimother and freethinker who dares to make life choices based on her own desire, thus condemning her son Don and ex-lover Larry Slade to lives of desperation and loneliness, and Evelyn Hickman, whose insistence on repeatedly forgiving her husband Hickey finally drives him to murder her. Mary Tyrone's lapse into morphine addiction propels the whole Tyrone family into a downward cycle of despair. Only Josie Hogan of *A Moon for the Misbegotten* escapes O'Neill's misogyny, but she is necessary to provide absolution to the tortured Jim Tyrone; it's clear that her primary function in that play is to serve the emotional and spiritual needs of the male protagonist.

Not surprisingly, O'Neill's view of the family constellation is equally gimlet-eyed. Although his male protagonists frequently long

18. In "The Politics of Intimacy," Wood writes that the "great antagonist" in Foote's theater is isolation. "To be fully satisfying, the characters' actions need to bring them into communion with their race or class, their place or religion, their loved ones. . . . With this connection, this sense of place, comes judgment and control, and the courage to be themselves and face death." Wood, "Politics of Intimacy," 50.

for the peaceful haven that the experience of family offers, except for the rosy-hued *Ah, Wilderness!,* this is an ideal gone a-glimmering. While it lures from the distance, like the promised kingdom of peace and harmony in Deborah Harford's tale of the banished prince, up close it proves to be unavailable, a mirage. Looking again at his final plays, the historical-autobiographical cycle, we see that Simon Harford cannot reconcile his wife and his mother; home becomes a battleground between the two women, competing for Simon's love. He at length is driven to despair, forced to choose one or the other—a dilemma only resolved when he falls and hits his head at the end of *More Stately Mansions* and, experiencing amnesia and regressing into his past, he calls Sara "Mother." In merging mother and wife, he is able to find peace at last, but at the cost of reality. The painful experience of family in *Long Day's Journey* hardly needs comment. It is perhaps no accident that the all-male family of boarders in *Iceman* and the two-man unit in *Hughie* strike us as more harmonious than O'Neill's other family units: with the exception of the three "tarts" in *Iceman,* who don't actually live in the hotel, there are no women to create discord.

Foote's women are presented much more sympathetically. While there are examples of self-absorbed and selfish women, like Horace's sister Lily Dale, weak ones, like his mother, and silly ones, like Mrs. Coons in *Lily Dale,* on the whole women in Foote's plays are seen as the source of goodness and strength. The example par excellence, of course, is Elizabeth, Horace's lodestar.[19] Her love transforms him, and their marriage becomes the source of his strength and happiness. This is perhaps nowhere more focused than in a speech Horace makes to Elizabeth in *Valentine's Day,* which in condensed form encapsulates the action of the entire *Cycle.* He has just told her a story about a wrenching episode from his childhood, when his mother, keeping a boardinghouse and having no food for the boarders, killed Horace's pet chickens to serve for Christmas dinner. He was so distraught that he became ill with a raging fever and nearly died. Speaking of his mother, he says, "She doesn't know the pain and the bitterness and the

19. The role of Elizabeth in the film versions of the *Cycle,* as well as the original stage productions, is played by Hallie Foote, the playwright's daughter, who bears a remarkable resemblance to her grandmother.

unhappiness she has caused me. Sometimes when I'm around her I have to walk out of the room to keep from telling her. I am no orphan, but I think of myself as an orphan, belonging to no one but you." He goes on to describe his newfound happiness and his dream of having a home of his own, where he will plant "growing things, fruitful things, fig trees, pecan trees, pear trees, peach trees" (*Three Plays* 103).

He has found his haven, Jung's green world, and it is located not in the past, but the present in his life with Elizabeth. "I do believe I might now have these things," he adds, "because you married me." He was afraid that Mr. Vaughn, a powerful man, would prevent their marriage, he says, "But he didn't stop us; you did marry me, and I tell you I've begun to know happiness for the first time in my life. I adore you. I worship you . . . and I thank you for marrying me" (*Three Plays* 83).[20] Family, rather than trapping Horace, liberates and sustains him. While examples of bad marriages abound in the *Cycle*—Foote is no sentimentalist—the trust, love, and mutual respect which ground Horace and Elizabeth's marriage sustain them through the hard times and enrich both their lives and the lives of those around them. Elsewhere in this play, Mr. Vaughn says of their one-room boardinghouse home, "There's peace in this room and contentment . . . They don't have much, but they're contented. You feel that" (*Three Plays* 103).

These differences in vision in the respective cycles of O'Neill and Foote are ultimately reflected in their dramatic structure. O'Neill's late plays, informed by a tragic sensibility, are shaped by a quest of some sort. In *More Stately Mansions,* for instance, Simon Harford's desire to write a book about the goodness of humanity is put aside as business success overtakes him and he thinks in terms of founding an empire. His son Ethan sets out to break the world record for a clipper ship voyage around Cape Horn to San Francisco. Con Melody tries desperately to maintain the aristocratic status into which he was born in the face of his present poverty. The American dream in O'Neill's cycle is defined in terms of conquest, mastery, wresting some trophy from the world. The scale of his action, accordingly, is immense; the

20. In an interview with Sheila Benson, Foote reveals that in writing that speech, he had in mind his situation with his wife, Lillian, who also had a powerful father who might have prevented their marriage. "That speech to Elizabeth was really for my wife," he says. Benson, "MM Interview," 57.

action in the completed cycle would have taken place in Rhode Island and San Francisco, New York, Paris, and Shanghai, encompassing the entire panoply of history for nearly two hundred years, including the American Revolution and the Napoleonic Wars.

Foote's canvas is much smaller, and his focus, inward. The farthest his characters get from Harrison is Houston, a few hours away. And while the *Cycle* as a whole can be regarded on one level as a quest, shaped by Horace's determination to belong to a family, as a genre the plays come closer to domestic drama. The focus is not on conquering the world or slaying dragons, large or small, but rather the living out of daily life, specifically in the context of relationships. The romance or quest archetype demands a larger-than-life hero. Odysseus and Aeneas and their counterparts do battle with the cosmos. At some point in their journeys, which range across time and space, they descend to the underworld, which is outside time as we know it, entering the forbidding realm of the nonhuman and emerging with a boon, some wisdom or crucial piece of information, that will enable them to found a new civilization (Aeneas) or restore order to chaos (Odysseus). The family drama is of a different order. The problems aren't "out there" in the world, but within the societal-familial context; they deal with interpersonal conflicts rather than human-divine ones. In an interview with Irv Broughton, Foote says simply, "I have enormous compassion for the human condition. A great admiration for what people have to put up with and endure—the way they survive or don't survive."[21] It is this mystery, why some survive and others don't, and a sense of wonder at the strength of the human will, that drives Foote's plays. If the works of O'Neill and Faulkner emerge from a sense of human limitation, Foote's plays are imbued with a sense of human potential. One way or another, some—not all—of Foote's characters will survive, defying all the odds. Our job as audience is simply to respect the enormity of the struggle.[22]

21. Broughton, *Writer's Mind*, 21.

22. It is interesting in this regard to compare the arc of the plots of Faulkner's family sagas with those of Foote's *Cycle*. In *The Bear* and *The Sound and the Fury*, for instance, we trace the dissolution of family in the lives of two young men: Ike repudiates his heritage, moving away from the McCaslin plantation and into a rented room in town, while Quentin, in despair over his familial history, commits suicide. *The Orphans' Home Cycle*, structured by the *creation* of family, tracks an opposite path: Horace's movement from orphan to husband and father.

Thus time and the past are embedded in the family rather than outside it. The goal is not to escape time or overcome it, but to live within its confines, learning from the past, embracing the present, and anticipating the future. Time in these plays is experienced as the unfolding of family history. It traces Horace's evolution from child and orphan to adult and husband/father. As we have seen, its dramatic presentation is fairly complex, encompassing both the linear paradigm of time with which we are most familiar, the individual life moving from childhood through adulthood to death, and a more arational understanding of time with the present containing the past and allowing for a kind of double vision, both on the part of the characters and, slightly differently, on the part of the audience. Like the Tralfamadorians in Kurt Vonnegut's *Slaughterhouse-Five*, who experience time like humans might see a stretch of the Rocky Mountains, taking in all of time at once, the *Cycle*'s structure allows us to see Horace's life as a whole—or at least twenty-six years of it, from childhood to adulthood. In both its manifestations, the function of time is a crucial component of these plays, and our understanding of it is essential to a full appreciation of Foote's artistry and vision.

7

AN ORPHANS' HOME

Family, Place, and Redemption

Foote's Academy Award–winning film *A Trip to Bountiful* opens with a beautiful shot of a mother running through a field of bluebonnets, chasing her young son, apparently in some sort of game. As the credits roll, she reaches him, catching him up in her arms in an exuberant embrace. In the background we hear a clear soprano voice singing the familiar Protestant hymn "Jesus Is Calling," with the haunting refrain "Come home, come home, ye who are weary, come home." This scene at first appears to have nothing to do with the action of the film, which takes place in a cramped apartment in Houston in the late 1940s. It's only after we reach the end of the film, which revolves around the elderly Carrie Watts's obsession with returning to her tiny hometown of Bountiful, Texas, that we understand that it reflects a memory of a happier time in Carrie's life, when she lived there with her son, Ludie. Carrie has to return to Bountiful in order to reconnect with her origins and her sense of herself as a valuable human being, something she has lost by living in Houston with Ludie and his self-absorbed wife, Jessie Mae. The theme of the movie as a whole is summed up in the repeated phrase which floats across the meadow of bluebonnets: "Come home." This is, indeed, a film about coming home. But what is the nature of home? In what does it consist and how does it function to bequeath or withhold integration and peace?

Just as it is a commonplace that Southern literature is concerned with the past and its impact upon the present, as discussed in the previous chapter, so too is it characterized by an awareness of place, of "home." More than any other body of regional American literature, it is indelibly stamped by its geographical moorings. It is impossible to think of the works of Faulkner or O'Connor, Williams or Wolfe, or any of the great Southern writers, for that matter, without visualizing their settings—whether Mississippi or Georgia, New Orleans or North Carolina. All are drenched with a sense of the local, a specific town or area or landscape which determines language, custom, and identity. Place is arguably such a trademark of Southern literature that when it is absent, it ceases to qualify as *Southern*. Flannery O'Connor's position on this matter is, I think, representative. In an address entitled "The Regional Writer," occasioned by receiving the Georgia Writers' Association Scroll for *The Violent Bear It Away,* O'Connor says, "I read some stories at one of the colleges not long ago—all by Southerners—but with the exception of one story, they might all have originated in some synthetic place that could have been anywhere or nowhere. These stories hadn't been influenced by the outside world at all, only by television. It was a grim view of the future." In "The Fiction Writer and His Country," she writes, "To know oneself is to know one's region."[1] For the Southerner, the two axes of identity are family and place.

Within the plantation tradition, of course, the two are so closely related as to be synonymous. In this tradition families occupy a piece of land for generation after generation, so that the name of the estate—Lionnet, Twelve Oaks—is sufficient to identify the family that lives there. More than just a backdrop, the site where one lives out one's life, the land itself is perceived as conferring identity and wholeness, even redemption. In *Gone with the Wind,* when all else fails, Scarlett O'Hara says reverently, "I'll go back to Tara," a refrain which becomes a leitmotif of the novel. As we watch the film version of this scene, with Scarlett digging down into the earth when she finally reaches the plantation, letting the soil sift through her fingers as the music swells in the background, the contribution of place to her sense

---

1. Flannery O'Connor, "The Regional Writer," in *Mystery and Manners,* ed. Sally and Robert Fitzgerald (New York: Farrar, Straus, and Giroux, 1957), 56; Flannery O'Connor, "The Fiction Writer and His Country," in *Mystery and Manners,* ed. Sally and Robert Fitzgerald (New York: Farrar, Straus, and Giroux, 1957), 35.

of wholeness is unmistakable. The land itself is seen as redemptive somehow, as if goodness and purification reside in the very soil.[2]

Although serious Southern literature tends to critique this and other elements of the plantation myth, the connection between place and identity cannot be ignored. In Faulkner's *Go Down, Moses,* for example, the destruction of the primeval forest is inextricably linked with the concept of the South's fall from grace. If there is an "original sin," it is the rape of the land as well as the rape of its people, black and red. The whine of the buzzsaw and the encroachment of railroad tracks into the pristine wilderness signal for Faulkner, as they did for James Fenimore Cooper a century earlier, the invasion of a civilization which, while necessary, will ultimately corrupt and destroy. Similarly, in *The Sound and the Fury,* the selling of Benjy's pasture so that Quentin can go to Harvard marks the beginning of the end of the Compson family. The novel, which traces the moral disintegration of the Compsons, tracks the gradual dissolution of the estate itself, from the selling of the pasture to Jason's breaking up the land into lots to parcel off to real estate developers. In the last analysis, the two processes are impossible to separate, as if the land and the family spring from the same matrix.

Another example of this phenomenon is Tennessee Williams's classic treatment of the legend of the Old South, *A Streetcar Named Desire.* Blanche DuBois, who arrives in New Orleans to stay with her sister Stella, cannot survive once the old plantation, Belle Reve, collapses. Without the cultural supports that the old way of life provided, she is only an aging spinster whose delicate beauty has faded; she has nothing to offer the world except her love of poetry and literature, a gift which a world "lit by lightning" (to quote *The Glass Menagerie*) no longer values.

Place also plays a critical role in the works of Horton Foote, as

2. As noted in Chapter 6, *Gone with the Wind* is perhaps the quintessential articulation of the Southern plantation myth. It took the entire country by storm when it was first published in 1936, selling one million copies in the first six months and six million copies by 1949. The premier of the film became a kind of ritualistic reassertion of the legend of the Old South, with people from the entire region making a pilgrimage to Atlanta for the event. See Thomas E. Porter, *Myth and Modern American Drama* (Detroit: Wayne State Press, 1969), 156.

critics inevitably mention in their response to his plays and screenplays. His terrain is that of Gulf Coast Texas, specifically his home
town Wharton, the source of his characters and themes. His comment to Samuel G. Freedman while home in Wharton is typical of his
attitude: "No matter how far away I've been—New York, London,
Hollywood—half of me is always thinking about Wharton, trying to
figure out some aspect of this life back here." An acute sensitivity to
place is so essential to his work that he insists on it in selecting directors for his films, which need special handling if they are to be successful in translating his unique vision to the screen. S. Dixon
McDowell points to this in his discussion of Foote's collaboration
with Bruce Beresford, the Australian director of *Tender Mercies.* Initially Foote had reservations about Beresford as a potential director,
since their backgrounds were so different. As Foote explained to Mc-
Dowell in a 1988 interview, when Beresford responded that he'd take
the job if he could get along with the writer, "he flew in, and we did
get along very well. I'm devoted to him. And I took him down to
Texas to look at the terrain. And he looked around, and he said, 'This
is just like Australia.' And felt immediate kinship with it."[3] It was essential that Beresford have a feel for the vast, empty plains of Texas
where the action takes place; without an appreciation for the land, as
McDowell explains, he couldn't fully grasp the story or the vision that
informs it. Their shared response to the land enabled writer and director to bridge what could have been an otherwise insurmountable
cultural barrier.

McDowell comments elsewhere in this article, "The fact that
Foote, even while living in the East, has written almost exclusively
about his hometown and its surroundings indicates the primacy of
setting in his work. The landscape and culture of rural southeast
Texas are not just the backdrops for his stories; in a way, they *are* his
stories." Again, he quotes Foote: "I go back South often, but I've
not consistently lived there . . . since I was seventeen or eighteen, and
yet I don't even question the fact that when I take up a piece of paper
and a pen or pencil I know that I have begun to think about the
South. . . . It isn't that I'm not fully aware of all the rich wonderful

3. Freedman, introduction to *Two Plays,* xix; S. Dixon McDowell, "Horton
Foote's Film Aesthetic," in *Foote: A Casebook,* 142.

life around me here in the East or all over America. I just don't think in those terms. I don't hear those voices.[4]

This vision marks Foote's work as quintessentially Southern. Indeed, in *The History of Southern Drama,* Watson remarks that "*The Orphans' Home Cycle* is the best and fullest recreation of the southern past by a recent dramatist."[5] But the meaning of place in his canon, specifically the concept of home and its relationship to family, sets Foote apart from other Southern writers in two important ways. First, Foote's emphasis is not so much on returning home or holding on to it as it is on leaving. Whether physically or psychologically, to achieve individuation and full personhood, characters in Foote's works must leave their family of origin and create a new family of their own. Secondly, home is not defined so much by a specific place or locale as it is by a network of relationships. Although there are exceptions, as we shall see, home, in his films and plays, for the most part means *people,* not a place. In this final chapter I would like to explore the concept of home from this perspective, first looking briefly at Foote's film *Tender Mercies* as a paradigm of this phenomenon, then examining the *Cycle* plays from this perspective, and finally considering a variation on this pattern in *The Trip to Bountiful.* The nature of home and family and their relationship to individual redemption lie at the heart of Foote's vision and provide a fitting conclusion to this study, which begins and ends with the concept of family.

Tender Mercies, Foote's acclaimed 1983 film starring Robert Duvall and Tess Harper, tells a story of degradation and redemption. It begins with a drunken binge of Mac Sledge, a has-been country western singer who has reached the nadir of his life. When he wakes up in a run-down motel in an isolated Texas town to discover that his buddy has deserted him, Mac finds himself with no job, no money, and no future. He offers to work off his bill and repay the damages done to the room by doing odd jobs for the proprietor, Rosa Lee, a single mother of a young boy, trying to make ends meet. The narrative revolves around the growing love of Mac for Rosa Lee and Sonny, her son, a love which ultimately redeems him. As the story unfolds, we learn that he had been a famous singer who wrote songs

4. McDowell, "Foote's Film Aesthetic," 146.
5. Watson, *History of Southern Drama,* 198.

for himself and his equally famous wife, Dixie, and that they had a daughter, now a troubled young woman. As Mac slowly begins to rebuild his life, putting in quiet days of mending broken furniture and helping Rosa Lee with her motel and gas station, he forms tentative relationships with both Rosa Lee and Sonny, taking his meals with them and gradually becoming a part of their lives. They eventually marry, and he even gets baptized in Rosa Lee's church. Meanwhile, equally tentatively, he begins to pick at his guitar in the evenings, teaching Sonny the rudiments and composing a few songs. His identity is discovered by a group of awestruck young men who are trying to break into the music world, and he and Rosa Lee frequent the local country western bar where they play, dancing to the music. Eventually Mac decides to take a new song he has written to Austin, where his ex-wife, Dixie Scott, is performing at the Grapevine Opera House, to see if she will buy it; he also gets drawn into a relationship with his daughter, who comes to visit him both before and after she runs away with a penniless musician in an act of rebellion against her overly controlling mother.

If this were a Hollywood movie, the story would end with Mac's being reinstated in the world of country music and playing a key part in turning around his daughter's life, but this is a Horton Foote film, and neither of those options occurs. Dixie's agent turns down Mac's song, telling him it's no good and sending him off on what looks to be his first binge since meeting Rosa Lee, and his daughter is killed in a tragic automobile accident. Mac isn't saved by an obvious, external circumstance like recovered fame or a reestablished career, but by his quiet, steady love for Rosa Lee and Sonny, with whom he builds a new family. Perhaps the film's most famous line occurs after he has returned from his daughter's wake, held in Dixie's ostentatious but empty house, as he and Rosa Lee are working in the garden. "I don't trust happiness," he says. "I never did, I never will."[6] Rosa Lee wisely says nothing, just listens. There are no happy endings, no simple solutions in this scheme of things. Nonetheless, he and Rosa Lee continue to till the soil, a gesture of faith and hope. The final scene, wordless except for a voice-over song, shows Mac and Sonny throw-

---

6. Horton Foote, *Three Screenplays: "The Trip to Bountiful," "Tender Mercies," and "To Kill a Mockingbird"* (New York: Grove Weidenfeld, 1989), 145.

ing a football back and forth as the camera pans out to reveal the vast sky and empty landscape behind their small home.[7]

That landscape is an inescapable presence throughout *Tender Mercies*. It would not be the same film—indeed, it is unimaginable—if set in New York or San Francisco. The loneliness and ruggedness of the terrain both reflect and shape the experience of those who live there; one thinks of McDowell's comment that in some sense the setting *is* the story. Yet what redeems Mac Sledge in the end is not his experience with the land per se, but his formation of a family with Rosa Lee and Sonny. This is his real homecoming. As he learns to trust, even in the face of life's arbitrary cruelties and injustices, he discovers within himself the potential to love. The conversion is interior, as it always is with Foote, and it takes place within the context of committed relationships and the creation of a family.

The creation of a family, of course, provides the spine for Foote's nine-play cycle. "All the world's an orphans' home," the epigraph states at the outset. We are all orphans, alienated and alone, desiring connection with the cosmos and one another but finding none. To the extent that we accept Horace Robedaux's experience as representative, *Roots in a Parched Ground,* the first play, establishes the human condition as one of orphanhood. If the ground is "parched," how is a young child to be nourished? How will he learn to love if there is a dearth of love around him? *Roots* can be seen as stating the problem which the rest of the *Cycle* will resolve. At its conclusion, Horace is left alone. His family has dissolved overnight, and there is as yet not another one to take its place.

With the next play, *Convicts,* we watch Horace begin life on his own. This play provides a particularly helpful illustration of the ways in which Foote's concept of the family and place differs from that of other Southern writers, since it is set against the backdrop of the traditional plantation milieu. The action takes place in Floyd's Lane in Coastal Texas on Soll Gautier's four-thousand-acre sugar cane plantation. Given Foote's minimal stage directions, we have no physical description of the estate or the mansion itself, which is simply referred

7. Setting this scene in the garden, which Mac and Rosa Lee tend together, links it with the scene earlier in the film when he proposes to her, which also takes place in the garden. Foote's use of symbolism is subtle, but powerful.

to as the "big house." But the social dynamics replicate those of ante-bellum plantations, except that the plantation is worked not by slaves but by black convicts. Soll is the undisputed master of the plantation, which is run by his overseer, Jackson; he is attended by two servants, Ben and Martha, who run the plantation store and see to his personal needs. All pretense of gracious living has long disappeared, however. Foote employs the plantation milieu ironically to bring into focus the moral poverty of a system whose existence depended upon the subjugation of an entire race.

In the idealized version of the plantation myth, the land is lush and fertile, producing an abundance of crops, as well as lush, flower-lined lawns which spill over in profusion from the house to the fields. The fecundity of nature is brought under control by the careful management of the master, who is not only competent and wise, a shrewd businessman-farmer, but benevolent, civilized, and cultivated. The fertility of the land is reflected in the fertility of the family: a gracious and accomplished wife, beautiful daughters, and gallant sons. This harmonious picture is completed by a group of happy, well-cared-for slaves, regarded as an extension of the family. The family's connection with the land goes back several generations, with each new generation taking up the responsibility for tending it wisely and passing it along to the next.

The portrait presented in *Convicts* presents a sharp contrast to this ideal. In the first instance, the lushness of the land has become a threat rather than a boon. There are repeated references, for example, to the fact that the cane, if left to itself, would take over the land. In the final scene, as they are burying Soll, Ben says of Soll's father's tombstone, "If the convicts didn't keep it weeded over there, you wouldn't be able to find it for the brush in a week" (*Four Plays* 162). He goes on, speaking of Asa's plans for the plantation, "She's gonna let the weeds and trees and the cane get this land. . . . 'Cane land' they called it once, cane land it will be again" (*Four Plays* 162–63).

In the figure of Soll Gautier, the master, we have a parody of the judicious, careful manager of the land. His erratic behavior and drunken ramblings establish an atmosphere of violent unpredictability. When he is out "hunting" with Horace, for instance, he shoots at random at what he believes to be convicts. "I'm gonna kill all them convicts," he says, handing the gun to Horace and telling him,

"Shoot you a convict" (*Four Plays* 128). The black convicts, who are treated with total disregard for their well-being, are kept from rebelling only by the remorseless cruelty of Soll's overseers, whom he selects on the basis of their toughness: the meaner they are, the more he likes them. Typically, when Sherman Edwards, one of the convicts, says that he is too sick to work, Soll insists that he work anyway; when he dies, Soll shows no remorse. Finally, the image of the happy family linked to and reflecting the fecundity of the land contrasts with that of the aging Soll, unmarried and alone, forcing young Horace, an employee whose name he has trouble remembering, to stay with him as he dies.

Against this backdrop we observe Horace form relationships and even a surrogate family by virtue of his kindness and sensitivity to the needs of others. The fact that he is alone, abandoned by his family, is established in the opening moments of the play, as Billy Vaughn says to Martha, "My God, I don't know what Horace's people are thinking of, letting him work out here in this Godforsaken place." When his wife, Asa, asks him what difference it makes, he replies, "It sickens me to see a boy abandoned this way" (*Four Plays* 94–95). Martha informs Billy, who inquires where Horace lives, that he didn't like it up at the "big house" with Mr. Soll, and instead sleeps on the floor of the plantation store, adding that when it's cold, she and Ben sleep there, too, to keep warm by the fire. The portrait is a fairly desperate one: a young boy, deserted by his family, without a home or a place to call his own. Yet when Horace appears, he seems anything but desperate. Committed to his goal of raising money to buy a tombstone for his father, a theme which is established in his first exchange with Martha and soon reiterated to the chained convict Leroy, he is unsentimental about spending Christmas with his extended family in Harrison, vowing instead to stay on the plantation until Mr. Soll pays him the salary he's owed. They don't care what he does, he tells Martha, and when she protests, he says simply, "No they don't. My daddy cared about me, but he's dead" (*Four Plays* 97). There is no self-pity in this statement, only an acknowledgment of his situation.

What is perhaps even more remarkable is that given this lack of familial love and nurturance, Horace is open to relationships with others. This is dramatized early in the play, as Ben asks Horace to stand guard over a convict who has murdered a fellow convict. Horace asks Ben if he can talk to the convict, and typically, strikes up a conversation, offering him a chew of tobacco. He asks the convict his name, and when he says "Leroy," Horace asks, "Leroy what?" When he learns that it's "Kendricks," he inquires about his kin, saying, "There are a lot of Kendricks [*sic*] out around Kendelton" (*Four Plays* 100). This is distinguished from idle talk both by the fact that Horace, a white boy, should be interested in Leroy's background (it's significant that no one else even asks his name, as we noted in Chapter 5) and that he begins by establishing his family origins. Horace, who knows no racial barriers, observes the same social conventions with Leroy that he would with one of his peers. As the conversation continues, they trade stories in a free and open manner, the boy and the murderer-convict: about their families, about the murder, about Leroy's past and Horace's running away once. Gradually and quietly, parallels between their lives begin to emerge. Horace, abandoned by his family, asks where Leroy's family is, to which he replies, "I don't know now. Used to be around New Iberia, Louisiana, last I heard" (*Four Plays* 102). In a few short lines, Foote limns the poignancy of Leroy's situation: his family doesn't know where he is and he can't reach them, since as he tells Horace, "I can't write and they can't read." With far graver consequences than Horace's, he is alone in the world. When he asks why Horace isn't with his mother and Horace explains the situation, Leroy says that he ran away from his home, to which Horace replies, "I ran away too, once. Did I tell you that? . . . I could run forever now and nobody would even know I was gone" (*Four Plays* 105).

The conversation then turns to running away, something Leroy is clearly considering, and as they speak hypothetically ("If you were running away from here, which way would you go?" Leroy asks), Horace provides him with information and advice, telling him to stay away from the river if he can't swim because of the alligators and suckholes. In just a few short minutes, Horace has been able to transcend the barriers of race, class, age, and situation and establish a connection based on simple, human need. He asks Leroy if he's afraid of dying, and then in the same spirit of kinship that he extends to Leroy, gets up to say a prayer over the grave of the convict Leroy has just killed. Horace's compassion and kindness are set off in stark contrast to the behavior of the sheriff, who enters at this point and says to

Leroy brusquely, "Are you the one?" When the convict, lying on the ground, doesn't respond, the sheriff kicks him and says, "Answer me when I speak to you," kicking him again, at which point Horace quietly leaves. A few minutes later, the sheriff comes into the store, saying offhandedly to Ben, "You won't have to go no place now, Ben. . . . he tried to overpower me and I kilt him. I missed him with the first shot, he was fighting so. It took three shots to kill him. I left him out on the road. You'll have to bury him." Then turning to Horace, he gives him an orange and a sack of hard candy from his Uncle Albert in town, and says, "Merry Christmas" (*Four Plays* 111).

Unlike the sheriff, who sees only a black convict, Horace sees an individual. This is illustrated once again in a conversation about another convict who is too sick to work. "Which one is it?" Horace asks the overseer, Jackson.

> JACKSON: The brother to the one that got killed.
> HORACE: Sherman Edwards. His daddy is a white man.
> MARTHA: How do you know that?
> HORACE: Leroy told me.
> MARTHA: Who is Leroy?
> HORACE: He is the convict that killed Jessie Wilkes.
> MARTHA: Who is Jessie Wilkes?
> HORACE: He's the brother of Sherman Edwards, whose father is white.
> (*Four Plays* 117)

This small, almost comic bit, though amusing on one level, demonstrates Horace's tendency to think in terms of human beings, not categories.

Horace's sensitivity is also evident in his close relationships with Ben and Martha, who function as a surrogate family for him. Martha clearly feels protective toward Horace and defends him against Mr. Soll's capricious demands. When Soll wants to send Horace out in the fields with a message to the overseer, Martha tells him to send Ben or Jackson instead rather than exposing Horace to the convicts. When Soll reneges on his promise to pay Horace's back salary, she takes his part, saying, "I'm disgusted. This poor boy is out here working to get a tombstone for his daddy's grave. And he's been here six months and you ain't paid him nothin' yet" (*Four Plays* 110). She realizes that it would upset Horace to see Leroy's body, and says to him, "You'd better go into the store if you don't want to see the convict. They are going to have to bring him by here" (*Four Plays* 114); Horace quietly does so.

These examples illustrate both Horace's desire for human contact and his considerable sensitivity and gentleness, to which people instinctively respond. Like Faulkner's Lena Grove in *Light in August*, he seems to create small families wherever he goes. We are not surprised when even Mr. Soll senses Horace's goodness and keeps him at his side through what will become his final night.

This sets the stage for the remaining plays of the *Cycle*, where Horace, now older, sets about creating a family for himself. Two points here. First, consideration of the role of place in *Convicts* reveals that for Foote, unlike many other Southern writers, though place and community clearly play a pivotal role in shaping identity, land itself— that is, a particular piece of land—is not ultimately what matters. In fact, *Convicts*, like *A Trip to Bountiful*, illustrates that the nature of the land itself shifts and changes. Left to itself, the cane will take over the land: "Cane land it will be again," Ben says. Carrie Watts returns to Bountiful, only to discover that the town has disappeared. What is essential transcends whatever territory human beings have carved out of the land, as Carrie explains to Ludie:

> MRS. WATTS: Pretty soon, all this will be gone. Twenty years, ten, this house, me, you . . .
> LUDIE: I know, Mama.
> MRS. WATTS: But the river will still be here. The fields, the trees, and the smell of the Gulf. I always got my strength from that. Not from houses, not from people.[8]

It is not the land itself that matters, but one's relationship to the land, internalized and integrated into one's sensibility and consciousness.

When Carrie says she does not get her strength "from people," she's referring to the townsfolk with whom she grew up. Ludie, her son, is at the center of her life. It is crucial to her (and, as we will see, to *him*) that she share this homecoming experience with him. Even

8. Foote, *Three Screenplays*, 213.

getting along with the difficult Jessie Mae, because she is Ludie's wife, is critical to Carrie. For Horace, too, family is everything. But "family" is not necessarily defined by biology, which is my second point. His only blood relative on the plantation, Uncle Albert, is less emotionally nurturing to him than Martha and Ben are. Though Billy Vaughn talks of adopting Horace, he, too, is disqualified as surrogate father by his lack of sustained commitment. In Foote's world, family is not so much about *coming* home as it is about *creating* a home, and that invariably means leaving one's family of origin, whether physically or psychologically. This play dramatizes a stage in Horace's life when, having left the security of his childhood days behind, he ventures out into the world. His defining mission, buying a tombstone for his father's grave, looks both backwards and forwards. He will honor his father's memory and preserve in as permanent a fashion as he can—names and dates carved on stone—the facts of his parentage, but to do so he must strike out on his own, entering uncharted territory.

Lily Dale, the following play, tells the story of Horace's last effort to be reincorporated into his family of origin, as Chapter 2 details. Now twenty, Horace travels to Houston to visit his mother and sister and look for a job or a business course, hoping to make a life there that will allow him to be a part of Corella's world. Foote's decision to begin and end this play with the train scenes with Mrs. Coons, first going to, then returning from, Houston, demonstrates once again Horace's instinctive ability to forge sustaining relationships— "families," if you will. In the final scene, rejected by his mother and sister, who for various reasons are not able or willing to make a place for him in their lives, Horace reaches out to Mrs. Coons, who recognizes him from the train ride three weeks earlier. After she unburdens herself to him (her husband has relapsed into alcoholism: "Mr. Coons got sick again," she says), she notices that he is not well, expressing concern and asking if he found out whether he was baptized. When Horace asks her to pray for him and Corella and Lily Dale in the closing lines of the play, we recognize both his generosity of spirit in forgiving his mother and sister and his ability to respond to warmth and affection, even from a relative stranger. Like Ben and Martha in *Convicts*, Mrs. Coons ministers to Horace, forging a bond based on simple human need. *The Widow Claire* takes the story one step further, revealing Horace at a critical fork in the road on his journey toward establishing a family, this time tracing a path not taken, in contrast with *Courtship,* which sets the stage for his marriage to Elizabeth.

The overarching action of these nine plays, then, is Horace's movement from orphan to husband and father, his establishment of a family of his own. Though place in the form of community is clearly a key factor in the formation of identity, as we have seen, land does not function in the same way here that Tara does in *Gone with the Wind* or Belle Reve in *Streetcar Named Desire* or the McCaslin estate in *The Bear.* The land-family nexus associated with the plantation way of life and the values with which it is associated do not inform these plays. In fact, one of the primary functions of *Convicts* is to critique the plantation myth, putting in perspective the cost in human life of maintaining it. It is no accident that the title of this play does not refer to Horace or even Mr. Soll, but to the convicts on whose sweat and blood the plantation is built.

What is redemptive, ultimately, is the formation of a family, which entails the leaving of home and then returning again, re-creating, redefining for oneself those relationships which will anchor life experience. This is something that Lily Dale, who moves from her sheltered existence within the Corella-Pete constellation to her marriage to Will Kidder, never experiences. For whatever reasons—and they are ultimately mysterious, as we see so consistently in Foote's canon—Lily Dale does not have the courage or the will to confront the facts of her life with honesty. She prefers to simply close off painful or frightening memories of her childhood, denying any connection with her father and identifying herself as pure "Thornton," thus foreclosing the growth that only comes through pain. Her marriage to Will, while it might seem like the formation of a new family, is really the continuation of her childhood state. It's revealing that she says to Corella, for instance, when discussing her pending marriage, "I'm never going to leave you, and you are never going to leave me." When Corella points out that Lily Dale will have to leave when she gets married, she asks why she and Will can't just move in with Corella and Pete. When Corella responds that wouldn't be practical, Lily Dale says, "Anyway, we'll get a house next door and if we can't do that, as close as we can" (*Four Plays* 247). As we learn in *Cousins,* Lily

Dale's unhealthy dependence on her mother does indeed continue throughout her marriage. Given her history of avoiding pain at all costs, we are not surprised when in *A Young Man from Atlanta,* she can't come to grips with the homosexuality and suicide of her only son.[9]

A variation on this theme seems to occur in *A Trip to Bountiful,* where Carrie Watts explicitly states that she draws her strength from the land, the trees, the smell of the Gulf. This play, as we noted earlier, is about coming home and what that means. There is no question that for Carrie Watts, the physical act of returning to Bountiful, the home of her youth, has taken on immense significance. When she is apprehended by the sheriff at the bus station in Harrison, just twelve miles from her home, and it appears that all her efforts have come to nought, she pleads, "Let me go those twelve miles . . . before it's too late. Understand me. Suffering I don't mind. Suffering I understand. I didn't protest once! Even though my heart was broken when those babies died. But these fifteen years of bickering, of endless, petty bickering. It's made me like Jessie Mae sees me. It's ugly. I will not be that way. I want to go home. I want to go home."[10] Carrie believes that returning to Bountiful will in some mysterious way be redemptive, restoring to her a sense of integrity and wholeness, and she's right. It is not the land itself that saves, however, but the land as it embodies memories from her past. This is revealed in a story she tells to Thelma, the young woman she meets on the bus, about Ray John Murray, the only man she ever loved, whom her father forbade her to marry.[11] Even after her own husband died and she had to move back in with her parents and Ray John married another woman, she says, "I used to sit on the front gallery every morn-

9. Laura Lee in *Night Seasons* is another example of a character who never finds the courage to leave home. See Horton Foote, *Four New Plays* (Newbury, Vt.: Smith and Kraus, 1993).

10. Foote, *Three Screenplays,* 203.

11. Carrie Watts's relationship with Thelma on the bus recalls that of Horace and Mrs. Coons in *Lily Dale.* By the time they part, they have formed a mini-family, however briefly. She says to Thelma before she leaves, "If my daughter had lived, I would have wanted her to be just like you" (ibid., 196). Like Horace, Carrie draws people to her—the sheriff and even the ticket agent in Harrison, to cite two more examples.

ing and every evening just to nod hello . . . as he went by the house to work at the store." She adds, "I don't think about those things now. But they're all part of Bountiful."[12]

As she sits on her front porch at last, listening to the birds singing, she recalls that her father wouldn't let any hunters shoot birds on their property. "I think the birds knew they couldn't be touched here," she says to the sheriff; "ours was always home to them." It is a small detail, perhaps, but one that conveys the sense of security she associates with this house, where her father was born before her, where she grew up and later returned to raise her own son. "You know it's funny," she says, "but ever since we've got here I just . . . I have half the feeling that my father and my mother would come out of this house, greet me, and welcome me home."[13]

Her need to return home before she dies, to reconnect with her past, contrasts dramatically with Ludie's determination to forget his former life. When he arrives to pick his mother up and take her back to Houston, he apologizes for not bringing her here himself, adding, "I just thought it would be easier if we never see [*sic*] the house again." It was in this same spirit that in the play's opening scene, he denies remembering the night years ago when Carrie woke him and dressed him and took him outside to look at the full moon. But as he sits on the porch with his mother, reflecting on his life and its disappointments—the fact that he hasn't had any children, for instance, or that he hasn't been able to provide for his wife and his mother as he'd hoped, he says, "Mama, I lied to you. I do remember, I remember so much. This house with the life here. The night you woke me up and dressed me and took me for a walk when the moon was full, and I cried because I was scared and you comforted me. Mama, I want to stop remembering. It doesn't do any good remembering."[14]

But, in fact, remembering can be restorative, as it is with Carrie, if one uses it to gather strength and return, renewed, to the present. As she reflects on the fact that the fields once planted with cotton are all woods now and that this cycle will probably be repeated years after they're gone, Carrie says, "We're part of all that. We left it, but we

12. Ibid., 188.
13. Ibid., 207–208.
14. Ibid., 210, 212.

can never lose what it's given us."[15] It is this internalization of the land and the values it represents, her individual and familial history, that allows her to tolerate Jessie Mae in the play's closing scene, acquiescing graciously to Jessie's list of "rules" and even spontaneously kissing her on the cheek. In returning to her past and re-experiencing via memory the sense of her own value, she is able to re-enter the present affirmed in her goodness. She is "herself" again, the self that has eroded over the past fifteen years of living in a two-room Houston apartment with a daughter-in-law who resents her. Though a ghost town physically, the spirit of Bountiful resides within Carrie and will sustain her until her death. When she says to the sheriff, standing on her porch at last, "I'm home. I'm home," we understand that home to Carrie is a state of mind and heart, not a physical location. A mingling of place and family, land and the people who live there, it is essential for wholeness, but it does not come without pain. In order to reap the rich bounty it holds forth, one must leave it, literally or figuratively, and come back again.

This movement of leaving and returning, the fundamental pattern which underlies not just *The Orphans' Home Cycle* but all of Foote's plays in one way or another, traces the path of the death-resurrection archetype which Jung, Frye, and Eliade, among others, have shown to be an ordering principle in all human experience. Redemption in Foote's drama comes only through the pain of leaving home, whatever form that takes, of confronting one's sense of loss and moving forward into the future, making new connections, finding new sources of meaning. It is, as we have noted from the outset, a mysterious process, one that defies precise explanation or empirical evidence.

Flannery O'Connor (whom Foote deeply admires) articulates the nature of this mystery and its relationship to writing as well as anyone. In "The Regional Writer," speaking of the truth writers aspire to, she says, "It lies very deep. In its entirety, it is known only to God, but of those who look for it, none gets so close as the artist." Later in that same article, she quotes Walker Percy's famous answer to a reporter's question about why there are so many good Southern writers: "Because we lost the War." O'Connor goes on to explain that Percy did not mean that the Civil War provided good subject matter, but that

15. Ibid., 213.

the South had experienced its own fall from innocence. "We have gone into the modern world with an inburnt knowledge of human limitations and with a sense of mystery which could not have developed in our first state of innocence," she writes, "as it has not sufficiently developed in the rest of our country." It is this sense of mystery, an awareness of the dimension of life that lies beyond rationality and cause and effect and all the other explanations we devise to account for the vagaries of fate, that informs the deepest and truest writing. "The writer operates at a peculiar crossroads where time and place and eternity somehow meet," O'Connor concludes. "His problem is to find that location."[16]

For Foote, that crossroads is located squarely in Harrison, Texas, the fictive terrain that he has mapped out and continues to explore with endless fascination, presenting us with real people dealing with the everyday-ness of life, simultaneously in time and in eternity.[17] In his perceptive analysis of Foote's themes and style, Gerald Wood refers to this blending of the mundane and the mysterious as "mythic realism." In explaining that artists working in the realistic tradition must both remain faithful to the minutiae of everyday experience and transcend the particularity and specificity that that entails, he points, also drawing on O'Connor, to the power of myths "held sacred by the whole community" to bridge that gap: "Mythic realism asserts the power of stories, when held sacred by their culture, to give order and meaning to human experience. In times of faith, literature bridges between the profane and the sacred, sanctifying life and offering models of morality and courage. When, as in the modern age, faith recedes and the material world feels disconnected from the purpose and contentment of a spiritual one, the reiteration of myth becomes a

16. O'Connor, "The Regional Writer," 58, 59.

17. It is worth noting that Foote's family has lived in Wharton (a.k.a. Harrison) for seven generations, which goes far toward explaining his linking of family and place. In a recent interview with *Fort Worth Star-Telegram*'s Jeff Guinn, Foote, who lives part of the year in New York and part in Wharton in the house where he grew up, said, "In New York, people act a little different towards me, very respectful. Here, they treat me just like someone they grew up with. Not that too many people I really grew up with are still present, but there's still the sense of just being home I don't have anywhere else." Jeff Guinn, "The Return to Wharton," *Fort Worth Star-Telegram*, June 27, 1999, p. G1.

source of imaginative healing."[18] Wood goes on to explain that when practiced in the contexts of the Judeo-Christian tradition, which Southern writing often is, the operative myth is one of the fall from grace, tracing this theme as it plays out in the work of Faulkner, Porter, and O'Connor. For Foote, Wood argues, unlike his fellow Southerners, the emphasis is not so much on the loss of grace but on its recovery, not from leaving home, though that is essential, but on finding new ways to return: "In Foote's plays the leave-taking . . . is eventually followed by a need to compromise one's autonomy for an equally archetypal reconnection. Going away for identity in Foote's mental theater is followed—in the best, most healthy scenario—by various roads to humankind's many homes,"[19] whether that be in creating a family (Horace in *The Orphans' Home*), community and religious tradition (Rose Lee in *Tender Mercies*), work (Will Kidder at the end of *Young Man from Atlanta*), or the land (Carrie Watts in *Bountiful*). What Wood refers to as "the divine cycle of going away and coming home" and I call the death-resurrection archetype leads to healing and to peace.[20]

Place, then, in the works of Horton Foote, takes many forms. Squarely in the Southern tradition, it is a bedrock value that shapes the world of all his characters, but it is not necessarily associated with a specific geographical location. Generally some combination of place and people, it will always involve the concept of committed relationships, of "family," broadly construed. We have traced this archetype of leaving and coming home in the life of Horace Robedaux, from his simple statement to his friends at the end of *Roots*, "I'm on my own," through his painful experiences in *Convicts*, his rejection by Corella and Lily Dale in the third play, and his saying good-bye to the Widow Claire, knowing he is not yet ready to assume the responsibilities of family. In all of these instances, Foote carefully selects stages of Horace's life to illustrate his willingness both to endure loneliness and accept the kindnesses of others—Ben and Martha and Leroy, Mrs. Coons, even Claire. Thus when he meets Elizabeth, he

18. O'Connor, *Mystery and Manners,* 202; Wood, "Old Beginnings," 364.

19. Wood, "Old Beginnings," 366.

20. Wood also treats this matter in Chapter 5 of his book *Horton Foote and the Theater of Intimacy.* See especially pp. 60–63.

is ready and able to say yes to their relationship, as she is to the love that he offers.

That, too, is a remarkable thing. That Elizabeth, in the face of her parents' disapproval and the alarming examples of Syd Joplin and Sybil Thomas, finds the courage to say quietly to her sister, at the end of *Courtship*, that she will marry Horace Robedaux, "if he asks me," is another of Foote's small miracles, as is her ability to open her heart to her new son in the midst of her deep pain at losing baby Jenny. It is the subject of all Foote's plays, as he himself has said many times: the mysterious, ultimately inexplicable courage and goodness of ordinary people living quiet, undramatic lives. Burkhart puts it well: "Foote," she says, "like Horace when he thinks of Elizabeth, is in awe before the mystery of human goodness."[21]

Not everyone, of course, rises to this level. The examples of Horace and Elizabeth are brought into sharp focus by the contrasting stories of their siblings, Lily Dale and Brother, both of whom are unwilling to face pain or accept adult responsibility. Unwilling to leave home, physically or psychologically, they remain children, dependent on others to take care of them and clean up their messes. This lack of courage leads to lives that are superficial and empty, at best (Lily Dale), and destructive, at worst (Brother). As we watch the trajectory of Brother's life, we see him progress from relatively harmless, adolescent rebelliousness, like flunking out of college, to more serious situations, like getting a girl pregnant and paying for her abortion, typical of his pattern of buying his way out of trouble. Thus in the final play, when Mrs. Vaughn turns over her dead husband's estate to Brother to manage, we know as surely as Elizabeth and Horace do that he's headed for disaster. Indeed, the final outcome of that play is far more destructive than even his dissipation of the family savings, built over the years by Henry Vaughn's careful and compassionate stewardship: he kills a man in a barroom brawl. Brother's life provides a stark contrast to that of Horace and Elizabeth. Unable or unwilling to separate from his family, preferring to fall back on the forgiveness and financial resources of his parents rather than face the consequences of his actions, he squanders the possibilities that life holds out to him. It is no accident that he ends up, symbolically, as

21. Burkhart, "Horton Foote's Many Roads Home," 113.

an orphan, "wandering around the world," as he puts it. In the closing scene of *The Death of Papa,* the *Cycle*'s final moments, he says to Horace, who used to be an orphan, "Now you have a home and I don't. I expect someday you'll even be living in my home while I'm wandering around the world" (*Two Plays* 194). It is an instructive contrast, and Horace's answer, though simple, contains all the wisdom of his life. "No, I won't," Horace says. "This is my home." Because he has been willing to leave home, to walk through his pain and see himself and others as they are, Horace has been able to create a new home, a new family.

In the concluding lines of her fine article "Horton Foote's Many Roads Home," Marian Burkhart speaks to the point I am making here. It is a passage worth quoting at some length. "How did Horace," she asks,

> who suffered more and received less than any other of the Cycle's principal characters, find his way to compassion, to joy, to generosity? Why is he scrupulously honest when in his need as a child he was cheated and cheated again?
>
> To these questions there is no answer. He just is, as Elizabeth just knew and just chose. Their goodness, their wisdom, remain a mystery. We can answer, of course, the grace of God, but if we have any understanding at all of what those words mean, we ought to realize that they merely restate the mystery theologically. We ought to realize, too, the magnitude of Horton Foote's achievement. In choosing to praise such gentle heroes, to give them the fame that is their due, Foote has assessed American character, American myth, and the American ambience more accurately than has just about any other figure in the American theater.[22]

These are, indeed, "gentle heroes." Their stories are about leaving home and returning again, about forming families, about redemption. Place, at the heart of this mixture, is ultimately redemptive only insofar as it is defined not in terms of a specific location but a geography of the heart.

In understanding this, in articulating in his plays and films the deeply felt need of anchoring individual experience in a network of

22. Ibid., 114–15.

committed relationships, Foote speaks powerfully to a culture buffeted by the seas of change and impermanence and bewildered by the loss of metamyths to serve as guides. His stories of redemption tap into the "mythic dimensions" O'Connor speaks about, "a story . . . which belongs to everybody, one in which everybody is able to recognize the hand of God and its descent." This, I think, will ultimately secure Foote's place in the canon of American literature, along with Faulkner and O'Neill, O'Connor and Williams. And at the center of his dramatic achievement will be these nine plays of loss and redemption, of orphans coming home. Reynolds Price acknowledges this when he says in his introduction to the *Cycle*'s second volume, "When all three volumes of the series have appeared, and *The Orphans' Home* can then be seen whole and entire, I'm confident it will take its rightful earned place near the center of our largest American dramatic achievements."[23]

I agree with both Burkhart and Price. As time passes, Foote's films and plays will continue to unfold wisdom and goodness and wonder to audiences seeking to understand their experience as individuals and as Americans. For Foote's voice is that not just of the South, but of America at large. In the tradition of American writers before him, he explores the relationship of the one and the many, the contradictions of self-reliance and mutual dependency, but with a twentieth-century understanding of alienation and loss of faith, of uncertainty and despair. Yet he does not leave us there. Willing to embrace the possibility of mystery, without attempting to fully account for their strength in adversity, Foote creates characters who manage somehow to endure. In tracking the lives of these gentle heroes, portrayed with such honesty and grace, we return to our own lives strengthened and renewed. It is his gift to us, and his legacy to the future.

23. O'Connor, *Mystery and Manners,* 202; Price, introduction to *Three Plays,* xiii.

APPENDIX

Table of Settings and Characters in *The Orphans' Home Cycle*

Play	Time	Place	Horace's age	Characters/ Families	Plot summary
Roots in a Parched Ground	1902–1903	Harrison, Texas	12	Thorntons and Robedauxs	Horace's father, Paul Horace, dies; his mother, Corella, remarries and moves to Houston with her new husband, Pete Davenport, and Horace's sister, LilyDale, leaving him behind.
Convicts	1904	Gautier Plantation, Floyd's Lane, Texas	14	Soll Gautier, Asa and Billy Vaughn, black servants and convicts, and Horace	Horace lives with his Uncle Albert (Thornton) on the isolated Gautier plantation, worked by black convicts who are treated like slaves. Hoping to earn money to buy a tombstone for his father's grave, he witnesses violence toward the convicts and the death of the besotted, racist plantation owner, Soll Gautier.
Lily Dale	1910	Railroad car and Houston, Texas	20	Corella, Lily Dale, Pete Davenport, and Horace	Horace travels to Houston in an unsuccessful attempt to become a part of his mother and stepfather's family. The play begins and ends on the train and in conversations with a Mrs. Coons.
The Widow Claire	1912	Harrison, Texas	22	Claire, her suitors and chidren, Horace's friends, and Horace	Horace courts the widow Claire, who at twenty-eight has two children, ages nine and ten. Despite their obvious mutual attraction, by the play's end, Claire has decided to marry Ned, a safe but older traveling salesman, and Horace will go to Houston to take a business course.
Courtship	1915	Harrison, Texas	25	The Vaughns (Horace's future wife and in-laws), Horace	Horace courts Elizabeth under her father's watchful and disapproving eye. By the play's end, Elizabeth has decided to marry Horace if he asks her.

Valentine's Day	1917	Harrison, Texas	Horace and Elizabeth, the Vaughns, and townspeople	Horace and Elizabeth have been married ten months, and Elizabeth is five months pregnant. The play recounts the reconciliation of Horace and Elizabeth with the Vaughns, who opposed their marriage, and tells the tragic stories of various townspeople, climaxing with the suicide of George Tyler, a friend of Horace's father. The play ends with Horace and Elizabeth planning their new home, a gift from the Vaughns, and awaiting the birth of their first child.
1918	1918	Harrison, Texas	Horace and Elizabeth, the Vaughns	In the midst of World War I and his looming induction into the army, Horace succumbs to the flu epidemic sweeping through Harrison. Horace lives and the war ends, but he and Elizabeth lose their infant daughter, Jenny, to the flu. At the play's bittersweet conclusion, Elizabeth has given birth to a son.
Cousins	1925	Houston and Harrison, Texas	Horace and Elizabeth, Corella and Pete, Lily Dale and Will, cousins	This play revisits characters and issues introduced in *Roots* and *Lily Dale*, as we see Horace at middle age, struggling to support his family as the proprietor of a dry goods store. A serious operation on his mother, Corella, brings Horace and Elizabeth to Houston, where they meet Lily Dale and her wealthy husband, Will; Horace's stepfather, Pete; and his cousins Monty and Lola. Back in Horace's store in Houston we encounter more cousins, including Cousin Gordon, Cousin Lewis, and Cousin Minnie. Minnie is still bitter about what she sees as Corella's treatment of Paul Horace and Horace himself. These stories provide the subtext of the play while linking Horace the "orphan" in almost comic fashion to a seemingly endless chain of family relationships.

Play	Time	Place	Horace's age	Characters/ Families	Plot summary
The Death of Papa	1928	Harrison, Texas	38	Horace and Elizabeth, Mrs. Vaughn and Brother, Corella, Horace, Jr., and Gertrude	The sudden death of Elizabeth's father, the "papa" of the title, causes shifts and realignments within the family and the town. Elizabeth's ne'er-do-well brother, Brother, in trying to modernize by turning from cotton to pecans and cattle, squanders his father's fortune with drink and bad decisions and ends up exiled for killing a man in a barroom brawl. Horace reluctantly moves toward the role of family patriarch, though he stubbornly refuses help from his wealthy mother-in-law. The bright, inquisitive ten-year-old Horace, Jr., Foote's counterpart in the play, observes it all, including the tragic drowning death of eighteen-year-old Gertrude, their black maid, as the cycle of family moves into the next generation.

BIBLIOGRAPHY

Aristotle's Poetics. Translated by S. H. Butcher. New York: Hill and Wang, 1961.

Benson, Sheila. "MM Interview." *Modern Maturity,* November–December 1996, p. 53ff.

Bogard, Travis. *Contour in Time: The Plays of Eugene O'Neill.* 1972. New York: Oxford University Press, 1988.

Brian, Crystal. " 'To Be Quiet and Listen': *The Orphans' Home Cycle* and the Music of Charles Ives." In *Horton Foote: A Casebook,* edited by Gerald C. Wood, 89–108. New York: Garland Publishing, 1998.

Briley, Rebecca. *You Can Go Home Again: The Focus on Family in the Works of Horton Foote.* New York: Peter Lang, 1993.

Broughton, Irv, ed. *The Writer's Mind: Interviews with American Authors.* Vol. 1. Fayetteville: University of Arkansas Press, 1990.

Burkhart, Marian. "Horton Foote's Many Roads Home: An American Playwright and His Characters." *Commonweal,* February 26, 1988, pp. 110–15.

Canby, Vincent. "For Horton Foote the Pictures Speak Volumes." Review of *Talking Pictures,* by Horton Foote. *New York Times,* October 2, 1994, p. H5ff.

Castleberry, Marion. "Remembering Wharton, Texas." In *Horton Foote: A Casebook,* edited by Gerald C. Wood, 13–33. New York: Garland Publishing, 1998.

Chappel, Joe Mitchell, ed. *Heart Songs.* Cleveland: World Publishing Co., n.d.

Davis, Ronald L. "Roots in Parched Ground: An Interview with Horton Foote." *Southwest Review* 73 (summer 1988): 298–318.

Dickinson, Emily. *Final Harvest: Emily Dickinson's Poems.* Edited by Thomas H. Johnson. Boston: Little, Brown, 1961.

DiGaetani, John L. "Horton Foote." In *A Search for a Postmodern Theater: Interviews with Contemporary Playwrights,* 65–71. Westport, Conn.: Greenwood Press, 1991.

Edgerton, Gary. "A Visit to the Imaginary Landscape of Harrison, Texas: Sketching the Film Career of Horton Foote." *Literature/Film Quarterly* 17, no. 1 (1989): 2–12.

Ellermann, Robert. Introduction to vol. 2 of *Horton Foote: Collected Plays,* by Horton Foote. Lyme, N.H.: Smith and Kraus, 1996.

Faulkner, William. *Go Down, Moses.* New York: Random House, 1940.

———. *Intruder in the Dust.* New York: Random House, 1948.

———. *Light in August.* New York: Random House, 1932.

———. *The Sound and the Fury.* Edited by David Minter. 2nd ed. New York: W. W. Norton, 1994.

Fergusson, Francis. *The Idea of a Theater.* Garden City, N.Y.: Doubleday, 1949.

Fitzgerald, F. Scott. *The Great Gatsby.* New York: Charles Scribner's Sons, 1925.

Flynn, Robert, and Susan Russell. "Horton Foote." In *When I Was Just Your Age,* 15–24. Denton, Texas: University of North Texas Press, 1992.

Foote, Horton. "The Artist as Myth-Maker." Unpublished lecture, University of Texas at Arlington, Arlington, Texas, November 16, 1988.

———. *"Courtship," "Valentine's Day," "1918": Three Plays from "The Orphans' Home Cycle."* New York: Grove Press, 1987.

———. *"Cousins" and "The Death of Papa": Two Plays from "The Orphans' Home Cycle."* New York: Grove Press, 1989.

———. *Four New Plays.* Newbury, Vt.: Smith and Kraus, 1993.

———. *Roots in a Parched Ground.* New York: Dramatists Play Service, 1962.

———. *"Roots in a Parched Ground," "Convicts," "Lily Dale," "The Widow Clair": Four Plays from "The Orphans' Home Cycle."* New York: Grove Press, 1988.

———. *Three Screenplays: "The Trip to Bountiful," "Tender Mercies," and "To Kill a Mockingbird."* New York: Grove Weidenfeld, 1989.

Freedman, Samuel G. Introduction to *"Cousins" and "The Death of Papa": Two Plays from "The Orphans' Home Cycle,"* by Horton Foote. New York: Grove Press, 1989.

Geffen, Arthur. "Profane Time, Sacred Time, and Confederate Time in *The Sound and the Fury." Studies in American Fiction* 2, no. 2 (autumn 1974): 175–97.

Guinn, Jeff. "The Return to Wharton." *Fort Worth Star-Telegram,* June 27, 1999, p. G2ff.

Hachem, Samir. "Foote-Work." *Horizon,* April 1986, pp. 39–41.

Mann, Ted. Interview by the author, January 8, 1999.

Martin, Carter. "Horton Foote's Southern Family in *Roots in a Parched Ground." Texas Review* 12, nos. 1–2 (spring–summer 1991): 76–82.

McDowell, S. Dixon. "Horton Foote's Film Aesthetic." In *Horton Foote: A Casebook,* edited by Gerald C. Wood, 137–50. New York: Garland Publishing, 1998.

Miller, Arthur. *The Crucible.* New York: Viking Press, 1952.

———. *Death of a Salesman.* New York: Viking Press, 1949.

———. *A View from the Bridge.* New York: Viking Press, 1955.

Moore, Marianne. *The Complete Poems of Marianne Moore.* New York: Macmillan-Viking, 1981.

O'Connor, Flannery. *Mystery and Manners.* Edited by Sally and Robert Fitzgerald. New York: Farrar, Straus, and Giroux, 1957.

O'Neill, Eugene. *Long Day's Journey into Night.* New Haven: Yale University Press, 1956.

———. *More Stately Mansions. Unexpurgated ed.* Edited by Martha Gilman Bower. New York: Oxford University Press, 1988.

———. *A Touch of the Poet.* New Haven: Yale University Press, 1957.

Porter, Laurin. *The Banished Prince: Time, Memory, and Ritual in the Late Plays of Eugene O'Neill.* Ann Arbor: UMI Research Press, 1988.

———. "An Interview with Horton Foote." *Studies in American Drama, 1945–Present* 6, no. 2 (1991): 177–94.

Porter, Thomas E. *Myth and Modern American Drama.* Detroit: Wayne State University Press, 1969.

Price, Reynolds. Introduction to *"Courtship," "Valentine's Day," "1918": Three Plays from "The Orphans' Home Cycle,"* by Horton Foote. New York: Grove Press, 1987.

Reinert, Al. "Tender Foote." *Texas Monthly,* July 1991, p. 110ff.

Rich, Frank. "1920s Lives That Leap into the Present." Review of *The Roads to Home,* by Horton Foote. *New York Times,* September 18, 1992, p. C2.

Sartre, Jean-Paul. "Time in Faulkner: *The Sound and the Fury.*" Translated by Martine Darmon. In *William Faulkner: Three Decades of Criticism,* edited by Frederick J. Hoffman and Olga W. Vickery, 225–32. East Lansing: Michigan State University Press, 1960.

Smelstor, Marjorie. "'The World's an Orphans' Home': Horton Foote's Social and Moral History." *Southern Quarterly* 19, no. 2 (winter 1991): 7–16.

Steinbeck, John. *Of Mice and Men/Cannery Row.* New York: Viking Press, 1945.

Sterritt, David. "Horton Foote: Filmmaking Radical with a Tender Touch." *Christian Science Monitor,* May 15, 1986, p. 1ff.

Underwood, Susan. "Singing in the Face of Devastation: Texture in Horton Foote's *Talking Pictures.*" In *Horton Foote: A Casebook,* edited by Gerald C. Wood, 151–62. New York: Garland Publishing, 1998.

Watson, Charles S. *The History of Southern Drama.* Lexington, Ky.: University Press of Kentucky, 1997.

Wood, Gerald C. *Horton Foote and the Theater of Intimacy.* Baton Rouge: Louisiana State University Press, 1999.

———. "Horton Foote's Politics of Intimacy." *Journal of American Drama and Theatre* 9, no. 2 (spring 1997): 44–57.

———. "The Nature of Mystery in *The Young Man from Atlanta.*" In *Horton Foote: A Casebook,* edited by Gerald C. Wood, 179–88. New York: Garland Publishing, 1998.

———. "Old Beginnings and Roads to Home: Horton Foote and Mythic Realism." *Christianity and Literature* 45, nos. 3–4 (spring–summer 1996): 359–72.

———, ed. *Horton Foote: A Casebook.* New York: Garland Publishing, 1998.

Wood, Gerald C., and Terry Barr. " 'A Certain Kind of Writer': An Interview with Horton Foote." *Literature/Film Quarterly* 14, no. 4 (1986): 226–37.

Index